Word and Music Studies

Essays on the Song Cycle
and on Defining the Field

WORD AND MUSIC STUDIES
3

Series Editors

Walter Bernhart
Lawrence Kramer
Suzanne M. Lodato
Steven Paul Scher
Werner Wolf

The book series WORD AND MUSIC STUDIES (WMS) is the central organ of the International Association for Word and Music Studies (WMA), an association founded in 1997 to promote transdisciplinary scholarly inquiry devoted to the relations between literature/verbal texts/language and music. WMA aims to provide an international forum for musicologists and literary scholars with an interest in interart/intermedial studies and in crossing cultural as well as disciplinary boundaries.

WORD AND MUSIC STUDIES publishes, generally on an annual basis, theme-oriented volumes, documenting and critically assessing the scope, theory, methodology, and the disciplinary and institutional dimensions and prospects of the field on an international scale: conference proceedings, collections of scholarly essays, and, occasionally, monographs on pertinent individual topics as well as research reports and bibliographical and lexicographical work.

Word and Music Studies: Essays on the Song Cycle and on Defining the Field

Proceedings of the Second International Conference
on Word and Music Studies at Ann Arbor, MI, 1999

Edited by
Walter Bernhart and Werner Wolf
in collaboration with
David Mosley

Rodopi

Amsterdam - Atlanta, GA 2001

The paper on which this book is printed meets the requirements of "ISO 9706:1994, Information and documentation - Paper for documents - Requirements for permanence".

ISBN: 90-420-1575-6 (bound)
©Editions Rodopi B.V., Amsterdam - Atlanta, GA 2001
Printed in The Netherlands

Contents

Introduction

The essays collected in this volume were presented at the Second International Conference on Word and Music Studies held at the University of Michigan in Ann Arbor in August 1999. The conference was also the second meeting of the International Association for Word and Music Studies (WMA), which was founded two years earlier during the preceding conference on Word and Music Studies held at Graz.

One focus of the Ann Arbor conference were general issues of word and music relations, which had already formed the thematic focus at Graz in 1997. Providing a platform for interdisciplinary discussions of interart or 'intermedial' relations between words/literature and music is indeed one of the principal *raisons d'être* for the WMA, whose aim it is to coordinate and connect the worldwide research in the field. This intermedial field is in fact so wide that even basic general perspectives on it, be it from a typological, semiotic, culturalist, or reception-aesthetic point of view, can hardly be adequately covered by one or two conferences. The discussion will consequently have to continue (at least) in the following conference organized by the WMA in Sydney in July 2001.

In addition, a second centre of interest of the Ann Arbor conference was the song cycle. It had been chosen from vocal music as an obvious area of word and music interaction. As a musico-literary genre, the song cycle not only elicits analyses of relations between text and music in individual songs but also raises the question if, to what extent, and under what conditions words and/or music contribute to creating a larger unity beyond the limits of single songs.

These two centres of interest of the conference also provide the bipartite structure of the present volume. The first section, entitled "**Defining the Field**", is a sequel to the same topic to which the entirety of volume 1 of the Word and Music Series was dedicated. The subjects discussed in this section of the present volume are threefold: issues linked with a culturalist approach to literature and music, the verbalization of music, and the cognitive and reception-orientated problem of what happens when a literary work attempts to imitate music.

The two opening contributions by John Neubauer and Michael Halliwell both deal with the culturalist issue, though from differing angles: **Neubauer** ("Organicism and Modernism / Music and Literature") addresses a very general topic: the problem of finding a common historical and theoretical terminology which besets all interart/intermedial reflections as opposed to 'internalist' ones. He illustrates this problem taking the example of 'organicism' as a widely recognized notion in musical as well as literary histories of Modernism. Referring, on the one hand, to contemporary musicological discussions by A. B. Marx, Schenker, Schönberg, Bartók and others and, on the other hand, to literary critics such as Rudolf Steiner, Günther Müller, I. A. Richards and Cleanth Brooks, Neubauer reveals with a remarkably deconstructive impetus that 'organicism' had different meanings not only in writings about music and literature but also in different cultures and for different authors and thus appears unsuitable as a term characterizing Modernism. Ultimately, by also including 'Modernism' in his terminological deconstruction, Neubauer leaves a vast space for alternative notions that could be devised for the project of a "culturally embedded histor[y] of music and literature" (22) as advocated by him. **Halliwell** ("'Singing the Nation': Word/Music Tension in the Opera *Voss*") concentrates on a more specific but no less interesting issue: the contribution of vocal music to the self-definition of Australia as a post-colonial nation. His case study focuses on the operatic version of the Australian epic *Voss*, regarded as the key work of the nobel prize winner Patrick White. Exploring the relation of the opera to the original novel as well as the interrelation between operatic text and music, Halliwell comes to the conclusion that *Voss* may not be a 'great national opera' in the traditional sense, but with its in-built tensions, its hybridity and eclecticism it expresses the contemporary uneasy state of Australian nationhood particularly well.

The next two essays, by Mary M. Breatnach and Peter Dayan, highlight the problem of verbalizing musical experiences, and they both do so with reference to nineteenth-century French culture, in which, notably in the context of Symbolism and Le Parnasse, music played an outstanding role.

While **Breatnach** investigates Charles Baudelaire's response to Richard Wagner, whose music became a catalyst for Baudelaire for formulating the essence of his own aesthetics and in particular his ideas about 'great art' ("Writing about Music: Baudelaire and *Tannhäuser* in Paris"), **Dayan** concentrates on Stéphane Mallarmé's comments on music in *Divagations*. In this essay Mallarmé suggests that individual musical compositions are examples of an ideally non-referential 'ethereal' art which resists verbalization, unless such comments centre on music in general, while verbal criticism can at least bring out the difference between actual literary works with their inevitably inadequate referentiality and the Mallarmean idea of an ideal book. According to Dayan, Mallarmé thereby foreshadows poststructuralist approaches of literature and at the same time highlights a problem that is still worth considering with regard to today's musicological discourse.

Finally, in this section, Frédérique **Arroyas**, in posing the question, "When is a Text Like Music?", investigates a crucial issue of all literature that purports to approach the condition of music. Her reception-orientated answer is based on a cognitive approach: a text appears to be musicalized if it elicits a reader response in which elements of the two cognitive fields 'novel' and 'music' produce a particular kind of 'blending'. The emergence of this cognitive 'blending', which is more that the sum of the component parts involved, does not exclusively depend on explicit references to music in the text but can also result from the foregrounding of the acoustic dimension of fictional language or from other unusual devices. This theory is convincingly illustrated by Roger Laporte's novel *Fugue*, a *nouveau roman* that blends the frames of reference 'fiction' and 'music' by combining experimental novelwriting with structural analogies to a fugue.

The second section, dedicated to "**The Song Cycle**", offers insights into generalities of the genre and the (problematic) coherence of song cycles, and into historical examples ranging, in chronological order, from Franz Schubert to Benjamin Britten and contemporary concept albums. According to Werner **Wolf** ("'Willst zu meinen Liedern deine Leier drehn?' Intermedial Metatextuality in Schubert's 'Der Leiermann'"), Schubert's *Die Winterreise* is a rare case of a nineteenth-century song cycle in which a truly cyclic unity is achieved – due to the metatextuality of the last song. This metatextuality allows a retrospective reading of the cycle as a 'self-begetting' work and provides a fictional motivation for it as a 'duo-dramatic' re-enactment of the experience of the wanderer, who appears to sing his story accompanied by the hurdy-gurdy man. In addition, it seems as if Schubert had answered the wanderer's question terminating Müller's text with his own composition, so that the intermedial reference to the "Leier" (the hurdy-gurdy) also appears to motivate the musical accompaniment of the wanderer's songs.

In partial contrast to this thesis of the achievement of cyclical unity at least by metatextual implication, Leon **Plantinga**, making ample use of contemporary evidence, warns against the unhistorical assumption, stemming from a later (Schenkerian) aesthetics, that nineteenth-century song cycles generally aimed at aesthetic unity through textual and musical devices, even if the mention of 'cycle' and similar ideas in some of their titles may suggest such unity to modern minds. Discussing "Design and Unity in Schumann's *Liederkreis*, Op. 39?", Plantinga emphasizes the narrow limits of such a quest for unity in Schumann's famous setting to music of Eichendorff poems and likens this song 'cycle' with its loose coherence more to a collection of pictures in a gallery. The same question of a possible coherence in Schumann's Op. 39 is addressed by Jürgen **Thym**, though from the perspective of the compositional genesis and the publication history of the *Liederkreis*. While not denying certain unifying devices, he, too, stresses the problematics of a quest for unity of a song cycle which appears with different beginnings in different editions and which all in all turns out to be more (as Thym's title has it) "A Cycle in Flux" rather than a static pre-conceived whole.

A rather different answer to the question of unity of a song cycle is provided by Harry E. **Seelig**. He regards "Hugo Wolf's Seventeen *Divan*-Settings" not only as "An Undiscovered Goethe-Cycle" but also as a thoroughly through-composed song cycle. According to Seelig, this unity derives largely from the fact that the *Divan*-settings respect the motivic coherence of Goethe's *West-östlicher Divan* and retain the duodramatic structure which is already present in Goethe's text and which is given additional relief by Wolf's treatment of the female voice of Suleika, a part that was originally inspired by Goethe's friend, Marianne von Willemer.

Again in contrast to the preceding contribution, Suzanne M. **Lodato**'s investigation into "Problems in Song Cycle Analysis and the Case of *Mädchenblumen*" continues the scepticism towards the unhistorical quest for unity already emphasized by Plantinga. Her main critical reference are pro-unity interpretations of Schumann song cycles by Patrick McCreless and David Neumeyer, to which she opposes a more balanced interpretation of Richard Strauss's *Mädchenblumen*, an 'experimental' song cycle whose compositional history challenges and even compromises assumptions of 'organic unity'. Walter **Bernhart**'s main focus is on a typology of song cycles which he develops from an analysis of "The Variety of Benjamin Britten's 'Charms'", that is, *carmina*, songs; yet the seemingly inevitable issue of coherence between songs in a song collection reoccurs in his contribution, too, namely in the guise of criteria for typological differentiations. Groups of songs to which such criteria do not apply are labelled 'editorial collections', to which Bernhart opposes three other kinds: a) 'loose song cycles' whose coherence rests on no more than the role of a unified lyric persona, b) song cycles unified by (further) predominantly literary means, and c) song cycles whose unity is based on a predominantly musical principle of coherence.

Markedly differing from the predilection of 'high art' of the past to which all the contributors to the section on the song cycle mentioned so far testify, Martina **Elicker** investigates a related form of vocal music in present day pop culture: "Concept Albums: Song Cycles in Popular Culture". After defining the genre 'concept album' and giving an overview of outstanding examples of this genre that have appeared since the inaugural Beatles's album *Sgt. Pepper's Lonely Hearts Club Band* of 1967 she presents Paul Simon's award winning album *Graceland* as a case study of the various textual and musical means used in concept albums to create coherence even among seemingly heterogeneous songs. The song cycle thus appears as a form which, in spite – or perhaps because of – its relative looseness and flexibility, is not confined to the nineteenth and early twentieth centuries but continues the tradition of word and music interaction in our day, albeit in another cultural context and in a different form.

Graz, March 2001   Werner Wolf

The editors want to thank the local organizer of the conference, Siglind Bruhn, without whose help the Ann Arbor conference would not have taken place and the present proceedings would consequently not have come into being in their present form. In addition, they are grateful to David Mosley for his valuable cooperation in the editorial work, and to Ingrid Hable, who was already responsible for the word processing and the layout of the two preceding volumes of the book series Word and Music Studies and whose expertise was a second *sine qua non* of the present volume.

The editors would welcome comments, suggestions and queries both concerning the present volume and the International Association for Word and Music Studies at their following email addresses:
Walter.Bernhart@kfunigraz.ac.at
Werner.Wolf@kfunigraz.ac.at

General Perspectives

Organicism and Modernism / Music and Literature

John Neubauer, Amsterdam

Organicist aesthetics holds that artworks are so tightly integrated that no part can be modified or removed without endangering the aesthetic structure; that works, artists and epochs go through organic cycles and developments; and that artworks are based on laws that may be compared to natural laws. Both literary scholarship and musicology have made heavy use of these and other organicist concepts. Recent criticism of this organicist aesthetics is largely justified, but it often falls prey to an organicist view of organicism by claiming that the theory is an internally consistent system. A closer look reveals 1) that Goethe's morphology and Coleridge's organicism significantly differ from each other, 2) that musicology made much heavier use of organicist aesthetics than literary scholarship, and 3) that the modernist uses of organicism differ from country to country and from discipline to discipline.

Learning a terminology, a historical periodization, and techniques of analysis is at the heart of the professional training and certification of musicologists and literary scholars. While no reasonable person would expect here the logical and semantic rigor of the natural sciences, neither field could survive without a modicum of consistency and intersubjective consensus. Such a consistency and consensus is needed even more in a plurimedial field like the joint study of word and music, and distinguished practitioners of the field have always put the question of terminological clarification high on their agenda. The following essay returns to this concern within the context of cultural studies.

One usual approach to the standardization of terminology is to insist that a field must use internal criteria to construct its history. Such an 'internalist' history is what René Wellek had asked for in the *Theory of Literature* he wrote with Austin Warren, a work that became the authoritative voice in mid-century European and North American literary studies:

Most leading histories of literature are either histories of civilization or collections of critical essays. One type is not a history of **art**; the other, not a **history** of art. (253)

Literary history has before it the analogous problem [compared to music and art] of
tracing the history of literature as an art, in comparative isolation from its social history,
the biographies of authors, or the appreciation of individual works. (254)
[...] the literary period should be established by purely literary criteria. If our results should
coincide with those of political, social, artistic, and intellectual historians, there can be no
objection. But our starting-point must be the development of literature as literature. (264)

Such an approach all but prohibits crossdisciplinary and cultural histories, for
one can hardly take seriously Wellek's hope that the results of an internalist
literary history may fortuitously coincide with those in other fields. Furthermore, one might object to Wellek's project by noting that neat surgical cuts
between the arts and between various fields of culture are both impossible and
undesirable. Indeed, most contemporary students of culture are preoccupied
with the 'rhizomatic' intertwining of phenomena and the inevitable 'contami-
nation' of disciplinary fields. Wellek himself had later given up the hope for
constructing a disciplinary history that unfolds the field in terms of an internal
development. Few people would set out today to seek "the development of
literature as literature".

What then are the alternatives, if 'internalist' histories of the arts are both
unfeasible and undesirable? Can we construct culturally embedded histories
by starting with a terminology and a historical vision that encompasses more
than a single field? While I see the great need for such new, broader histories,
in this paper I wish to caution that cultural histories of the arts run great
dangers if they adopt as their premise Hegelian or similar models of history
that postulate an organic unity between the cultural phenomena of an age,
subordinating them to a common Zeitgeist. Cultural textures are too complex
and contradictory to allow for such kind of homogenizing and reductive
generalizations. While this is something of a truism today, the "Ghost of
Geistesgeschichte", as I called it elsewhere ("Cultural Analysis and the Ghost
of Geistesgeschichte"), still haunts our histories.

I want to tackle this general issue by taking a look at Modernism in literature and music. More specifically, I shall look at the use of a single concept in
both fields, and I shall ask whether this common use allows us to postulate a
transdisciplinary cultural field. To complicate (and perhaps slightly confuse)
matters, I have chosen the term *organicism* for my case study, for ever since
Romanticism it has served as a key concept in unifying works of art and
periods of history. I shall ask then 1) whether modernist music and literature

were conceived as organic unities, and 2) if this should indeed be the case, whether one can attribute therefore to Modernist culture itself an organic unity. To anticipate my results: organicism and its cognate concepts were indeed used in modernist discussions of literature and music; these concepts must therefore play a role in histories of Modernism in these two disciplines. Yet widely differing meanings of organicism were circulating, and we cannot use the term as some kind of glue for piecing the various disciplines into a single, organic period called Modernism. Furthermore, pace Wellek, the faultlines run between national traditions and other strands of culture as well as between music and literature. While transdisciplinary histories will have to make use of terms like 'organicism', they should not assume, as they often do, that such terms span the cultural field in a consistent way. We must first deconstruct the organic unities of past historiography before constructing new, more complex and tension-filled notions of culture.

1.

Organicism, with its various meanings and variants, has come under heavy attacks in recent decades. Michel Foucault, Jacques Derrida, Paul de Man, Stephen Greenblatt, Jean-François Lyotard and other leading thinkers of postmodernity have criticized it from various angles, often defining their own thinking in opposition to it. Organicism is usually seen as a 'romantic heri-tage' that perpetuated itself in Modernism. Seen from this angle, one could say that postmodernists tend to define themselves as postorganicists; they attempt to differentiate themselves from the modernists by projecting unto the latter an organicist ideology. By questioning this identification of Modernism with organicism, I implicitly question this postmodernist self-stylization as postorganicism – but working this out falls beyond the confines of this essay.

What then is organicism? Since I am unable to start with a consistent and comprehensive definition, I must start empirically, by selecting a few concepts that postmodern critical theorists reject: unity, harmony, truth, essence, wholeness, totality, progress, development. The list could be extended; I make no claim as to its adequacy. But I want to suggest that ever since Romanticism these and similar terms have belonged to the orbit of organicism. I propose to associate three types of arguments with it: 1) a structural, 2) a narrative, and 3) an ontological one.

1) The **structural** argument holds that parts of a whole are not just mechanically adjacent to each other but dynamically and organically inter-related. Organic structures constitute one single unit. In aesthetics and criticism this yields two widely accepted assumptions. The first, hermeneutic, assumption proclaims that the parts mirror the whole and that interpretation should repeatedly refocus our attention from part to whole and back. A second, metaphysical, assumption of organicism holds that changing a part, or changing the number of parts will affect all others. More specifically, any change or intervention will diminish the value of a great (or perfect) artwork (cf. Lord 263, following Harold Osborne). In Stephen Pepper's formulation: a whole is called an organic unity, when "no detail can be removed or altered without marring or even destroying the value of the whole" (79).

2) The **narrative** argument claims that organic structures develop from a seed or kernel that already contains the essence of the organism. Older, mechanistic theories of biological preformation (*Einschachtelung, emboite-ment*) claimed that all descendants were present in the oldest ancestor as miniatures. At the end of the eighteenth century, the theory of epigenesis replaced preformation and allowed for a greater autonomy of the individual; it became essential in romantic and idealist philosophies (cf. Müller-Siever). Theories of organic development provide the foundation for genetic approaches to the arts. They may refer 1) to the work's development in the mind of the artist, 2) to the artist's personal development, or 3) to the development of art and of history in general. Such genetic theories of development tend to conceptualize temporality in terms of causal explanations (cf. Wellek 70-71) and continuous processes. For this reason they are attacked by those contemporary theorists that are concerned with ruptures, traumas, and processes of *longue durée*. However, they are capable of accomodating violent breaks, and Rothstein, for one, goes even so far as to claim that "'organicism' cherishes continuities with natural ruptures between them" (588).

3) The **ontological** argument holds that artworks and cultural products have laws, and that these laws are comparable to the laws of nature. According to a radical version of this argument, often but erroneously ascribed to Goethe, aesthetic laws and natural laws coincide: rules in the arts are based on

laws in nature. As we shall see, this claim is more frequently made with respect to music than with respect to literature.

Now if these are indeed features by which we identify organicism, then key works of the broadly conceived modernist canon violate its principles. Recall the role of chance in the work of Mallarmé, Valéry, and the dada artists, the deliberate chaos in Eliot's *The Waste Land*, the heterogeneous profusion in Joyce's *Ulysses* and Musil's *Mann ohne Eigenschaften*, the foregrounding of geometry in cubism and of the mechanical in futurism, or the role of automatism in surrealist experiments. As for theory: Wilhelm Worringer's *Abstraction and Empathy* (1908) reaffirmed the "urge to abstraction" against the hitherto dominating Western empathy for the organic (14); Shklovsky, Tynjanow and the other Russian formalists affirmed 'alienation' and discarded the notion of a natural literary evolution; Walter Benjamin reaffirmed allegoric art against the organic-symbolic conception that dominated German aesthetics and art criticism ever since Goethe. The list could be extended. Postmodern theoreticians are not unaware of these cases. But facing them, they tend to save their organicist conception of Modernism by coopting the non-organicist modernists into the postmodernist camp, leaving behind a presumably consistent organicist Modernism. Would they carry out this strategy with a modicum of consistency and comprehensiveness, the modernist ranks would be all but depleted.

An encyclopedic and statistical survey of the modernist artforms would be both impossible and inappropriate here. Concerned, as we are, with word and music, I want to make only three points with respect to the function of organicism in Modernism: 1) Organicism was both more powerful and somewhat different in music than in literature. 2) In the German-speaking countries most artists and theoreticians adhered to a special form of organicism, which they derived from Goethe and the revival of his biological studies towards the end of the nineteenth century. As far as I can see, this German ideology and aesthetics of morphologism has no equivalent in France, the English-speaking countries, and the Mediterranean cultures. 3) Organicism outside the German sphere differed from morphologism. A rereading of Cleanth Brooks's classic article, "The Poem as Organism", suggests that in New Criticism the organic had social rather than natural associations.

2.

Joseph Kerman writes: "None of the arts has been affected more deeply than music by the ideology of organicism; its baleful influence is still very much with us" (*Musicology* 65). Christopher Norris remarks that the "powerful ideology" of organic form "acquired a central – well-nigh unquestioned – prominence in the thinking of 19th-century composers, critics and music theorists" (110). Norris cites in support of this claim Goehr, Solie, Street, Subotnik, as well as Kerman; he could have cited also Lotte Thaler, whose *Organische Form in der Musiktheorie des 19. und beginnenden 20. Jahrhunderts* (1984) is the most thorough historical study of the subject, and possibly also Judith Frigyesi, whose *Béla Bartók and Turn-of-the-Century Budapest* (1998) makes, to my knowledge, the largest claims for the role of organicism in Modernism. Looking at these two works, Kerman's and Norris's neat generalizations become problematic. For Thaler's study is limited to German theoreticians, while Frigyesi extends organicism from music and its theory to a variety of other modernist fields of culture. Where exactly are the national, historical, and disciplinary boundaries of organicism's empire?

Thaler intelligently and carefully traces the organicist music theories from their origin in the writings of Adolf Bernhard Marx, via Hugo Riemann's theory to Heinrich Schenker, August Halm and Hans Mersmann in the early twentieth century. But the burden of her history is that musical organicism possesses no organic core and development, for although Goethe's morphology inspired the German approaches to music theory (cf. 7, 55-75), organicism acquired a different meaning in the work of each theoretician. For Marx, whose *Lehre von der musikalischen Komposition* explicitly relies on Goethe, organicism was a 'study of form' (*Formenlehre*), and the supreme organic structure in music was the sonata, as exemplified by Beethoven. Thus, Thaler notes, organicist music theories emerge with Viennese classical music to replace extra-musical references with an internal system of relations: organicism is linked to the theory of pure instrumental (i. e. absolute) music (cf. 12). The appearance of the musical concept of organicism may be regarded as the "emancipation [...] of musical technique and musical form in general" (56). Thaler perceives this already in Heinrich Christoph Koch's *Handbuch bey dem Studium der Harmonie* (1811), which upgrades, as it were, the *elaboratio* with respect to the *inventio* by demanding that young composers follow the "right organic form", the "correct organic development" of the musical material (56).

As we move from A. B. Marx to Riemann, the meaning of organicism shifts from constructive thematic elaboration to the inner logic of a movement based on an eight-measure unit (cf. Thaler 31f.). By the time we come to August Halm, music teacher at Gustav Wyneken's famous reform school at Wickersdorf, organicism becomes a law of the theme that is quasi-independent of the composer's will:

> Ob ein Thema gut gewachsen oder verkümmert ist, das sagt es uns schon selbst; nicht der Autor, nicht der von ihm gewollte Charakter gibt hier den Maßstab, sondern der Keim des Themas, seine Urform könnte man auch sagen. (Halm 245f.; quoted from Thaler 105)[1]

The pendulum has swung a full turn away from Marx's notion of free elaboration. The scale, called by Halm also 'primordial form' (*Urform*), contains a will to melodic appearance (cf. Thaler 107). And this abstract, impersonal will acquires a dangerous ideological weight when Halm develops by means of his musical organicism the notion of a 'musical state' (*Musikstaat*). Music becomes a means of education, but only for an elitist minority that voluntarily subordinates its individuality to the community. An organically developed theme is 'inhuman, and hence also superhuman, because it produces work of cosmic necessity' (cf. Thaler 116).

Heinrich Schenker's 'doctrine of organic interconnections' (*Lehre vom organischen Zusammenhang*) is rightly regarded usually as the most important and most complex organicist music theory, in part because it has had an enormous impact on music analysis as practiced in the United States and Britain[2]. But, as William A. Pastille has shown, the young Schenker was not yet an organicist, for he declared in 1895:

> In der That ist kein musikalischer Inhalt organisch. Es fehlt ihm ein jeglicher Kausalnexus [...] der Componist [verschafft] von seiner Phantasie sich mehrere

---

[1] 'A theme itself will tell us whether it is well grown or withered, not the author, not his willed character gives here the yardstick, but the germ of the theme, its primordial form as it were.' (My translation)

[2] The literature relating to Schenker and Schenkerism is enormous. For the purposes of this article I found Solie, Kerman, Narmour, and Pastille most useful.

Ähnlichkeiten und Contraste, [...] um schliesslich die beste Wahl zu treffen. (Schenker, "Geist" 309)[3]

Schenker may have written this in reaction to Riemann, probably unaware that by rejecting Riemann's organicism he was embracing that of A. B. Marx. Be it as it may, Schenker soon moved to the position of Riemann and beyond, by severely curtailing the composer's creative freedom and attributing musical form to the organic power inherent in the musical material. The transition was facilitated by Schenker's adoption of a Kantian concept of genius, which allowed for attributing natural forces to the artist:

> Großen Talenten und Genies nämlich ist es oft eigen, Nachtwandlern gleich den rechten Weg zu gehen [...] Es ist als komponierte geheimnisvoll hinter ihrem Bewußtsein und in ihrem Namen die weit höhere Macht einer Wahrheit, einer Natur, der es gar nichts verschlägt, ob der glückliche Künstler selbst das Richtige wollte oder auch nicht. (Schenker, *Harmonielehre* 76-77)[4]

It is this organicist theory of music, which has strong affinities with Halm's position, that made Schenker famous. Like Halm, Schenker attempts to understand composition and analysis as activities in pursuit of organic laws given by nature. According to him, the overtones give music a natural foundation; each piece of music organically unfolds a 'primordial line' (*Urlinie*). The task of musical analysis is to destill from the complex musical texture its primordial line. Schenker stresses "die biologischen Momente im Leben der Töne" (ibid. vi)[5], and he argues: "[...] die Töne [haben] ein wirkliches Eigenleben [...], das in seiner Animalität vom Künstler unabhängiger erscheint, als man es sich anzunehmen getraute!" (ibid.)[6] Thus, in Schenker, as in Halm, the musical material has an inherent natural will and independence, and this

---

[3] "[...] musical content is never organic, for it lacks any principle of causation [...] the composer draws from his imagination various similarities and contrasts, from which he eventually makes the best choice." (Trans. in Pastille 31)

[4] "A great talent or a man of genius, like a sleepwalker, often finds the right way [...] The superior force of truth – of Nature, as it were, – is at work, mysteriously behind his consciousness, guiding his pen, without caring in the least whether the happy artist himself wanted to do the right thing or not." (Schenker, *Harmony* 60)

[5] "the biological factor in the life of tones" (Schenker, *Harmony* xxv)

[6] "[...] tones have lives of their own, more independent of the artist's pen in their vitality than one would dare to believe." (Schenker, *Harmony* xxv)

inverts the organic freedom that Marx perceived in the shaping of the development section of the sonata.

Thaler gives considerable attention to the literary, philosophical, and cultural embedding of organicist music theories, but she curiously ignores the composers themselves, for all her authors – Marx, Riemann, Schenker, Halm, and Mersmann – are scholars. Frigyesi fills this gap by discussing Schönberg and Webern, as well as Bartók[7]. Her aim is to show that although all of Modernism is characterized by an organicist worldview (Chapter 1: "Organic Artwork or Communal Style?"; 19-42) Bartók's music can only be understood in terms of its specifically Hungarian variant (Chapter 4: "Hungarian Modernism and the Organicist Theory of Art"; 89-115). By studying Bartók in his cultural milieu, Frigyesi thus takes a crossdisciplinary approach to Modernism as well as organicism.

What is the specific meaning of the "and" that conjoins the subject with its cultural embedding, the music with the literary and verbal world around it? Can Frigyesi escape the problem that has plagued many culturally 'thick' studies that conjoin the specific and the general by resorting to reductive interpretation of either or both? Can she link Bartók to "Turn-of-the-Century Budapest" without imputing to the music, to the culture, and to the relation between them organic systems?

Since I have reviewed Frigyesi's book elsewhere (cf. Neubauer, "Overtones"), I shall comment here only on those aspects that are relevant for our context. The answers to the questions I have just raised are not unequivocally positive. Frigyesi is so eager to distinguish Bartók's organicism from those of his Western contemporaries that she offers a reductive image of Western (mostly German) Modernism, and she washes out some of the distinctions that Thaler's historical overview had established. As to Bartók, she gives detailed and interesting analyses of the *First Piano Concerto* and *Bluebeard's Castle*, but her links from here to Ady, Lukács, and the writers of the journal *Nyugat* (*West*) are not always convincing, and the image of Hungarian culture that emerges is at times too 'organically' consistent to accout for the tension between orientation towards the West (Ady towards Paris, Lukács towards Heidelberg) and a search for native 'organic' roots. By locating Bartók decid-

---

[7]   Frigyesi's scholarly sources (cf. 301-303) are M. H. Abrams, Carl Dahlhaus, and Ruth Solie; she does not mention Thaler.

edly towards the latter end of the spectrum, Frigyesi follows traditional approaches; she stresses his emotional and conceptual ties with folkmusic at the expense of the modernist and Western elements in his personality and art. Discussing his national and organic views, she rightly claims that Bartók rejected the chauvinism of the Hungarian populists, but she passes over the more problematic aspects of Bartók's organicism: he idealized the peasants by claiming in 1943 (!) that there has never been "the slightest trace of hatred or animosity against each other among those people. [...] There is peace among the peasants; hatred against their brothers is fostered only by the higher circles!" (Bartók 34) His moral admiration led him to regard folkmusic as a product of nature:

> Peasant music, in the strict sense of the word, must be regarded as a natural phenomenon; the forms in which it manifests itself are due to the instinctive *transforming power* of a community entirely devoid of erudition. It is just as much a natural phenomenon as, for instance, the various manifestations of Nature in fauna and flora. (321)
> [...] peasant music of this kind actually is nothing but the outcome of changes wrought by a natural force whose operation is unconscious in men who are not influenced by urban culture. (6)

Now Frigyesi is surely right to insist that this admiration for peasant culture separates Bartók from Schönberg. The Hungarian composer himself remarked once that Schönberg "is free from all peasant influence and his complete alienation from Nature, which of course I do not regard as a blemish, is no doubt the reason why many find his work so difficult to understand" (Bartók 326).

Yet, beyond this obvious contrast, Bartók's and Schönberg's organicism may have affinities. The opening pages of Schönberg's *Harmonielehre* (*Theory of Harmony*) reject the notion of "eternal laws" in music (Frigyesi 303; Schoenberg, *Theory* 8); more precisely, they reject the claim, descending from Rameau, that the rules of harmony were based on the overtones and hence radicated in nature: "I say: tonality is no natural law of music, eternally valid" (Schoenberg, *Theory* 9).

Indeed, Schönberg's 'de-naturalization' of tonality must be reconciled with the organicism he expressed elsewhere, for instance, in his well-known article in *Der blaue Reiter* (1912), which restates old organicist commonplaces on poetry and its relationship to music in a lied (cf. "Das Verhältnis zum Text"). Schönberg claims here that he used to be ignorant of what many Schubert songs said; once he looked at them, he discovered that he possessed an intuitive grasp which was superior to any understanding that analysis could have yielded. Indeed, whenever he set texts to music without understanding the words save the very first ones, the result was always a perfect match. This proved to him that the first words of (good?) poems contained a perfect organic image of the whole, and that the music of songs (his own? all good ones? all?) organically related to the words:

> Mir war daraus klar, daß es sich mit dem Kunstwerk so verhalte wie mit jedem vollkommenen Organismus. Es ist so homogen in seiner Zusammensetzung, daß es in jeder Kleinigkeit sein wahrstes, innerstes Wesen enthüllt. Wenn man an irgendeiner Stelle des menschlichen Körpers hineinsticht, kommt immer dasselbe, immer Blut heraus. Wenn man einen Vers von einem Gedicht, einen Takt von einem Tonstück hört, ist man imstande, das Ganze zu erfassen. Genauso wie ein Wort, ein Blick, eine Geste, der Gang, ja sogar die Haarfarbe genügen, um das Wesen eines Menschen zu erkennen. (Schönberg, "Verhältnis" 74)[8]

Frigyesi assumes too quickly that Webern's organicism was a direct (organic?) unfolding of these views of Schönberg. Indeed, Webern's *Wege zur neuen Musik* – a series of private lectures given in 1932/1933, reconstructed from the notes of a listener and posthumously published – is one of the most explicit organicist manifestos of Modernism, derived from Goethe's aesthetics and morphology, which Webern discovered in the 1920s (cf. Wübbolt 104f.). According to Webern, Goethe saw art 'as product of general nature in the special form of human nature':

> Goethe sieht die Kunst als Produktion der allgemeinen Natur in der besonderen Form menschlicher Natur. – Das heißt, daß zwischen Naturprodukt und Kunstprodukt kein wesentlicher Gegensatz herrscht, sondern daß es dasselbe ist, daß das, was wir als Kunstwerk sehen und so nennen, im Grunde nichts anderes ist als ein Produkt der allgemeinen Natur. (Webern 10)[9]

---

[8] 'This made it evident to me that artworks are like all perfect organisms. They are so homogeneous in their composition that every smallest detail reveals their true inner essence. [...] Hearing a line of a poem or a measure of a piece of music one can grasp the totality. Just as a word, a glance, a gesture, a gait, even the color of the hair, is sufficient to recognize the essence of a person.' (My translation)

[9] 'This means that no significant contrast exists between products of nature and products of art, but that they are one and the same, that what we regard as an artwork and call by that name is basically nothing else but a product of general nature.' (My translation)

In works of art, as in those of nature, there is necessity, law: "Wir werden uns bemühen müssen, das Notwendige in den Meisterwerken festzustellen. Keine Spur von Willkür! Nichts Eingebildetes!" (Webern 11)[10] Indeed, Webern declares that the system of overtones provides a natural foundation for Western tonal music (cf. 13). This explicitly contradicts Schönberg's quoted view, but Frigyesi, who wants to set an organically consistent western musical organicism against Bartók's Hungarian one, papers over the differences (cf. 38).

Where exactly does that leave us? For a comprehensive assessment of the role of organicism among modernist composers much more work will have to be done; limiting the discussion to Schönberg, Webern, and Bartók, as Frigyesi does, is clearly inadequate. But even if we focus our attention to these composers we shall have difficulty in constructing a common modernist platform on organicism. Frigyesi's somewhat obscure formula is that Bartók "superposed a second organicist paradigm on the idea he shared with Schönberg and Webern. He thought not only of the individual artwork but of style too in organicist terms, as if style were an artwork" (107). Leaving aside Webern's differences with Schönberg, one may suggest that Schönberg and Bartók both appealed to organicism for different reasons but in pursuit of comparable strategic aims, namely to 'pull the rug' from under the opponent: Schönberg denied that tonal music was natural, because he needed space for atonal music; Bartók declared that urban (gipsy and other) music was 'rootless' in order to sublimate the rural to the natural.

3.

We may now begin to broaden our perspective by noting that, apart from Bartók, we have considered German composers and theoreticians only. Frigyesi also mentions in passing Busoni, but, as far as I can see, organicist ideas do not play a comparably important role in his writing. The focus on German texts is neither accidental nor explainable by the dominant position of nineteenth- and early-twentieth-century German music theory. It has to do with a German tradition that originates around 1800 with Romanticism,

---

[10] 'We shall have to make efforts to ascertain what is lawful in masterworks. No trace of arbitrariness! Nothing imaginary!' (My translation)

idealist philosophy, and, above all, with Goethe's notion of morphology. The latter was, as Thaler has indicated, a motivating force in A. B. Marx's organicist ideas. In the mid-nineteenth century, interest in Goethean morphology waned, but it experienced a tremendous revival when in the wake of the German unification Goethe became the canonized national poet and monumental editions of his works started to appear.

Reworking and reopening Goethean science was at the heart of his canonization. The young Rudolf Steiner became editor of Goethe's scientific writings for the *Nationalausgabe*, a monumental library of German literature, and the equally monumental *Weimarer Sophien-Ausgabe* of Goethe's oeuvre. He subsequently published in 1897 a monograph on Goethe's morphological worldview and initiated the anthroposophic movement, in part on allegedly Goethean principles. By the mid-1920s, Wilhelm Troll, Lothar Wolf, and Wilhelm Pinder developed a new morphological biology based on Goethean principles. This revival of Goethean morphology, which had tenuous links with Goethe's own ideas (cf. Neubauer, "Morphological Poetics?" and "Organic Form"), gave rise to a broad spectrum of morphologist cultural and artistic studies, of which the theories of Halm, Schenker, and Webern are outstanding examples. Webern, as we have seen, explicitly cites Goethe and fully relies on his ideas. Schenker is less explicit, but his concepts of *Urlinie* and *Ursatz* are surely indebted to Goethe's *Urpflanze* – or rather early-twentieth-century reinterpretations of it. Indeed, it would be worthwhile to consider, whether Schenker's shift from anti-organicism to organicism that Pastille describes may not have been stimulated by the publication and reinterpretation of Goethe's morphology. Be it as it may, the motto of the first section of his mature, organicist work *Der freie Satz* (1923) is taken from Goethe's *Farbenlehre* (Goethe, *Werke* 10: 11).

Since I have already discussed elsewhere the massive 'biologization' or 'morphologization' of German culture during the early half of this century (cf. "Organic Form"), a few examples must suffice here. There is, to begin with, Oswald Spengler's *Der Untergang des Abendlandes* (*Decline of the West*), subtitled *Umrisse einer morphologischen Weltgeschichte* (*Outlines of a Morphological World History*), which proposed nothing less than a theory of history with 'predictive power' (cf. 3), based on a Goethean notion of morphology:

Was er die **lebendige Natur** genannt hat, ist genau das, was hier Weltgeschichte im weitesten Umfange, **die Welt als Geschichte** genannt wird. [...] Und so wie er die Entwicklung der Pflanzenform aus dem Blatt, die Entstehung des Wirbeltypus, das Werden der geologischen Schichten verfolgte – **das Schicksal der Natur, nicht ihre Kausalität** – soll hier die Formensprache der menschlichen Geschichte, ihre periodische Struktur, ihre **organische Logik** aus der Fülle aller sinnfälligen Einzelheiten entwickelt werden. [...] man sehe in den Worten Jugend, Aufstieg, Blütenzeit, Verfall, die bis jetzt regelmäßig und heut mehr denn je der Ausdruck subjektiver Wertschätzungen und allerpersönlichster Interessen sozialer, moralischer oder ästhetischer Art waren, endlich objektive Bezeichnungen organischer Zustände; man stelle die antike Kultur als in sich abgeschlossene Erscheinung, als Körper und Ausdruck der antiken Seele neben die ägyptische, indische, babylonische, chinesische, abendländische und suche das Typische in den wechselnden Geschicken dieser großen Individuen, das Notwendige in der unbändigen Fülle des Zufälligen. (35-36)[11]

Goethe, who was skeptical about laws in history, would have agreed with Karl Popper that such theories reveal the 'poverty of historicism', for he was wary of transcendental laws in science and he repeatedly rejected the reification of cultural products. The view that Goethe had "naturalizing ambitions" in the realm of art and culture (Rothstein 590) is based on the early-twentieth-century reception of his scientific writings. That reception has engendered, as I have shown elsewhere (cf. "Organic Form"), not only Spengler's concept of history, but also Erwin Kolbenheyer's 'biological metaphysics', which argued that individual minds had to be subordinated to racial and volkish forces, for only the latter could fight to adopt to the environment and to reach new levels of development (cf. 19). Poets were forces rooted in the volk instead of inspired geniuses (cf. 452).

The ideological taint of 'morphological poetics' (cf. my article with that title) is more complicated than Kolbenheyer's proto-nazi philosophy. Its main theorist was Günther Müller, a discriminating critic and a leading Germanist of his generation. His idea of a *morphologische Literaturwissenschaft*, a study of the formal and poetic properties of literary texts, gave important impulses

---

[11] 'What he [Goethe] called **living nature** is precisely what is called here world history in the widest sense, **the world as history**. [...] just as he followed the development of plant forms from the leaf, the origins of the vertebrate type, the becoming of geological layers – the fate of nature, not her causality – so shall we develop here the form language of human history, its periodic structure, its **organic logic**, from the plenitude of all the striking details. [...] One must finally see in the words youth, ascendance, flowering, decay [...] objective designations of organic conditions. One should posit ancient culture as a self contained phenomenon, as body and expression of the attic soul, next to the Egyptian, Indian, Babylonian, Chinese, and Western one, and seek the typical in the alternating fortunes of these great individuals, the necessary in the intractable plenitude of the accidental.' (My translation)

to the practice of 'close reading' (*werkimmanente Interpretation*) in post-war Germany and to the study of time in narrative structures. And yet, in 1941 Müller had hailed Franz Koch's admiring account of Kolbenheyer's theory as 'decisively important' for combining literary studies and biology (cf. Müller 364). This intrusion of biologism into formalist literary scholarship was a result of Müller's attribution of natural force to poetic texts (cf. 226); apparently concerned that the nazis may accuse him of formalism, he declared in 1944 that the study of formal properties ultimately aimed at showing 'whether and how it [a poetic text] originated from a healthy volkisch life-force, whether and how it represents the values of a nation, and whether and how it furthers life and belongs to the vital context [*Lebenszusammenhang*] of the volk through this representation' (my translation):

> Nicht ob und auf welche Weise ein Dichtwerk formale Reize oder Vorzüge besitzt, ist uns wichtig, sondern ob und wie es aus gesunder völkischer Lebenskraft entstanden ist, ob und wie es Kräfte und Werte der Nation darstellt und ob und wie es durch dieses Darstellen lebenfördernd wirkt und in den Lebenszusammenhang des Volks gehört. (Müller 152: "Die Gestaltfrage in der Literaturwissenschaft und Goethes Morphologie"; first published in *Die Gestalt. Abhandlungen zu einer allgemeinen Morphologie*. Heft 13, 1944)

Morphological approaches to literature are prominent in a number of still widely read studies from the 1920s, '30s, and '40s, including Hermann Pongs's *Das Bild in der Dichtung*, whose first volume is subtitled *Versuch einer Morphologie der metaphorischen Formen* (*Attempt at a Morphology of Metaphoric Forms*), André Jolles's *Einfache Formen*, which proposed a Goethean study of gestalt in legends, fairy tales, myths, and other simple forms, and Horst Oppel's *Morphologische Literaturwissenschaft* (subtitle: *Goethes Ansicht und Methode* [*Goethe's View and Method*]). Although these works contain, as far as I can judge, no incriminating passages, their authors all sympathized with the nazis. Jolles comitted suicide at the end of the war. Morphologism in literary scholarship had a fatal tendency to convert culture into nature and to ascribe racial features to culture thus 'naturalized'.

4.

The organicism of Anglo-American modernist literary criticism did not lead
to such biologistic reifications of literature. I. A. Richards, Cleanth Brooks,
and other New Critics adopted the notion of organism as a metaphor to
characterize poems and the role of tradition in literary history, but none of
them ever claimed seriously that poems were products of nature or that
literary history displayed inevitable universal laws.

Take for instance Cleanth Brooks's "The Poem as Organism", which
distinguished poems as organism from "poetry as statement" (20). The latter
amounted to a "denaturing of poetry" (21), because mere statements reduce
rich poetic language to some logical, prose, or biographical content. Thus, for
Brooks, keeping to the 'nature' of poetry had nothing to do with natural laws
and plant structures; it meant, as in the case of William Empson's criticism,
an appreciation of the suggestive, connotative, and associative power of
poetic words. For Empson, in contrast to [Dr. Samuel] Johnson, "words are
plastic, their meanings much less definite, and as a consequence the relations
among them are almost limitless in their complexity" (Brooks 23). Brooks
considers 'organic' as a valid modern critical term to characterize poetry
because "the relations between the various elements in the poetic context are
so intimate, so fluid, and so complex that, beside them, the relations which
Johnson emphasized seem mechanical" (ibid.). As an illustration, Brooks
cites I. A. Richards's, discussion of the word 'intrinsicate' in Shakespeare's
Anthony and Cleopatra: it brings together half a dozen meanings from 'intrinsic' and 'intrinse', but in such a way that none of the constituents exhausts the
meaning of the composite (cf. 23f.). Hence, for Brooks, 'fluid' and 'complex'
organic poetry has a meaning that is diametrically opposed to the notion of a
morphological form that is patterned after biological organisms and is strictly
lawful. Poems are organic precisely because their meaning cannot be laid
down by law; they resist reduction to a statement, remaining open and
infinitely interpretable[12].

---

[12]   It would require another context to show that Brooks's and Richards's notion of poetry as
an inexhaustible source of meaning generation harks back to Kant's notion of 'aesthetic ideas'
and Goethe's notion of the symbol. It is precisely here that Goethe's own morphology is
diametrically opposed to certain twentieth-century interpretations of morphology.

Though Brooks sides with Romanticism and Richards's reinterpretation of it by rejecting what is mechanical in Johnson and the earlier eighteenth century, he carefully defines also his difference from certain strands in romantic criticism. And his first target is precisely the kind of mysticism that Schönberg embraced by claiming that intuition could better grasp the organic relations between words and music than analysis. Brooks's polemical words against F. L. Lucas's *Decline and Fall of the Romantic Ideal* could just as well be directed against Schönberg's organicism:

> But the typical Romantic critic avoids Coleridge's discussion of interconnections. He honors the unconscious, but he wants to keep it unconscious. He praises the magic power of certain lines, but he becomes annoyed if one tries to discover the source of magic. (25f.) [...] it is a Romantic perversion of the organic concept of poetry which causes the alarm. This perversion would remove the poem from the purview of criticism – it gives us, not an organism, but a mystic entity which eludes examination because it is plastic to the point of haziness. (27)

Defenders of organic poetry usually respond to the charge of mysticism by claiming that the poem's 'organic' cohesion is by design rather than magic. Walter Pater, for instance, insisted that poetic creativity involved "analysis"as well as "calculation": "By exquisite analysis the artist attains clearness of idea; then, through many stages of refining, clearness of expression. He moves slowly over his work, calculating the tenderest tone, and restraining the subtlest curve" (5: 81). Hence Pater would have objected to Halm's and Schenker's organicist view that the creative process was driven by forces within the material itself, and in fact he objected to Coleridge's use of the plant metaphor because he thought that it attributed a mechanical process to writing: "[What makes Coleridge's] view a one-sided one is, that in it the artist has become almost a mechanical agent: instead of the most luminous and self-possessed phase of consciousness, the associative act in art or poetry is made to look like some blindly organic process of assimilation. The work of art is likened to a living organism." (5: 80)

Brooks carefully navigates between the extremes, between the personal and the impersonal, the expressive and the plant concept of creativity. In a lengthy discussion of T. S. Eliot's "Tradition and the Individual Talent" (cf. 27-30) he supports the view that we must detach the poem from the personality of the poet in order "to allow us to inspect the poem as a structure"

$(30)^{13}$. But in entertaining the notion that the poet has no "complete control over his words" (31) he silently departs from Eliot's position by suggesting that the poem's organic structure is due partly to accidents in its genesis and partly to the constructive activity of the reader. While some of the complexity in poetry is by design, much of it is due to "happy accidents", those "fortunate printers' errors which occasionally lift a dull line into radiance and beauty or those effects too subtle and too complicated to have been deliberately planned" (32). Yet other instances of poetic complexity are constructs of the reader, for "words continually invite and stimulate the word-drenched human mind to arrange them in manifold patters – logical, grammatical, metaphorical" (ibid.). Poems are living organisms because words and their combinations are unceasingly producing new meaning via reading and criticism: "Whose poem is it, anyway, the reader's or the poet's?" (33) Thus Brooks's organic poetry harks back to Kant and Goethe, both of whom regarded aesthetic objects as inexhaustible sources of meaning; at the same time it anticipates reader-oriented criticism and the deconstructive foregrounding of opacity in language[14].

Brooks, the New Critic who "most consistently held a strictly organic view" (Wellek 95), would rightly protest that today's critics of organicism couldn't possibly mean the brand he shared with William Empson and I. A. Richards. Indeed, we may question whether English-speaking Modernism ever entertained organicist ideas comparable to those inspired by morphologism. The leading textbook of mid-century, Wellek and Warren's *Theory of Literature*, may have talked about literary evolution in the sense of the Russian formalists, but it does not attribute organic structures to poems, and it is highly critical of biologistic histories by Nadler, Spengler, Brunetière, Symonds, and others (cf. 52, 236, 255-257). Wellek's skeptical position with respect to evolutionary literary histories in *Theory of Literature* originates in

---

[13] What Pater attacks here (the alleged romantic surrender of control) is almost identical with what Eliot affirms in attacking Romanticism (the true poet is a mere catalyst). It makes little difference that Pater's metaphor comes from biology and Eliot's from chemistry – both stress the involuntary.

[14] Unfortunately, Brooks severely compromises his insight with an illustration of the limits of interpretation: he regards the poetry of Ella Wheeler Wilcox so irremediably dull that we "cannot fairly father [sic!] the ambiguity upon her; more important, the context will not support the ambiguity for those who discover it and try to press it upon the poem" (34).

his writings from the 1930s and assumes a radical form in his late essay "The Fall of Literary History", which declares that "attempts at an evolutionary history [including his own] have failed" (77). The modernist persuasions of Wellek come to coincide here with those postmodern theorists he otherwise so vehemently attacks.

By 1970, another leading American literary theorist, William Wimsatt, explicitly questioned whether the growth of a poem resembles that of a plant and whether the poem as a hypostasized verbal and mental act has an organic structure (cf. 66-71). Arguing against the dogma that in great works of art no part can be changed or moved without ruining it, Wimsatt reminded the audience at the 1970 MLA Convention that many poets "continue to revise their poems assiduously, to remove parts, to add others, to replace others – even to the last gasp of their deathbed editions" (74), and he claimed that the "wider stretches of poetry" are often no more than "atmospheric, or virtual context for local episodes of the most intense aesthetic quality" (73). K. K. Ruthven's more recent critique of organicism is not more than an extension of Wimsatt's view.

5.

What conclusions can we draw from this all too short examination of organicist theories in Modernism? On the word/music relationship in texted music – subject of several other essays in this volume – I have touched only lightly, in connection with Schönberg's essay, but my discussion of Brooks and the New Critics suggests that Schönberg's obscurantist organicism is not representative of Modernism in general.

What then may be the modalities of a history in an age 'beyond formalism'? The enormous importance of organic theories in music illustrates that, for the better or worse, the arts and sciences are no secluded islands. As Thaler concludes, the organic model of music emerges as an aspect of the notion that music is autonomous, but it is woven into a tissue of extra-musical ideas. The concept is not specific to music; as a concept of musical form it is loaded with non-musical content (cf. 130). This suggests that 'internalist' disciplinary histories (exemplified by the passages from Wellek at the outset of my essay) are difficult to come by. Yet internalist histories in the arts and the sciences cannot simply be replaced by transdisciplinary or interdisciplinary histories based on 'organic' relations between the cultural phenomena. Organicism may have acquired different meanings in music and literature, but it also meant different things within different national traditions, and must also be differentiated within each of the national traditions in music and literature. Some of these meanings, like morphology, cut across the disciplines and the arts but are language specific. Deconstructing Modernism (and organicism itself) is a precondition of culturally embedded histories of music and literature.

References

Abrams, M. H. *The Mirror and the Lamp*. London: Oxford Univ. Press 1953.
Bartók, Béla. *Essays*. Sel. and ed. Benjamin Suchoff. London: Faber & Faber, 1976.
Brooks Jr., Cleanth. "The Poem as Organism: Modern Critical Procedure", *English Institute Annual* (1940): 20-41.
Burwick, Frederick, ed. *Approaches to Organic Form: Permutations in Science and Culture*. Dordrecht: Reidel, 1987.
Dahlhaus, Carl. *The Idea of Absolute Music*. Trans. Roger Lustig. Chicago, IL: Univ. of Chicago Press, 1989.
—. *Nineteenth-Century Music*. Trans. J. Bradford Robinson. Berkeley, CA: Univ. of California Press, 1989.
Eagleton, Terry. *Literary Theory*. Oxford: Blackwell, 1983.
Eliot, T. S. "Tradition and the Individual Talent" (1920). T. S. Eliot. *The Sacred Wood*. London: Methuen, 1960. 47-59.
Forte, Allen. "Heinrich Schenker". *The New Grove Dictionary of Music and Musicians*. London: Macmillan, 1980. 16: 628.
Foucault, Michel. *The Order of Things* (French orig. *Les Mots et les choses* 1966). New York, NY: Vintage Books, 1973.
Frigyesi, Judit. *Béla Bartók and Turn-of-the-Century Budapest*. Berkeley, CA: Univ. of California Press, 1998.
Goehr, Lydia. *The Imaginary Museum of Musical Works: An Essay in the Philosophy of Music*. Oxford: Clarendon Press, 1992.
Goethe, Johann Wolfgang von. *Die Schriften zur Naturwissenschaft*. Leopoldina-Ausgabe. 12 vols. Weimar: Böhlau, 1947-.
—. *Sämtliche Werke*. 22 vols. Munich: Hanser, 1985-1999.
Halm, August. *Von zwei Kulturen der Musik* (1913). Stuttgart: Klett, [3]1947.
Jolles, André. *Einfache Formen* (1930). Tübingen: Niemeyer, 1958.
Kerman, Joseph. "A Few Canonic Variations". *Critical Inquiry* 10 (1983): 107-125.

—. *Musicology*. London: Fontana, 1985.

Koch, Franz. "E. G. Kolbenheyers Bauhütte und die Geisteswissenschaften". *Dichtung und Volkstum. Neue Folge des Euphorion* 41 (1941): 269-296.

Kolbenheyer, E. G. *Die Bauhütte*. Rev. 2nd ed. Munich: Albert Langen, 1940.

Lord, Catherine. "Organic Unity Reconsidered". *Journal of Aesthetics and Art Criticism* 22 (1964): 263-268.

Marx, Adolf Bernhard. *Die Lehre von der musikalischen Komposition*. Leipzig ⁴1852.

Mersmann, Hans. *Angewandte Musikästhetik*. Berlin: Hesse, 1926.

Müller, Günther. *Morphologische Poetik*. Ed. Elena Müller. Darmstadt: Wissenschaftliche Buchgesellschaft, 1968.

Mueller-Siever, Helmut. *Self-Generation. Biology, Philosophy, and Literature Around 1800*. Stanford, CA: Stanford Univ. Press, 1997.

Narmour, Eugene. *Beyond Schenkerism: The Need for Alternatives in Musical Analysis*. Chicago, IL: Univ. of Chicago Press, 1977.

Neubauer, John. "Morphological Poetics?" *Style* 22 (1988): 263-274.

—. "Organic Form in Romantic Theory: The Case of Goethe's Morphology." Larry H. Peer, ed. *Romanticism Across the Disciplines*. Lanham: Univ. Press of America, 1998. 207-230.

—. "Cultural Analysis and the Ghost of Geistesgeschichte". Mieke Bal, ed. *The Practice of Cultural Analysis*. Stanford, CA: Stanford Univ. Press, 1999. 287-302.

—. "Overtones of Culture". *Comparative Literature* 51 (1999): 243-254.

Neue Hefte zur Morphologie. Weimar: Böhlaus Nachfolger, 1954 -.

Norris, Christopher. "Deconstruction, Musicology and Analysis: Some Recent Approaches in Critical Review". *Thesis Eleven* 56 (1999): 107-118.

Oppel, Horst. *Morphologische Literaturwissenschaft: Goethes Ansicht und Methode* (1947). Darmstadt: Wissenschaftliche Buchgesellschaft, 1967.

Pastille, William A. "Schenker, Anti-Organicist". *Nineteenth-Century Music* 8 (1984): 29-36.

Pater, Walter. *Works*. 8 vols. London: Macmillan, 1900-1905.

Pepper, Stephen. *The Basis of Criticism in the Arts*. Cambridge, MA: Harvard Univ. Press, 1946.

Pinder, Wilhelm, Lothar Wolf, Wilhelm Troll. *Die Gestalt: Abhandlungen zu einer allgemeinen Morphologie*. Leipzig: Becker & Erler, 1940.

Pongs, Hermann. *Das Bild in der Dichtung*. Vol. 1: *Versuch einer Morphologie der metaphorischen Formen*. Marburg: Elwert, 1927.

Riemann, Hugo. *Die Elemente der musikalischen Ästhetik*. Berlin: Spemann, 1900.

Rothstein, Eric. "Organicism, Rupturalism, and Ism-ism". *Modern Philology* 85 (1988): 588-609.

Rousseau, G. S., ed. *Organic Form: The Life of an Idea*. London: Routledge, 1972.

Ruthven, Kenneth Knowles. "Organic and Inorganic Form". K. K. Ruthven. *Critical Assumptions*. Cambridge: Cambridge Univ. Press, 1979. 16-32.

Schenker, Heinrich. "Der Geist der musikalischen Technik". *Musikalisches Wochenblatt* 26 (1895): 245-246, 257-259, 273-274, 279-280, 297-298, 309-310, 325-326.

—. *Harmonielehre* (1906). Vienna: Universaledition, 1978.

—. *Harmony* (German orig. 1906). Oswald Jonas, ed., Elizabeth Mann Borgese, trans. Chicago, IL: Univ. of Chicago Press, 1954.

—. *Neue musikalische Theorien und Phantasien.* III: *Der freie Satz.* Oswald Jonas, ed. Vienna: Universal Edition, ²1956.

Schönberg, Arnold. "Das Verhältnis zum Text". Wassily Kandinsky, Franz Marc, eds. *Der blaue Reiter.* Munich: Pieper, 1912. 60-75.

Schoenberg, Arnold. *Theory of Harmony* (1911/1940). Trans. Roy E. Carter. London: Faber, 1978.

Solie, Ruth. "The Living Work: Organicism and Musical Analysis." *Nineteenth-Century Music* 4 (1980): 147-156.

Spengler, Oswald. *Der Untergang des Abendlandes: Umrisse einer morphologischen Weltgeschichte* (1917-1923). 2 vols. Munich: Beck, 1981.

Steiner, Rudolf. *Goethes Weltanschauung* (1897). Berlin: Philosophisch-Anthroposophischer Verlag, 1918.

Street, Alan. "Superior Myths, Dogmatic Allegories: The Resistance to Musical Unity". *Music Analysis* 8 (1989): 77-123.

Subotnik, Rose Rosengard. "Toward a Deconstruction of Structural Listening: A Critique of Schoenberg, Adorno and Stravinsky." Eugene Narmour, Ruth Solie, eds. *Explorations in Music, the Arts, and Ideas: Essays in Honor of Leonard B. Meyer.* Stuyvesant: Pendragon, 1988. 87-122.

—. *Developing Variations: Style and Ideology in Western Music.* Minneapolis: Univ. of Minnesota Press, 1991.

Thaler, Lotte. *Organische Form in der Musiktheorie des 19. und beginnenden 20. Jahrhunderts.* Munich: Katzbichler, 1984.

Troll, Wilhelm, Karl Lothar Wolf. *Goethes morphologischer Auftrag* (1942). Tübingen: Neomarius, ³1950.

Webern, Anton. *Wege zur neuen Musik.* Ed. Willi Reich. Vienna: Universal Edition, 1960.

Wellek, René, and Austin Warren. *Theory of Literature* (1948). New York, NY: Harcourt, Brace, ³1956.

Wellek, René. *The Attack on Literature and Other Essays.* Chapel Hill, NC: Univ. of North Carolina Press, 1982.

Wimsatt, William. "Organic Form: Some Questions about a Metaphor". Rousseau, ed. 61-81.

Worringer, Wilhelm. *Abstraction and Empathy* (1908). Cleveland, OH: World, 1967.

Wübbolt, Georg. "Weberns Goethe-Rezeption: Ein Beitrag zum Thema Natur und Kunst". Dieter Rexroth, ed. *Opus Anton Webern.* Berlin: Quadriga, 1983. 103-107.

'Singing the Nation'
Word/Music Tension in the Opera *Voss*

Michael Halliwell, Sydney

The conflict between words and music is as old as opera itself and, indeed, has been the
subject of several operas. An outstanding contemporary Australian composer, Richard
Meale, and celebrated Australian novelist, David Malouf, in their adaptation of Nobel
Prize winning author Patrick White's seminal Australian novel *Voss* have chosen to
explore, as one of their themes, the nature of words, particularly writing, in the construction of personal as well as national identity. The opera explores the limitations of
words as an effective means of communication, contrasting the spoken and written
word's limitation when compared with the ability of music to transcend both time and
space. The opera also explores the tension between words and music in larger terms:
namely, the tension between the western and the aboriginal worlds. This paper investigates the notion of post-colonial opera and argues that the opera *Voss* exemplifies many
issues current in the post-colonial debate in Australia.

> [...] he would hear the stubborn music that was waiting for release.
> Of rock and scrub. Of winds curled invisibly in wombs of air.
> Of thin river struggling towards seas of eternity.
> All flowing and uniting. (White, *Voss* 446)

As Australia approaches two important nation-defining millennial events:
the 2000 Olympics and the centenary of Federation in 2001, there is much
debate concerning questions of national identity, reconciliation, multi-
culturalism, social justice, racism and, in fact, what the term 'Australia'
actually means. It is a country seeking to define its place and identity in an
increasingly globalised region and world. The arts in general, as one would
hope and expect, are in the forefront of this endeavor and the relatively
small but thriving Australian operatic scene is no exception[1]. Two recent

---

[1] Opera Australia, the national company, is the third largest company in the world in
terms of the number of performances per year. It has an interesting mix of standard
repertoire balanced with more unusual works. Like most companies which depend on the
box office for a large percentage of its financial operating base, it seems to be moving more
and more into the standard popular repertoire but does still occasionally commission works
by Australian composers.

Australian operas in particular have grappled with this issue. *The Eighth Wonder*, with music by Richard Mills and libretto by Dennis Watkins, took as its subject the almost operatic controversies surrounding the building of the Sydney Opera House, probably Australia's most instantly recognisable icon. The opera deals with the political, artistic and personal intrigues which dominated the lengthy construction period and indirectly focused on wider issues of national identity. This opera was given a lavish production and enjoyed considerable success at its premiere in 1996 (appropriately enough in the Sydney Opera House) and is due for a revival in 2000. The work that I wish to discuss investigates similar issues but in much greater depth, and has as its central figure an even more enduring and central Australian icon: the explorer[2].

The opera *Voss*, with music by the highly regarded Australian composer, Richard Meale, and libretto by the award-winning Australian poet and novelist, David Malouf, was premiered to great acclaim in Adelaide in 1986 and received subsequent performances in Melbourne and Sydney. It was broadcast on national television, recorded by Phillips, and released on video as well. The opera is written in a relatively conservative idiom but its outstanding reception at the time of its first performance posed the question whether the 'Great Australian Opera' had arrived.

---

[2]   Roslyn D. Haynes traces the changes in perception that the figure of the explorer has undergone in Australia:

> Each generation reinvents its myths according to its particular needs. In Australia this has been particularly evident in the recasting of the explorers. The heroic figures of nineteenth-century literature and art who carried with them the hopes of the colony for expansion were constructs of desire – desire not only for more pastoral land but for inspiring models of valour and resourcefulness. In the twentieth century the requirements were different. At first the new nation needed internationally acknowledged heroes to establish and adorn its identity. Subsequently it needed to demote these role models because they were not Australian but European. By the 1950s the notion of any kind of heroism was regarded with cynicism, and psychoanalysis of these figures, to unearth their unacknowledged motives and their existential despair, was more intellectually respectable. Later still, towards the turn of the twentieth century, in a materialist culture where it is nevertheless fashionable to bemoan materialism and search for a new spirituality, the explorers have again been pressed into service by writers and artists as our representatives. What they are now shown as seeking in the desert is not land or colonial power but spiritual enlightenment and wholeness, a purging of wrong priorities and the discovery of cosmic meaning. (226)

Questions of national identity were prominent at the time of the opera's premiere (Australia celebrated the bi-centenary of European settlement in 1988). In this paper I will attempt to argue that a central thematic concern of the opera – the concept of verbal and non-verbal communication – can be seen as part of this debate concerning national identity as well as part of wider issues of post-colonialism. Of course, this is also closely linked to the old operatic controversy concerning the primacy of words or music.

The opera also tangentially raised issues such as the role in a post-colonial society like Australia of the essentially European art form of opera. Richard Dellamora and Daniel Fischlin argue that "[o]pera as genre stages the epic of imperial culture. The epic requirements of the materials of operatic production are correlative with its place in the symbolic landscape of nation. It is no accident that there is no such thing as Third World grand opera" (8). While not disagreeing with this assertion, one could argue that there are works that might be labeled 'post-colonial'. Indeed, all opera written outside of the European tradition could, perhaps, be regarded as post-colonial in the broadest sense of the term. In this paper, I would apply the term only for those operas that deal thematically with issues prominent in post-colonial studies. This concept is embodied particularly well in the opera *Voss*[3].

The opera is an adaptation of the novel of the same name by the Nobel Prize-winning Australian writer, Patrick White, published in 1957. Many still regard it as one of the greatest Australian novels and it is certainly piv-

---

[3] The question of opera as a reflection of nation is the subject of several essays in Fischlin and Dellamora. They argue that

> [n]ations embody and refract desire; that is, like opera, they give shape to the pleasures and pains, the mystifications and material effects that are a product of desire. But desire, like opera, is mediated by the politics of community and the individuals who articulate the apparent collectivity of the desires that constitute nation. The potent seductions of nationhood entail a symbolic discourse by which an apparently natural will (of the people, of a leader) – deemed the national, formed of shared language, common geography, ethnicity, vision of the future, and so forth – produces the phantasm of collectivity that becomes nation. Thus nation is illusion materialized and requires a symbolic language by which the imagination of nation becomes thinkable and enters into the realm of representation. (2)

otal in the Australian literary canon[4]. Something of the novel's centrality in Australian literature as well as the national psyche can be gauged by Roslyn D. Haynes's assertion that the "historical novel can only 'represent' ideas and stereotypes" of that past but that White has managed to create "a protagonist and imagery that for subsequent Australians **became** history" (239).

Both novel and opera have the theme of failure, albeit heroic failure, at their core. The expedition into the interior of Australia led by Voss, judged in objective terms, accomplishes none of its purported aims. The central relationship between the two protagonists, Voss and Laura, can, on a superficial level, be judged as a failure. After their initial uncomfortable meetings in Sydney, there are no more physical encounters, letters fail to reach their intended recipient, Voss dies in the desert a few months later, and the final image of Laura is as a rather staid 'old maid'. One can argue that failure is central in Australian mythology. The origins of the nation as a penal settlement and the unforgiving nature of the land and climate have contributed to a sometimes bleak and often cynical *weltanschauung*. Perhaps the most potent myth of all, and one that seems continually to increase in importance, is evoked by the term 'Anzac' – epitomised by the disastrous campaign at Gallipolli during the First World War in which Australian and New Zealand troops (as part of the British Army) were conspicuously unsuccessful in dislodging the Turkish army but engendered a legend of comradeship, bravery and 'mateship' which is seen as fundamental to the national psyche (although there is currently a lively debate about the validity of the idea of 'mateship' – a particularly charged word in Australia at present). The First World War as a whole has also been seen as a defining moment during which the nation lost its innocence and came of age. However, the sense of a truly distinctive Australian national identity remains elusive[5].

---

[4] William Walsh sees Australia as central to the novel:

Australia is almost another character in the novel, certainly an impressive and influential force, the complex presence of which affects the organization and the feeling of the novel at many different points. Australia is the sole opponent worthy of Voss's will. The will to know Australia is the initiating impulse of the novel. (38)

[5] Ashcroft/Griffiths/Tiffin, eds. (1995) have elaborated on the difficulties faced by the settler colonies seeking to define their own national identity:

Settler colony cultures have never been able to construct simple concepts of the nation, such as those based on linguistic communality or racial or religious homogeneity. Faced

I will not attempt to delimit or define the term 'post-colonial'[6]. There is a danger that the term has come to embrace almost any concept that is desired[7]. In simple terms, post-colonialism can be distinguished by a dialectic between the centre and the margins, metropole and colony. Ashcroft, Griffiths and Tiffin, in their influential study of post-colonial literature, *The Empire Writes Back* (1989), argue that fundamental to the idea of post-colonialism is the notion of "place and displacement" and a concern with the "development or recovery of an effective identifying relationship between self and place" (8-9). It is within this search for both personal and national identity that White's *Voss* can be located. Obviously the range of subject-matter in post-colonial fiction is vast but among the

---

with their 'mosaic' reality, they have, in many ways, been clear examples of the **constructedness** of nations. In settler colony cultures the sense of place and placelessness have been crucial factors in welding together a communal identity from the widely disparate elements brought together by transportation, migration and settlement. At the heart of settler colony culture is also an ambivalent attitude towards their own identity, poised as they are between the centre from which they seek to differentiate themselves and the indigenous people who serve to remind them of their own problematic occupation of the country. The process of effecting justice, restitution and reconciliation with the indigenous peoples is now crucial to any notion of creating an effective identity, and the issue of how nationalism may continue to function to elide and obscure such important constitutive 'differences' has been at the heart of the debate in all ex-settler colony cultures in recent years. (151-152).

[6]   Ashcroft/Griffiths/Tiffin, eds. (1995) acknowledge the problem of defining the field, including the dispute between the terms 'postcolonial/post-colonial':

These terms [...] encapsulate an active and unresolved dispute between those who would see the post-colonial as designating an amorphous set of discursive practices, akin to postmodernism, and those who would see it as designating a more specific, and 'historically' located set of cultural strategies. Even this latter view is divided between those who believe that post-colonial refers only to the period after the colonies become independent and those who argue [...] that it is best used to designate the totality of practices, in all their rich diversity, which characterise the societies of the post-colonial world from the moment of colonisation to the present day, since colonialism does not cease with the mere fact of political independence and continues as a neo-colonial mode to be active in many societies. (xv)

[7]   Ashcroft/Griffiths/Tiffin, eds. (1995) offer a general definition which is useful:

Post-colonial theory involves discussion about experience of various kinds: migration, slavery, suppression, resistance, representation, difference, race, gender, place, and responses to the influential master discourses of imperial Europe such as history, philosophy and linguistics, and the fundamental experiences of speaking and writing by which all these come into being. None of these is 'essentially' post-colonial, but together they form the complex fabric of the field. (2)

recurring themes that have been identified by Ashcroft, Griffiths and Tiffin (1989), are those of "exile, the problem of finding and defining 'home', physical and emotional confrontations with the 'new' land and its ancient and established meanings" (27). Most of these themes are central to *Voss*, but the characteristic most pertinent to this discussion is what is described as "the journey of the European interloper through unfamiliar landscape with a native guide" (ibid. 28). This kind of journey gives *Voss* its basic structure.

Linda and Michael Hutcheon argue the case for the term 'postnational' rather than post-colonial as more appropriate to describe certain contemporary Canadian operas. They maintain that "in the contemporary world of economic and political globalization, Canada, unlike other parts of the world, shows little sign of any revitalized nationalist impulses" (237). However, in the case of Australia, there certainly is considerable evidence of a people attempting to define nationhood – perhaps best exemplified in the current lively debate on whether Australia should sever all constitutional ties with Britain and become a republic with its own head of state. While it would be simplistic to describe the opera *Voss* as grappling directly with these issues, it could be argued that they are a recurring subtext through the work.

* * *

In the central character of the explorer Voss, two potent European concepts are united: the hero and the quest. The title character is based on the historical figure of Ludwig Leichhardt, the German explorer, whose third expedition across Australia disappeared without trace in the 1840s. Voss combines aspects of the tragic hero of Western epic tradition such as Odysseus, Heracles, and Jason with strong elements of the grail legend that developed during the Middle Ages. The strongly Christian and mythical structures of the novel have been noticed by several commentators, and Joan Newman sees the journey as "both a physical and a spiritual one, not only an expedition into the interior of the continent, but a quest into the inner being of his own self" (109). She draws interesting parallels with Dante's *Divine Comedy* where, she argues, "the protagonist's self is an inner essence, the soul, which must journey through Hell and Purgatory towards a revelation of divine love". However, she qualifies Voss's journey as commencing with his characterisation as "a modern existential hero for whom the soul is in doubt and the psychic self a wasteland" (109).

In the first scene of the opera, before the expedition has set out, Voss is forced to reply to repeated questions from the principal sponsor of the expedition, the merchant Mr Bonner, about the importance of maps[8]. Voss exclaims:

> I do not need a map. The map is in my head [...] I have imagined it. Now it must be found. It is a country in search of its spirit. I am that spirit. I will make my own map. The country is mine. I have only to walk into my kingdom. (Meale/Malouf 39-41)

For Bonner, maps are a physical entity representing something which can be valued in terms of profit, whereas for Voss they are an irrelevance; whether mapped or not, the country is a space to be explored and dominated spiritually. Bonner, as the representative of pragmatic mercantile colonial values, is out of his depth in a metaphysical discussion of this kind and attempts to convince Voss of the fact that names have already been impressed on the land. Voss's response is typical:

> Names are nothing. We do not possess things by giving them a name. We must become them. (43)

This exchange is emblematic of the wider post-colonial debate that concerns the construction of 'place' and the ability of the 'old' language of the settlers to describe the new and unfamiliar conditions[9]. Roslyn Haynes traces a

---

[8] David Malouf, the librettist, has also been strongly concerned in his own novels with the symbolism of maps. Amanda Nettelbeck discusses this theme in relation to several of Malouf's novels and remarks that the term 'Australia' suggests that

> its geographical location on the world map merely touches the surface of a more complex question of definition. This is a question which is rooted in Australia's memory of white settlement, and which has to do with the ways in which its territory is mapped out in the minds of those who inhabit it. (2)

[9] As Ashcroft/Griffiths/Tiffin (1989) express it: "[t]he gap which opens between the experience of a place and the language available to describe it forms a classic and all-pervasive feature of post-colonial texts" (9). Nettelbeck remarks that "[t]he crisis of 'place' and belonging [...] reflects the colonial legacy of a perspective divided between the edge of Australia and the somehow more real norm of Europe" (2). Malouf, in an interview with Paul Kavanagh (in Nettelbeck), remarks:

> What we had was a highly developed sense of language and names for everything, and a reality in front of us that did not fit [...]. It does throw us back on a very keen sense of

progression in the novel from the colonial to the post-colonial, arguing that "[i]n post-colonial terms, *Voss* retraces European attitudes to the land, from desire for conquest, whether scientific or geographic, and ownership of the land, to appreciation of the Aboriginal understanding of being owned by the land" (240). For the title figure it is a journey of self-understanding which he has to undergo and which will change his desire to possess the land to his being ultimately (literally as well as figuratively) possessed by it.

This theme is further expanded in the opera when Bonner pleads with Voss that "men need a map" (48)[10]. Described as "breaking out of his dream", Voss turns to Bonner and says: "If I fail, Mr Bonner, I will write your name and your wife's name on a paper, seal it in a bottle, and bury it beside me. So that your name will be perpetuated in Australian soil" (49). In musical terms this is declaimed over orchestral silence with a directionless vocal line[11]. This lack of orchestral comment reflects something of the meaninglessness of the gesture and draws particular attention to the words of Voss's promise with its implicit mockery of colonial aspirations[12]. For Mr Bonner the act of naming something is, in some sense, an act of taking possession. The futility of this action that Voss describes and the mocking tone that he uses, deflate the pomposity and arrogance of the settlers' attitudes to the new country. Bonner's insistence on naming things betrays an insecurity and lack of understanding on the part of the settlers which will

---

loss [...]. If there is anything like the fall that I believe in, it is that fall which is peculiar to Australia in which the landscape and the language are not one. (Quoted ibid.)

[10] Haynes remarks:

Voss's own desire for conquest re-enacts the ambition of Western culture to colonise the continent intellectually by locating it within an explanatory scientific ideology [...]. As an essential part of [this attempt] Voss proclaims himself the map-maker of the continent [...]. However, during the expedition such simplistic notions of owning and mapping territory are subverted. White insists on a more complex arena of exploration that encompasses the internal, the spiritual. In this sense *Voss* can be seen as a precursor of revisionist and particularly feminist geographies with their insistence on the inadequacy of the grid map as an explanation of the land. (241)

[11] For a discussion of the use of the orchestra as narrator see Halliwell, "Narrative Elements in Opera".

[12] This orchestral 'silence' can further be seen as symbolic of the "profound silence between cultures which [...] cannot be traversed by understanding" (Ashcroft/Griffiths/Tiffin [1989] 86); the 'gap' between Mr Bonner's world and that of the desert cannot be bridged.

only be overcome when they, like Voss and Laura, identify both physically and spiritually with the land rather than seeing it purely as something to be exploited. Voss's gesture also looks forward to the fate of his letter to Laura that is torn up by the expedition's aboriginal guide, Dugald. Later, Laura's prayers for Voss's safety are described by Voss in the novel as "little pieces of white paper [...] fluttering" (90). This accumulation of imagery illustrates the ironic scrutiny to which language and writing are subjected in both novel and opera, a process that locates both works within post-colonialism[13].

* * *

> No libretto can reproduce the novel from which it is drawn. A novel, especially a great one, is itself unique, irreplaceable. The best a libretto can do is reproduce the experience of the book in a new and radically different form. (Malouf, "Essay")

This is how David Malouf articulated the challenge he and composer Richard Meale faced in adapting the novel for the lyric stage. The opera itself can, in wider terms, also be seen as a meditation on many of the problems of the operatic adaptation of literature in general. Music is both symbolic and semiotic and opera operates on the edges of language – it is simultaneously a verbal construct as well as transcending verbal communication. The words in opera are both language and music – in effect, a metalanguage. The music amplifies the meaning of the libretto by helping to extend the context of the verbal text in creating the unique world of the opera. It has been argued by Ashcroft/Griffiths/Tiffin (1989) that it is primarily through language and writing that post-colonialism defines itself by "seizing the language of the centre and re-placing it in a discourse fully adapted to the colonized place" (38). Language and the possibilities of its transcendence are vital thematic

---

[13] Just as language is a central theme in *Voss*, so it is in the fiction of Malouf. Nettelbeck remarks:

> Language in particular plays an important role in his novels as the means by which the world is imagined in terms of the speaker's experience. In Malouf's fiction, the disabling aspect of inheriting a language which doesn't fit the landscape is turned around to become an enabling aspect: the process of mapping out and naming the world in terms of experience allows for new kinds of maps to be drawn, for old myths to be revised and updated. (4)

concerns of both novel and opera. However, the opera further extends this investigation into the viability of traditional operatic discourse in the post-colonial situation. If anything, the librettist Malouf has more strongly focused the theme of language than was evident in White's novel[14].

The libretto concentrates the focus on Laura and Voss, using a method comparable to the novel's in its construction. The opera follows the broad outline of the novel with, obviously, much detail being left out, and it reveals a flexibility of construction in its deployment of the original text of the novel. The text of the libretto is almost wholly taken from the novel but lines and scenes from different parts of the novel are merged in a similar way to the novel's method of counterpointing 'reality' with dreams and visions. What Walsh has described as the novel's characteristic "freedom from realistically objective description" (34) is particularly amenable to opera's fundamentally anti-mimetic bias and especially to this opera's insistence on absolute flexibility in temporal and spatial representation.

White's novel already possessed certain features that facilitated its trans-lation from page to stage. Veronica Brady notes qualities in White's novels which distinguish them from most others and which suggest their potential suitability for operatic adaptation. Characters in most novels, she argues, are motivated by "social ambition and erotic desire" while the motivating force in White's novels, and particularly in *Voss*, she suggests, is a "heroic long-ing" which calls upon characters to "contest the normal conditions of exis-tence" and which lends these figures "epic stature" (113). Music has the power to amplify mundane characters and Laura and Voss, who in the book start out as larger-than-life characters, assume an almost heroic aspect in the opera[15]. They both dominate the opera, perhaps even more than they do the novel. Both the heroic aspects, and certain melodramatic elements in the novel, are important factors in its suitability for operatic adaptation. In many

---

[14] Malouf's own concerns with the concept of language are well known. In an interview (in Nettelbeck) he articulates his view, stating that "the medium through which we finally understand things and make them available to ourselves as areas of action is language itself – the articulating of spaces is what allows us to move" (44).

[15] Opera's inherently magnifying properties facilitate the translation of figures in literature exhibiting these characteristics. Gary Schmidgall notes that operatic characters generally tend to "test, force, sometimes violate [...] the standards of normal customary behaviour. They show us the unimagined possibilities for good and evil" (9).

ways these are characters in a novel who 'cry out' for their translation into opera.

In a sense the structure of the novel can also be seen as 'operatic'. Although divided into sixteen chapters which first alternate between Laura's 'world' and that of Voss, and then merge these two locations, there is a fluidity and a resistance to linearity which finds a particularly operatic parallel in the vertical operatic ensemble. The fictional structure also reflects aspects of the Aboriginal concept of time as cyclical with the past being recoverable in the present, and it is in the realm of dream where the European and the Aboriginal systems are synthesised. It is this aspect of communication that the opera is able to effectively explore in music, with elements of the past and present seeming to co-exist[16].

The issue of language and communication becomes even more explicit as the opera proceeds. In the first act of the opera, the title character sings a song in German[17]. Laura's reaction to the song, and the subsequent exchange, is ambiguous: "That was very – German, sir" (Meale/Malouf 86), she says. Voss counters with the remark: "There is no translation", to which Laura replies: "I know. Poems will not bear it. They remain themselves. We

---

[16] White himself commented that he was determined to prove that the Australian novel was "not necessarily a dreary, dun-coloured offspring of journalistic realism", maintaining that in the novel he attempted to create "the textures of music, the sensuousness of paint [...] to convey through the theme and characters of Voss what Delacroix and Blake might have seen, what Mahler and Liszt might have heard" ("Prodigal Son" 40). John Weigel, employing an appropriate musical analogy, remarks that incidents are "treated polyphonically rather than chronologically; that is, events happen simultaneously in different places" (49). As the physical distance between Laura and Voss increases so too does their sense of closeness. The opera is able to achieve this with an astonishing simplicity and directness.

[17] This is, of course, an ideal opportunity for the composer and librettist to provide a song for Voss as an equivalent of the poem he reads in the novel. What is used is Goethe's poem, "Jäger's Abendlied", which is, of course, a well known text in its own right as well as being better known in the famous setting by Franz Schubert. Many in the audience will recognise the words of the song, even though they are in German, but not the melody as they will have the melody of the Schubert setting in their mind's ear. Here is a deliberately reflexive moment even though the song springs out of the action. Voss is, at this moment, a singer performing to an 'audience' – Laura (and, of course, the 'real' audience) – executing a song that seems to be well known but is not. And the words of the song have a prophetic quality in that the narrative of the poem has implications concerning the situation facing Laura and Voss themselves. It is a moment of reflexivity which Dallenbach describes as "the *mise en abyme*, as a means by which the work turns back on itself, appears as a kind of reflection", and which functions as an "internal mirror that reflects the whole of the narrative" (48).

lose the words but catch the music" (ibid. 86f.), thus succinctly articulating the opera's concern with the power and 'truth' of non-verbal communication compared with the unreliability of words. This is underlined by Voss's remark "I try to catch your music" (ibid. 87), and is an indication that the real communication between them occurs on some level beyond the purely verbal, even when face to face. (In fact, the exchanges in their three brief encounters in the novel are characterised by extreme awkwardness on both a verbal and physical level, although one is aware of the beginning of a psychic communion.) Music in itself is not a discrete 'language', but the fusion of words and music into operatic discourse is a kind of metalanguage that transcends both the purely verbal and musical, more connotative than denotative. In this opera the music in which these characters exist, is analogous to the dreams and visions in the novel through which the main communication between Voss and Laura takes place.

At the beginning of Act Two Voss once again sings a song in German. This is taken from the novel where it is described in vivid musical terms:

> He was singing, too, in his own language, some shining song, of sunlight and of water-falls. As the words of the song were few, or those with which he was familiar, they would recur, which stressed their shape, and emphasized their mystical errand in the silence of the gray bush [...]. Voss was jubilant as brass. Cymbals clapped drunkenly. Now he had forgotten the words, but sang his jubilation in a cracked bass, that would not have disgraced temples, because dedicated to God. (White, *Voss* 143-144)

Here White seems again to allude to the impotence of words which, in this passage, are superseded by purely musical vocalisation. One has a sense of the potency of the raw sound of the voice as opposed to its use as a means for communication[18]. The fact that both songs are in German and were

---

[18] Jeremy Tambling describes the grain of the voice as encompassing the "materiality of the voice itself, the sense of the body in the voice as against its use as an instrument for communication purposes" (51). This points back to a continual tension between words and music. One can see in this tension an analogy with what Michel Poizat describes as the conflict between reason and emotion in the appreciation of opera where one feels a "radical antagonism between letting yourself be swept away by the emotion and applying yourself to the meaning of each word as it is sung". Poizat explains moments of *jouissance* as those instances when "language disappears and is gradually superseded by the cry, an emotion which is expressible by the irruption of something that signals the feeling of absolute loss, by the sob; finally a point is reached where the listener himself is stripped of all possibility of speech" (199).

probably unintelligible to most of the Australian audience emphasises Malouf's and Meale's similar concern with the limits of language as communication. Even though they can converse perfectly well with each other, Voss and the settler community of Sydney do not have a 'language' in common – effectively they cannot communicate. However, although the expedition members and the two aboriginal guides do not have a 'verbal' language in common, this does not limit their ability to communicate non-verbally. There is a great irony in Voss addressing Dugald in German, a language which is 'twice removed' from his comprehension. Voss says, "Wörter haben keine Bedeutung" ('words have no meaning'), they are "Irrsinn" ('madness'); this is a word Voss utters frequently in the opera when under physical or psychological stress. His path back to sanity, humility and wholeness is not through verbal communication but through his psychic exchanges with Laura[19].

Later in the act Voss once more addresses Dugald in German:

Carolyn Abbate describes the autonomization of the human voice that occurs in all kinds of vocal music, remarking that

> the sound of the singing voice becomes, as it were, a 'voice-object' and the sole center for the listener's attention. That attention is thus drawn away from words, plot, character, and even from music as it resides in the orchestra, or music as formal gesture, as abstract shape [...]. When opera allows itself to project this voice-object, it also runs into peril – for [...] the 'presence of the performer' may well suddenly emerge to impede the listener's contemplation. We are aware at these junctions – painfully, if the high C is missed – that we witness a performance. (10)

Catherine Clément describes the music in opera as "the word's unconscious", and claims that

> in a world where the unconscious takes up so little room, where so much is made of spoken words, as if they meant what they said, with no past and no roots, we have the opera, where the conscious part, the part played by words, is forgotten. No doubt it is because opera is the place for unformulated dreams and secret passions, a place Brecht saw as the link between pleasure and unreality. Consequently, the less one hears the words, the greater the pleasure. (21)

[19] Joan Newman has described how White, in the novel, has in the character of Laura embodied

> the various elements to be found in the wise guide of ancient legends and great epics. In Jungian terms, Laura is Voss's anima, the female aspect of his own personality which he initially denies, but eventually accepts. In acceptancing her tenderness and humility he becomes complete. (111)

Dugald, hör wohl zu. Tomorrow you will leave for Jildra. Verstanden? I write paper. I give letter. Verstanden? (Meale/Malouf 221)

Voss persists in speaking to Dugald and Jackie in broken German and English, making verbal communication almost farcical in this situation. What now occurs, in a mime sequence, is stated in the stage directions:

> During the following duet [Dugald] begins to dance as if in a trance. He casts off his frock coat, he opens the bag he carries and takes out the letters. Slowly he tears them up and scatters them. (222)

In the opera it is solely through gesture that Jackie and Dugald communicate and their dances assume a ritualistic quality which can be seen in relation to the larger structures of ceremonial movement which characterise the opera[20]. (The sedate quadrilles which open and close the opera are counterpointed with the wild, distorted dances which occur both in Sydney and the desert during Voss's and Laura's psychic disturbances – emblematic, perhaps, of atavistic instincts that are suppressed by the European settlers.) Dugald's dance is part of the metalanguage of the opera[21]. The fact that both characters are mute in the opera – although not in the novel – seems to be a telling commentary on the status of aboriginal people in contemporary Australia. The composer and librettist portray them as 'voiceless' in terms of their political and social situation in the country, yet able to communicate in ways that remain closed to the whites, although Voss and Harry gain some insight towards the end[22]. The opera seems to take up issues of social justice, land rights, and other burning issues in contemporary Australia

---

[20] In the novel, the songs of the aboriginal guides feature prominently and Voss is aware of the ability of the aboriginals to communicate without words:

> Voss [...] [was] sustained by a belief that he must communicate intuitively with these black subjects, and finally rule them with a sympathy that was above words. In his limpid state of mind, he had no doubt that the meaning of the song would be revealed, and provide the key to all further negotiations. (334)

[21] These dances can be interpreted as part of the aboriginal's "unique conception of textuality" wherein the "land itself is constituted as a text of the dreaming" (Ashcroft/ Griffiths/Tiffin [1989] 144).

[22] The depiction of the aboriginal characters in the opera is an expansion of their role in the novel where they "serve to emphasize the differences between white forms of land-possession – philosophical projection or verbal claim – and actual understanding" (Scheckter 138).

which were not as pronounced during the period of the gestation of the novel[23].

In the novel, the main avenue of communication between Voss and Laura, once the expedition has left Sydney, is through the dreams and visions that both experience. It is through the music that this essentially non-verbal form of communication is successfully conveyed in the opera where the interweaving of their distinctive musical identities in the form of duets, which occur more frequently as the opera progresses, suggests that their mental empathy becomes so complete that it transcends the need for physical or verbal communication. In the novel, by far the most significant development of the relationship between Voss and Laura takes place in dreams and visions, and their metaphysical and psychic union precludes the necessity for physical contact. Such a relationship would obviously lend itself to musical amplification, which conveys the emotional and the psychological so much more effectively than the physical. As Annie Patrick points out, one of the strengths of opera lies in its "challenge [to] narrative convention" in which the "spiritual dimension is an inbuilt component of the art form, as independent vocal lines can be voiced simultaneously in a vertical ensemble that communicates over individual boundaries as well as time and space" (137). Malouf notes that the "problem for a librettist is that it is too natural. What was daring in the novel might seem, on the stage, to be merely conventional"[24].

---

[23] In many ways both these incidents as portrayed in the opera encapsulate several important post-colonial themes in White's novel while, at the same time, pointing towards the fundamental word/music debate that has concerned operatic practitioners since the origins of the art form in the late sixteenth century. It is the successful fusion of these two elements that is the ultimate goal of composers and librettists – a fusion that seeks a different level of communication, a realm beyond the purely verbal and the purely musical – a metalanguage.

[24] Malouf has articulated what it is in the novel that facilitated its translation into opera:

[T]he relationship between Voss and Laura Trevelyan [...] has always seemed to me to be essentially operatic. They meet only three times. Their communion after that is entirely by letter or (and this is one of the book's most daring moves) in some spiritual dimension where space, time and the barriers of the individual soul are immediately dissolved.

I call this daring because it is, in fictional terms, non-realistic and challenging of the normative narrative conventions. But music is itself such a dimension. Voices exist in it with no question about the physical distance between them or whether they are audible to one another [...]. This unique characteristic of opera – its ability to give voice

The second act of the opera is increasingly characterised by episodes
where music explores the space between the social realism of Sydney and
the quasi-religious intensity of the occurrences in the outback. Laura's
moment of epiphany during the funeral of Rose, where she experiences an
essentially religious oneness with the land, is counterpointed with the
Christmas Day celebrations in the outback where Voss is unable to accept
the 'eucharistic' offering of Judd, symbolic of the loss of a potential
moment of 'communion' between the men. The ritualistic deaths of
Palfreyman and Le Mesurier (with their echoes of Amfortas and the grail
legend in Wagner's *Parsifal*, a seminal work in the operatic tradition which
adumbrates many themes in Meale's *Voss*) also have obvious religious connotations, an important aspect of the strongly developed ritualistic element
in the opera culminating in the ceremonial death of Voss himself. The
physical horror of their deaths is subsumed in a transcendental spiritualisa-
tion. Jackie, Judas-like, severs the head of Voss with the knife he had
received from him. Voss's cry: "*Oh Jesus, rette mich nur. Du lieber*"
(Meale/Malouf 320), has some of the despairing quality of Christ on the
cross and the ritualistic quality of Laura's words:

When man learns that he is not God,
then he is truly nearest God.
And Man is God decapitated. (Ibid. 321)

The ritual is emphasised in visual terms through her standing behind Jackie
and seeming to 'assist' him in the decapitation. As Voss 'achieves' a final
transcendental humility, the ultimate stage of "God into Man. Man. Man
into God" (ibid. 322), he becomes visual myth in a spectacular 'coup de
theatre'. The statue of Voss, in a moment reminiscent of *Don Giovanni*,
suddenly 'appears' at the back of the stage and dominates the final scene of
the opera. Man has become colonial myth – he has become 'God'.

* * *

simultaneously, in vertical ensemble, to characters who may be speaking out of
different worlds and different world views, and from different places – makes the long-
distance communication of Voss and Laura the most natural thing possible. ("Essay")

However, it is in the epilogue of the opera where many of the themes touched on in the earlier part of the work are most fully explored. This scene captures much of the spirit and substance of the final chapters of the novel and is a recreation of the party set in the house of Belle and Tom Radclyffe on the day of the unveiling of the statue of Voss, twenty years after the disappearance of the expedition. It is a scene reminiscent of the typical final transformation scene of comedy where tangled strands of the plot are unraveled and this analogy is heightened by the pervasive presence of theatrical imagery. At the centre of proceedings is Belle, who, in both novel and opera, is developed as a transitional figure between the colonial and the post-colonial state. She obviously does not endure the same transcendent experiences as Laura, but she is treated with a degree of sympathy and respect which acknowledges a greater dimension to her than that granted to the other members of Sydney society[25]. Belle welcomes the assembled guests with a strange, yet significant speech:

> I have asked you all tonight because I value each of you for some particular quality. Is it not possible for each to discover, and appreciate, that same quality in his fellow-guests, so that we may be happy together in this lovely house? (White, *Voss* 435)

This speech is incorporated verbatim into the opera but with the important addition of the final phrase, "and in this country of ours" (Meale/Malouf 326). This suggests that composer and librettist were fundamentally concerned with the concept of national identity and inclusivity, an issue even more current in the '80s and '90s than in the '50s of the novel. This investigation of the concepts of aboriginal land rights and the status of the settler community firmly locate the opera in the post-colonial realm.

The use of the chorus in the final scene of the opera is significant. The chorus music is, at times, deliberately banal – most frequently they sing along to the authentic dances by the nineteenth-century Australian composer, William Ellard, whose contemporary quadrilles Meale has incorporated into the opera and which were first heard in the opening scene. These are accompanied by a piano and the quotidian quality of this instrument and

---

[25] Brian Kiernan remarks that Belle "grows to experience fulfilment of self within the social and natural world, instead of standing off from life, as Laura does, or escaping from it, as Voss (ironically) does" ("The Novelist and the Modern World" 13).

the simplified choral writing, when contrasted with the power of the full orchestra, deliberately produce the aural effect of a shallow society which is smug and secure in its attitudes – completely at odds with Voss and Laura, and certainly with the country 'out there' (the banal rhymes they sing further contribute to this effect). In the final scene, the choral music of the opening scene is repeated, suggesting that nothing in this society has really changed in the intervening twenty years, its values are still fundamentally the same[26]. It will erect a statue of Voss but it has come no closer to understanding him. The children play a game of "blind man's buff", symbolic of the fact that their adult society is still 'blind' to the realities of the country in which they live: they have not yet awakened to its possibilities as Belle has, and remain huddled on the periphery – 'fringe-dwellers'. As in earlier sections of the opera, the blandness of the music immediately warms when Laura (or Voss) becomes engaged in proceedings. The chorus can be seen as the dominant voice of society while Voss and Laura remain clearly identified as the 'other'[27].

This final scene also functions as a re-evaluation of the status of Voss himself. Judd, who is the sole survivor of the expedition, describes the end of the expedition to Laura. He confuses Palfreyman's death with that of Voss, which he did not witness, and in the process helps to establish the myth that will take root. As Newman observes: "although the facts of the story are incorrect, the myth, it would seem, is true [...] perhaps it would be truer to say that the myths and legends pretexts the events and give them a

---

[26] Linda and Michael Hutcheon note a similar use of chorus in the opera *Louis Riel* by Harry Somers and Mavor Moore. They observe that political scenes set in Ottawa are "accompanied by a kind of banal dance music, as if to underline the manipulative political dance under way. This contrasts sharply with the highly lyrical and melismatic arias of the visionary poet and leader Riel" (239).

[27] Richard Dellamora and Daniel Fischlin argue that

[o]pera frames its narratives in a collective imaginary that follows a particular logic dependent upon a vision of nation as the imagination of a collective will yoked to the common goal of production [...]. Opera produces [...] the public realm of nation, insofar as opera voices an archetypal model of what nation is: a chorus, not always harmonious, against whose backdrop a small oligarchy of soloists intone the desires that give nation its illusory meaning. (3)

Anthony Arblaster, in discussing Verdi's use of chorus, describes how "[i]n it we hear the collective voice of a people, a nation, a community" (99).

shape, a coherence, and a meaning" (116). Laura's comment would seem to endorse this view:

> Knowledge was never a matter of geography. Quite the reverse, it overflows all maps that exist. (446)

The unveiling of the statue elicits the remark from Laura that Voss "is safe now [...] He has been hung with garlands of newspaper prose", deftly joining the two strands of writing and language and their inadequacy to reveal truth, with the wider issue of national identity and the creation of national myths. Laura's comment is in reply to the question of a reporter who suggests that "there are people out there who want to know the truth". Her response is that "all truths are particoloured, save the greatest truth of all. I know nothing" (Meale/Malouf 341). Truth is discoverable only by those who open themselves to the country[28]. The opera intimates that perhaps truth is to be found beyond the verbal and is something which might be communicated through music; the implication is that although music is anchored in the ordinary, it is able to achieve a transcendence which goes beyond purely verbal signification.

Laura's speech to the group assembled round her further draws different thematic strands together. The reporter remarks: "Ah, yes. A country with a future. But when does that future become the present?" (Ibid. 355) The answer to that question is found in Laura's final 'benediction':

> Now. Now. Every moment that we live, and breathe, and love and suffer. Now. Now.
> *(As the others have been moving back, the shadow of Voss's statue falls across the stage. Laura is alone with it.)*
> Voss. Johann, Ulrich my love. You are there still, in the country your legend will be written in the air, in the sand, in thorns, in stones by those who are troubled by it. And what we do not know the air will tell us, the air will tell us. (356-358)

The 'truth' of the country is to be found in complete identification with the land in all its aspects. Voss has been unable to keep his promise to Bonner that his name will be 'written' into the landscape – an empty and meaningless wish in any case. However, Voss himself is now both literally and figu-

---

[28] Kiernan suggests that in the novel the "true nature of Voss's quest remains uncommunicated except to the few who know that the absolute is discoverable within the ordinary universe" (*Patrick White* 64).

ratively 'written' into that landscape, something Bonner will never achieve. The implication is that the colonial quest of possession is fundamentally doomed, truth and knowledge of a country, and, ultimately, possession, can only be achieved by becoming part of that country as Voss, Laura and Belle are able to do[29].

The focus of the scene gradually isolates Laura more and more from those around her and has a similar musical quality to the end of the first act, employing what seem to be similar life-affirming triads in the orchestra, suggesting infinite space and timelessness[30]. This ending provokes Michael Ewans to suggest that the librettist "makes an unequivocal bid to canonise the story of Voss as an emblematic legend of the conquest of Australia"[31]. However, this is somewhat of a simplification as the ending is more equivocal than he supposes. While not denying an element of the celebration of the colonial experience in the verbal text (taken directly from the novel, however, without White's ironic qualifications), one must note that it is not necessarily 'supported' by the music, which is less than celebratory and which seems less 'secure' in its assumptions – the ending is, in fact, somewhat problematised. In this sense, the opera engages in a debate similar to that discussed by Linda and Michael Hutcheon in their article on contemporary Canadian opera. Richard Dellamora and Daniel Fischlin, in their commentary on this article, observe that "the very moment when state patronage

---

[29] Brenda Bosman maintains that in the novel

Laura speaks to the 'pioneers' about speaking – about the languages of art set free from both patriarchy and imperialism, languages, in effect, of a native culture. These are to be part of the country's future, but, predictably, Laura dates that future from the 'now' of the closure of the narrative, in this way subverting the narrator's stated intention to close. Perhaps the story of Voss has already been freed from its confines and made 'native' – the reader cannot fail to recognise the author of *Voss* as foremost of those who, Laura predicts, will write down the legend because they "have been troubled by it" (448), and who have "found the answers to their questions in their native air" (127).

[30] Annie Patrick suggests that "Malouf's epilogue [...] presents Laura as a Straussian heroine, a dramatic soprano evoking the image of her spiritual lover" (139).

[31] Michael Ewans describes the audience reaction to the first performance in Sydney in 1986 as possessing a "tangible feeling of self-satisfaction" (521). He acknowledges the fine performances of cast, orchestra and conductor and suggests that in both audience and performers there was an element of "self-congratulation". He continues: "[i]f we have not just witnessed the Great Australian Opera that will finally establish our nation on the operatic map of the world, we have seen a work that gives good cause to hope that it may be just around the corner." (Ibid. 522)

promoted the development of specifically Canadian opera during the nation's centennial in 1967, Canadian composers were at pains to write operas, admittedly on national subjects, that contest ethnic and linguistic chauvinism" (17). What these operas offer is "an apt warning [...] of the dangers posed by populist nationalism" (ibid. 18). What Meale and Malouf attempt in *Voss* is a similar critical engagement with the idea of nation, however, with a somewhat different view of the future. True nationhood has not been achieved, but the opera depicts a post-colonial nation in the process of constructing a viable identity for itself.

The ending of *Voss*, viewed in conventional operatic terms, is under-stated, in the sense that there is no great choral finale or any of the other traditional climactic and affirming devices. One has the impression that, much as in the novel, the operatic ending resists closure, that the questions which have been raised in the opera have no easy answers, and that it is left to the audience to construct their own 'meaning' from the open-ended nature of this text. One has a sense that the ending of the opera is equivocal in its attitude to what constitutes the nation[32]. The statue of Voss dominates this final tableau as he had dominated everyone while he was alive. Although this seems to realign the focus on Voss and Laura, Laura's words direct the attention away from Voss and herself back towards Australia. The ending of the opera attempts to offer insights into what the term 'Australia' actually means.

Perhaps the main insight is that there is no single meaning, that there is a necessary ambiguity, and that the term finally signifies a typical post-colo-nial hybridity. In a sense the achievement of the novel lies in its synthesis of several binary discursive systems: British – Colonial; Colonial – Aboriginal; social comedy – religious quest. Meale's opera exemplifies this hybridity in offering a parallel attempt at a synthesis of similar binary discursive sys-tems: speech – singing; musical quotation – composition; social dancing – aboriginal dance. As we have seen, some of the debate around the initial reception of the opera concerned whether one could describe Voss as 'the

---

[32] However, there is not the same level of distrust as described by Linda and Michael Hutcheon in their discussion of contemporary Canadian opera which, they maintain, "reflect[s] a deep suspicion of unitary national narratives of identity and an even deeper distrust of the emotional power of nationalism" (238).

Great Australian Opera'. Perhaps this is, ultimately, futile as it can be argued that opera itself is not essentially Australian. Nor would the solution have lain in Meale's incorporating Aboriginal music into his opera. As Michael Ewans maintains, Australians "cannot lay claim to this continent by simply appropriating the music of a vastly different culture. Precisely because [they] are fringe-dwellers – perhaps forever? – the Great Australian Opera cannot be written" (525)[33].

However, I would argue that *Voss* could best be described as a successful post-colonial opera: an eclectic mix of elements drawing upon a four hundred-year-old operatic development and forging a sometimes uneasy synthesis. In countries that have no authentic operatic traditions of their own, any operatic output must naturally draw upon a wide variety of outside sources until an authentic 'voice' can develop. Ewans criticises the opera by contrasting what he sees as White's success in idiomatically evoking the interior of Australia with the opera's lack of a similar evocation of an authentic Australian voice. He remarks:

> White's descriptions were denounced as geographically inaccurate by some early critics of the novel; but his prose is at its most powerful in its evocation of the country that Voss and his party explore. Just like his hero, White invents and creates an interior for Australia – one that is [...] more true to the reality than any geographically literal descriptions could ever be. (Ibid. 523)

Because of the lack of an Australian operatic tradition, Ewans argues, the Australian composer "faces a choice of evils. He or she can adapt an avant-garde idiom [...] or write [...] in a tonal idiom [...]. [This] would leave the composer vulnerable to charges of eclecticism" (ibid. 524). Of course the great operatic composers have grown out of a long tradition that has built upon what had gone before or developed a unique style by drawing upon elements of their own national music, and Ewans's point is correct that this "essential sense of tradition is lacking outside Europe" (ibid. 524). Devel-

---

[33] Australia, as a post-colonial nation, is attempting to find a distinctive voice in the arts as elsewhere, and it is perhaps appropriate that as the last vestiges of colonialism are thrown off with the prospect of republic, opera which is so implicated in the grand imperial narratives, should also be a means whereby the nation finds its identity. Linda and Michael Hutcheon note how the "historical moment of the rise of nationalism in Europe coincided [...] with the moment of European imperialism. In opera as in other art forms, Europe defined itself against its non-European other" (236). In a sense then, one could argue that in an opera such as *Voss*, Australia is defining itself against the European other.

oping a distinctive national 'voice' in opera is a lengthy process, and perhaps is not even possible today in our global village. Eclecticism and hybridity is part of the postmodern and post-colonial condition and one could even argue that there is no longer a distinctive Italian, German or French operatic tradition.

However, one can argue that *Voss* can be seen as a typical product of the post-colonial condition. Its hybridity and eclecticism is its strength rather than a weakness. It participates in the post-colonial process of abrogation and appropriation during which the metropolitan discourse is transformed into one appropriate to the new situation. It looks forward, in perhaps a somewhat idealised way, to a time when a complete artistic fusion between an essentially European art form and the indigenous cosmology might be possible. Its refusal to appropriate elements of Aboriginal music (which has been seen by several critics as a major shortcoming) is perhaps a sensitive recognition that an artificially contrived combination of Western and Aboriginal elements is not the solution. The achievement of an authentic Australian 'voice' is an evolutionary process. For the present, the actual achievement of Meale's and Malouf's opera is to have dramatised the tension between worlds, exploring the space between them.

References

Abbate, Carolyn. *Unsung Voices: Opera and Musical Narrative in the Nineteenth Century*. Princeton: Princeton Univ. Press, 1991.

Arblaster, Anthony. *Viva la Libertà: Politics in Opera*. London: Verso, 1992.

Ashcroft, W. D. "More Than One Horizon". R. Shepherd, K. Singh, eds. *Patrick White: A Critical Symposium*. Adelaide: CRNLE, 1979. 123-134.

Ashcroft, Bill, Gareth Griffiths, Helen Tiffin. *The Empire Writes Back: Theory and Practice in Post-Colonial Literatures*. London: Routledge, 1989.

—, eds. *The Post-Colonial Studies Reader*. London: Routledge, 1995.

Bosman, Brenda. "Alternative Mythical Structures in the Fiction of Patrick White". Unpublished PhD Thesis. Rhodes Univ. 1989.

Brady, Veronica. "The Novelist and the Reign of Necessity: Patrick White and Simone Weil". R. Shepherd, K. Singh, eds. *Patrick White: A Critical Symposium*. Adelaide: CRNL, 1978. 108-116.

Clemént, Catherine. *Opera, Or the Undoing of Women*. Transl. Betsy Wing. London: Virago, 1989.

Dallenbach, Lucien. *The Mirror in the Text*. Transl. Jeremy Whitely with Emma Hughes. Cambridge: Polity, 1989.

Dellamora, Richard, Daniel Fischlin, eds. *The Work of Opera: Genre, Nationhood, and Sexual Difference*. New York: Columbia Univ. Press, 1997 ("Introduction" 1-23).

Ewans, Michael. "*Voss*: White, Malouf, Meale". *Meanjin* 48 (1989): 513-524.

Halliwell, Michael. "Narrative Elements in Opera". Walter Bernhart, Steven Paul Scher, Werner Wolf, eds. *Word and Music Studies: Defining the Field*. Amsterdam: Rodopi, 1999. 135-153.

Haynes, Roslyn D. *Seeking the Centre: The Australian Desert in Literature, Art and Film*. Cambridge: Cambridge Univ. Press, 1998.

Hutcheon, Linda, Michael Hutcheon. "Imagined Communities: Postnational Canadian Opera". Dellamora/Fischlin, eds. 235-252.

Kiernan, Brian. *Patrick White*. New York, NY: St. Martin's Press, 1980.

—. "The Novelist and the Modern World". John McLaren, ed. *Prophet from the Desert: Critical Essays on Patrick White*. Melbourne: Red Hill Press, 1995. 1-23.

Malouf, David. "Essay on the Libretto". D. Malouf. *Voss: The Australian Opera Programme*. Sydney: Australian Opera, 1986. [N.p.]

Meale, Richard, and David Malouf. *Voss*. Sydney: Sounds Australian, 1986.

Nettelbeck, Amanda. *Reading David Malouf*. Sydney: Sydney Univ. Press, 1995.

Newman, Joan. "The Significance of Christian Myth Structures in *Voss*". John McLaren, ed. *Prophet from the Desert: Critical Essays on Patrick White*. Melbourne: Red Hill Press, 1995. 106-117.

Patrick, Annie. "David Malouf the Librettist". Amanda Nettelbeck, ed. *Provisional Maps: Critical Essays on David Malouf*. Perth: The Centre for Studies in Australian Literature, 1994. 133-147.

Poizat, Michel. *The Angel's Cry: Beyond the Pleasure Principle in Opera*. Ithaca: Cornell Univ. Press, 1992.

Scheckter, John. *The Australian Novel 1830-1980: A Thematic Introduction*. New York, NY: Peter Lang, 1998.

Schmidgall, Gary. *Literature as Opera*. Oxford: Oxford Univ. Press, 1977.

Tambling, Jeremy. *Opera, Ideology and Film*. Manchester: Manchester Univ. Press, 1987.

Walsh, William. *Patrick White: Voss*. London: Edward Arnold, 1976.

Weigel, John A. *Patrick White*. Boston: Twayne, 1983.

White, Patrick. "The Prodigal Son". *Australian Letters* 1 (1958): 37-40.

—. *Voss*. Harmondsworth: Penguin, 1974.

Writing About Music
Baudelaire and *Tannhäuser* in Paris

Mary Breatnach, Edinburgh

Baudelaire wrote extensively about painting and literature, and in both types of criticism musical analogies occur with great frequency. They occur in such a way that the meaning attributed to certain key words ("harmonie", "mélodie", "mélodieux", "dissonance") is clear and consistent. It was not until 1861, however, that Baudelaire wrote for the first time about music itself. The essay entitled "Richard Wagner et *Tannhäuser* à Paris" has been hailed as the finest summary of all the tenets of Baudelaire's own aesthetic, and as a fascinating exposition of all the recurring issues of the literary response to Wagner.

Baudelaire identified in Wagner's work an extraordinary affinity with his own. 'It seemed to me', he wrote to Wagner, 'that this music was *my own*'. This paper takes this aspect of Baudelaire's reaction as its starting point. From the opening plea to be allowed 'to speak often in [his] own name' to the final challenge: 'Where have you ever read that great causes were lost in a single round?', an acute awareness of the new ground he is treading informs the work. My purpose is to look in detail at Baudelaire's presentation of arguments and ideas, suggesting that the terms of his presentation are inextricably linked to the particular project of writing a piece of criticism whose point of reference, by its very nature, resisted verbalisation.

"Remontons, s'il vous plaît, à treize mois en arrière, au commencement de la question, et qu'il me soit permis, dans cette appréciation, de parler souvent en mon nom personnel"[1] (*Œuvres complètes* vol. 2, 779). That is the opening sentence of Baudelaire's famous essay, "Richard Wagner et *Tannhäuser* à Paris", which was first published in the *Revue européenne* of April 1, 1861, under the simple title "Richard Wagner". I should like to begin by looking at the second part of Baudelaire's plea, the request to be allowed to speak personally, and I want to look at it in light of a letter which the poet wrote to Wagner on the 17th of February 1860. The subject of the letter is a series of three concerts which had taken place a few weeks earlier at the Theâtre-Italien in Paris. There, on the 25th of January, the 1st of

---

[1] 'Let us, if you please, retrace our steps back over thirteen months to the beginning of the question and may I be permitted, in this critique, to speak often in the first person.' (This and all subsequent translations are my own.)

February and the 8th of February 1860, Wagner had conducted extracts from four of his operas: *The Flying Dutchman, Tannhäuser, Tristan and Isolde* and *Lohengrin*. The occasion marked Baudelaire's first encounter with Wagner's music and was thus, in a very tangible sense, 'the beginning' to which he refers in the opening sentence of his article. Unlike the article, however, which is a thoroughly thought-out and closely-argued piece of musical and aesthetic criticism, written, as Baudelaire makes clear, some thirteen months after the event, Baudelaire's very personal letter to Wagner allows us to share the thoughts and feelings the poet experienced in the immediate aftermath of the concerts.

For obvious reasons, the use of the first person in the context of such a letter can be allowed to pass without comment. On the other hand, the striking mixture of diffidence and confidence with which we are confronted in the opening paragraph merits closer attention. It does so not only because it illuminates some of the ideas discussed in the later essay, but also because it is a very important facet of the private individual for whom Baudelaire asks indulgence in the sentence quoted at the beginning of this essay. Both from the poet's letters and from biographical sources, we know that this mixture was a fundamental aspect of his make-up. T. S. Eliot, for example, considered it to be an intrinsic part of his genius. Writing about him in the 1930s, Eliot said that

> he had the pride of a man who feels in himself great weakness and great strength. Having great genius he had neither the patience nor the inclination, had he had the power to overcome his weakness; on the contrary, he exploited it for theoretical purposes. (231-232)

The ability and, as importantly, the determination to capitalise on his weakness in the way Eliot suggests is without doubt a driving force behind Baudelaire's writing both in his letter to Wagner and in the *Tannhäuser* essay. One might even say it is the main driving force, and certainly in the context of an attempt to understand the significance for the poet of his encounter with Wagner, full recognition of it is of the utmost importance.

To illustrate the point, I want to look first of all at Baudelaire's awareness of his own musical shortcomings. The poet had no technical knowledge of music, and he makes no attempt to hide or minimise that fact. Rather the contrary: he is at pains to underline it. But far from seeing it, or indeed allowing it to appear, as a handicap or as something that might in some way call the validity of his viewpoint into question, he carefully and very consciously presents it as something that lends weight to what he has to say. In the letter, his way of doing so is rather ingenious. Having spoken in very personal terms of his feeling of affinity with the music he had heard, he suggests an equation between superior perceptiveness and a capacity to recognise and appreciate the pertinent nature of that feeling:

> Pour tout autre que pour un homme d'esprit cette phrase serait immensément ridicule [...] surtout écrite par quelqu'un qui, comme moi, *ne sait pas la musique,* et dont toute l'éducation se borne à avoir entendu (avec grand plaisir, il est vrai) quelques beaux morceaux de Weber et de Beethoven[2]. (*Correspondance* vol. 1, 673)

At one stroke, and with consummate skill, Baudelaire achieves three aims. First, he confronts and, by the same token, fends off the danger of being dismissed as inept or presumptuous. Second, he singles Wagner out, paying him a compliment (which is all the more charming for being oblique) by clearly implying that he is a person who possesses the requisite wit and intelligence. Third, and perhaps most important of all, by leaving an unarticulated but none the less powerful suggestion of a kind of kinship between himself and the nameless "homme d'esprit" hanging in the air, he touches on what for him is clearly a momentous matter: the possible existence of an aesthetic bond between himself and Wagner. Having thus established his platform, the poet proceeds without further ado to discuss what had struck him most about the music itself.

In the essay, he adopts a more discursive approach. Having made the initial request for tolerance, he devotes a good deal of the first paragraph to pointing out the possible advantages pertaining to the use of the first person. Far from being irrelevant or unworthy of notice, views expressed from such a personal point of view are, he submits, likely to voice the responses of others who, being quite unknown to the author, may safely be assumed to have arrived freely at the same conclusions. The evident impartiality of these unknown, like-minded persons may indeed serve to neutralise the

---

[2] 'For any but a man of wit and intelligence, this sentence would be immensely ridiculous [...] especially written by someone who, like me, *has no knowledge of music,* and whose entire training is limited to having heard (admittedly, with great pleasure) a few beautiful pieces by Weber and Beethoven.'

writer's inexperience. Furthermore, by implication or association, the latter's independence of mind may actually offset the subjectivity of his approach:

> Ce *Je*, accusé justement d'impertinence dans beaucoup de cas, implique cependant une grande modestie; il enferme l'écrivain dans les limites les plus strictes de la sincérité [...]. Il n'est pas nécessaire d'être un probabiliste consommé pour acquérir la certitude que cette sincérité trouvera des amis parmi les lecteurs impartiaux; il y a évidemment quelques chances pour que le critique ingénu, en ne racontant que ses propres impressions, raconte aussi celles de quelques partisans inconnus[3]. (*Œuvres complètes* vol. 2, 779)

This "*Je*" is, of course, the same 'I' who, in the letter to Wagner, spoke first of a profound sense of coming in contact with something he already knew, and second of an equally strong sense of having a very direct personal relation to the music he had heard. "D'abord", he wrote, "il m'a semblé que je connaissais cette musique, et plus tard, en y réfléchissant, j'ai compris d'où venait ce mirage; il me semblait que cette musique était *la mienne*"[4] (*Correspondance* vol. 1, 672-673).

These claims have given rise to much critical comment, and one reason for that is the way in which they echo the poet's much earlier response to one of his great literary heroes, Edgar Allen Poe. Indeed, it is clear from his correspondence that the feelings he experienced on first discovering Poe's poetry and theoretical works were very similar to those inspired by Wagner's music. For instance, in a letter to his mother in 1854, he spoke of "la ressemblance intime [...] entre mes poésies propres et celles de cet homme [Poe]"[5] (ibid. 269). Even more reminiscent of his reaction to Wagner are the following remarks made in 1864 in a letter to the art critic, Théophile Thoré. Referring to the fact that he had been accused of imitating Poe, Baudelaire talks of certain 'astonishing geometric parallelisms' that can occur in nature,

---

[3] 'This *I*, in many cases justly accused of impertinence, implies however a great modesty; it confines the writer within the strictest limits of sincerity [...]. It is not necessary to be a consummate probabilist to be certain that this sincerity will find friends among impartial readers; there is clearly a chance that the inexperienced critic, in recounting only his own impressions, may also recount those of some unknown supporters.'

[4] 'At first it seemed to me that I knew this music, and later, on reflection, I understood the provenance of this mirage; it seemed to me that this music was *my own*.'

[5] 'the intimate resemblance [...] between my own verse and this man's poems.'

and of his own shock when, on reading a book by the American poet, he recognised in its pages some of his own innermost dreams and thoughts:

> La première fois que j'ai ouvert un livre de [Poe], j'ai vu avec épouvante et ravissement non seulement des sujets rêvés par moi mais des PHRASES pensées par moi et écrites par lui vingt ans auparavant[6]. (*Correspondance* vol. 2, 386)

One can of course read all these statements quite simply as symbolic and somewhat hyperbolic attempts on Baudelaire's part to communicate the intensity of the impression made upon him by what he read or, in the case of Wagner, heard. To take such a view, however, would be to risk mistaking not only the source of the fervour with which the poet set about promoting the reputations of both artists in France, but, more significantly, to underestimate the importance of these encounters for the development of his own artistic vision. A close look at the syntax of the sentence quoted from the letter to Wagner will serve to illuminate the extent to which such personal and apparently subjective reactions informed his aesthetic and were in turn informed by it.

On one level, Baudelaire appears simply to be identifying two equally illusory beliefs: first, the certainty that he was already familiar with the music he was listening to ("que je connaissais cette musique"), and second, the conviction that in some sense he owned that music, that he might somehow have written it himself ("que cette musique était *la mienne*"). Moreover, what on first reading may very well seem to be a straightforward sequential relationship between the two illusions reveals itself, on closer examination, as something quite different. By means of the syntax, the poet edges his readers towards a novel and somewhat unsettling perception: that what he or she first took to be a second illusion is, for the writer at any rate, the reality behind or, perhaps more accurately, beyond the original one. A relation of cause and effect is implied. In Baudelaire's mind, the initial thought that he recognised this music quickly gave way to acknowledgement of a complex psychological truth behind that belief, namely that there existed a very particular, deeply personal connection between him and the

---

[6] 'The first time I opened a book by [Poe], I was both horrified and enraptured to find not only subjects I had myself dreamed of, but SENTENCES conceived by me and written by him twenty years earlier.'

music he had heard. In the context, the use of italics is compelling: it serves to highlight the gravity, the depth, the visceral singularity of the poet's insight. Featured and characterised through the typography, the poet's claim becomes an emblem of the overwhelming and inviolable nature of the feelings aroused in him by this music. To put it more plainly, when Baudelaire says that 'it seemed to [him] that this music was *his own*', he is not only identifying a very real, very private sense of the affinity between his work and Wagner's: he is verbalising what for him had clearly been a momentous flash of aesthetic insight. Entering a realm where thought and feeling are inextricably linked, he is attempting to articulate a belief in an identity at some deep, ontological level, not only between Wagner's creation and his own, but between the creative, aesthetic and imaginative world inhabited by Wagner and the poetic world he himself inhabits. In the essay as a whole, as in his writings about other fellow-artists, in particular Poe and Delacroix, it is clear that the qualities the poet chooses to emphasise are those which, for him, are the hallmarks not only of great art, but, more specifically, of modern art. By the same token, they are qualities with which he seeks tirelessly to imbue his own work. It is thus no exaggeration to say that, through this encounter with Wagner's music, Baudelaire the creator was revealed to himself.

His remarks also fulfil an important purpose in the context of his immediate project. Through them, he succeeds in putting forward a grand proposition, one which will inspire and underpin his argumentation throughout the essay. The proposition is this: artistic experience per se is essentially something that transcends the boundaries imposed by the practice of each individual art form. It is possible, Baudelaire implies, to break free from traditional modes of aesthetic discussion by acknowledging this possibility of transcendence as a reality. Or, to put it differently, it is possible momentarily to peel away technique and technical mechanisms, to penetrate beyond form, beyond all outward appearances, and thus to lay bare the aesthetic common ground of which all artistic endeavour is a creative exploration.

In terms of our understanding of Baudelaire's project, such a reading is illuminating. We are, on the one hand, confronted with a critic who has no knowledge of music – "quelqu'un", as he tells Wagner in the letter, "qui [...] *ne sait pas la musique*" (*Correspondance* vol. 1, 673). But we are also confronted by a critic who is a poet, and for Baudelaire the poet is the best

of all critics. As he says later in the essay: "Tous les grands poètes devien-
nent naturellement, fatalement, critiques […]. Je considère le poète comme
le meilleur de tous les critiques"[7] (*Œuvres complètes* vol. 2, 793). This
belief[8] is one Baudelaire had formulated many years before, when, in his
Salon de 1846, he went so far as to suggest that the ideal critique of any
work of art is its transposition into an alternative art form:

> Je crois sincèrement que la meilleure critique est celle qui est amusante et poétique; non
> pas celle-ci, froide et algébrique […] qui, sous prétexte de tout expliquer, n'a ni haine ni
> amour […] mais – un beau tableau étant la nature réfléchie par un artiste, – celle qui
> sera ce tableau réfléchi par un esprit intelligent et sensible. Ainsi le meilleur compte
> rendu d'un tableau pourra être un sonnet ou une élégie[9]. (Ibid. 418)

The reasons for this conviction are complex and the poet's decision to write
the *Tannhäuser* essay is closely related to them.

The essay is Baudelaire's first and only attempt to write about music, and
the fact that he chose, at such a late stage in his career, to turn his hand to an
entirely new field of criticism is worth dwelling on for a moment. After all,
by 1860, his aesthetic ideas and theories were fully formed, his poetic output was virtually complete, and he had written and published a considerable
body of criticism in the fields of painting and literature. (He had, of course,
started out as an art critic.) That he should write a letter to a composer
whose work he admired and who had, in his view, been treated cruelly and
disgracefully by the French is not in itself surprising: he clearly felt passion-
ately about the hostile press Wagner had received. Furthermore, it was in
character for him to take issue with what he saw as the lack of taste shown
by his fellow-countrymen in artistic and aesthetic matters. But why go
further? Why go out of his way, as indeed he did, to examine Wagner's

---

[7] 'All great poets naturally, inevitably, become critics […]. I consider the poet to be the
best of all critics.'

[8] For an original and illuminating discussion of this aspect of Baudelaire's thought, see
Margaret Miner, *Resonant Gaps: Between Baudelaire and Wagner.*

[9] 'I believe sincerely that the best kind of criticism is that which is amusing and poetic;
not the kind that is cold and mathematical […] which, ostensibly in order to explain everything, contains neither hatred nor love […] but – since a beautiful picture is nature reflected
by an artist, – that which will be a reflection of this picture produced by an intelligent and
sensitive mind. Thus, the best review of a picture may well be a sonnet or an elegy.'

theoretical works in detail and write a lengthy, analytical essay on the basis of his findings?

It has been suggested that what drove him to this was, at least in part, his recognition of a threat posed by Wagner's work to the supremacy of poetry (cf. Lacoue-Labarthe 6-7). But that perception, and certainly the real anxieties pertaining to it, surfaced primarily in the next generation of French poets, in Mallarmé's generation. Baudelaire's purpose in this essay was not to protect the status of poetry or defend it against music. It was rather to examine, in a new context, the criteria pertaining to great art, whatever the medium. What we find here is not a preoccupation with poetry, music or painting as separate practices, but an obsession, first of all, with art as an essential, and essentially multifaceted, human activity, and then with creation and criticism as complementary aspects of the artistic personality. Baudelaire's study of Wagner as an artist in whose work creative and critical faculties are manifestly related is also, and not just incidentally, an exploration and affirmation of the tenets of his own aesthetic. This is the aesthetic of which he was convinced Wagner's work was a magnificent realisation and there can be no doubt that the conviction lies at the root of the poet's very personal reactions to the composer's work.

In a letter written to his publisher, Auguste Poulet-Malassis, on about the 10th of February 1860, Baudelaire goes some way towards confirming this: "Si vous aviez été à Paris, ces jours derniers, vous auriez entendu les ouvrages sublimes de Wagner; ç'a été un événement dans mon cerveau"[10] (*Correspondance* vol. 2, 667). The word "événement'" is significant. In certain contexts – the theatre, for example – it is used to indicate a point of climax or culmination and it is quite plain that the situation Baudelaire describes in his letter to Poulet-Malassis is one in which such connotations apply. The English word 'milestone' might serve well as a translation. Often used abstractly to signal a stage in a process or a turning-point in a life – in other words, to mark some change or event which lends drama to a situation – it has many of the emotional implications of the French *événement*. For Baudelaire, the encounter with Wagner's work was such a milestone. Through it, he reached an entirely new and infinitely deeper level of under-

---

[10] 'If you had been in Paris in the last few days, you would have heard Wagner's sublime works; that was a milestone in my intellectual life.'

standing of the nature of artistic experience, an 'event' whose character he had spent his life trying to penetrate. What Baudelaire needed to do – and here I use the word 'need' to signify an absolute, existential necessity – was to articulate his new-found understanding. In order to do so, he needed to make his own of what he had heard: he needed to take possession of it psychologically.

I said earlier that, until he heard Wagner, Baudelaire never attempted to write any music criticism. That is not, of course, to say that music was unimportant to him, or indeed insignificant in the development of his aesthetic thinking. Far from it. There is a good deal of evidence, both in his prose and in his poetry, to suggest that music aroused in him an intense depth of feeling. The sonnet "La Musique" (*Œuvres complètes* vol. 1, 68), an extraordinary and wonderfully moving hymn to music, gives an especially vivid sense of how Baudelaire was affected by music:

La musique souvent me prend comme une mer!
Vers ma pâle étoile,
Sous un plafond de brume ou dans un vaste éther,
Je mets à la voile;

La poitrine en avant et les poumons gonflés
Comme de la toile,
J'escalade le dos des flots amoncelés
Que la nuit me voile;

Je sens vibrer en moi toutes les passions
D'un vaisseau qui souffre;
Le bon vent, la tempête et ses convulsions

Sur l'immense gouffre
Me bercent. D'autres fois, calme plat, grand miroir
De mon désespoir!

[Music often overwhelms me like a sea!
Towards my pale star,
Beneath a ceiling of mist or in a vast sky,
I set sail;

Chest forward and lungs filled with air
Like canvas,
I scale the back of the gathering waves
That darkness hides from me;

I feel quivering within me all the passions
Of a toiling vessel,
The good wind, the storm and its spasms

Upon the immense gulf
Cradle me. At other times, utterly calm, great mirror
Of my despair!]

In a certain, quite important sense, this poem occupies a unique position in *Les Fleurs du mal*: it is the only poem in the collection whose subject is real music and whose purpose is to communicate a sense of music's effect on the poet as listener. The majority of musical references in Baudelaire's poetry work the other way round: they assume familiarity with the experience of real music and seek, by means of an analogy with it, to convey a sense of some non-musical experience. But in spite of this difference, "La Musique" resembles poems containing such references in one highly significant respect: the fundamental underlying principle is the same in all of them. Functioning on the basis of an explicit analogy or parallel, they oblige us to enter into a kind of pact with the poet. As readers, we are required to accept and relate to the terms of Baudelaire's analogy and our ability to understand the poems is, at least to some extent, dependent on our willingness to do so. In the case of "La Musique", we reach an understanding, first of the feelings aroused in the poem's speaker by real music and then, by extension, of the experience of music itself, through acceptance of the extended analogy drawn between music and the sea.

The role played by musical concepts in Baudelaire's critical writing illuminates and complements that played by music and musical analogies in his poetry. A small group of words occur repeatedly in his discussions of art and literature and constitute an important part of what might appropriately be called his aesthetico-critical vocabulary. Those occurring most frequently are "harmonie", "mélodie" and "mélodieux"; others, such as "dissonance", "dissonant", "discordant" and "mélopée", occur less often. It is clear that Baudelaire's use of these words lay at the heart of his search to illuminate what he considered to be the fundamental problem for artist and art critic alike: the problem first of understanding and then of defining in some precise way how art functioned. By scrutinising the practice even briefly, we can come a little closer to understanding what it was, first about music, but also, and even more importantly, about Wagner that so enthralled him.

I shall illustrate the point by looking at a short passage from the *Salon de 1846*. It comes from the section entitled "De la couleur", in which Baudelaire explores what he calls the 'theory of colour':

> L'harmonie est la base de la théorie de la couleur.
>
> La mélodie est l'unité dans la couleur, ou la couleur générale[11]. (*Œuvres complètes* vol. 2, 425)

Any suspicion one might have that Baudelaire intended these words to refer to sound must quickly vanish in the face of these statements. The deliberate nature of his attempt to put them forward as visual rather than aural concepts cannot be ignored. Yet the connotations of sound do not simply disappear. Baudelaire was undoubtedly aware of this, and if, as his definitions suggest, his use of these words was inspired by a desire to isolate and abstract a quality or qualities shared by the aural and visual experiences of art, it is also safe to assume that he was deliberately exploiting their aural connotations. It is as if he believed he could count on the obstinacy of the sound association to enable him to communicate an experience of colour that was, in some abstract but none the less real and potentially definable way, akin to the experience of musical phenomena such as harmony and melody. This takes us to the very heart of the analogical approach that is the core of Baudelaire's celebrated theory of *correspondances* and indeed of his whole aesthetic. His definition of "mélodieux" a few lines later carries this analogical project even further:

> La bonne manière de savoir si un tableau est mélodieux est de le regarder d'assez loin pour n'en comprendre ni le sujet ni les lignes. S'il est mélodieux, il a déjà un sens, et il a déjà pris sa place dans le répertoire des souvenirs[12]. (Ibid.)

For Baudelaire, the quality of melodiousness is thus one that emanates from a certain use of colour. It comes into existence, not because an artist chooses to paint a certain subject, but because of the way the artist treats that subject,

---

[11] 'Harmony is the basis of the theory of colour. / Melody is unity of colour, or overall colour.'

[12] 'The best way to tell whether a picture is melodious is to look at it from such a distance that one can neither grasp the subject nor the outlines. If it is melodious, it will already have meaning, and it will already have taken its place in the repertory of memories.'

because of the way he applies his paint. This in turn is dictated by a purpose beyond both subject and treatment: art's *raison d'être*, Baudelaire insists repeatedly upon it, is to translate "tout ce qu'il y a d'excessif, d'immense, d'ambitieux, dans l'homme spirituel et naturel"[13] (ibid. 785). It is to reflect "le cœur universel de l'homme" and relate "l'histoire de ce cœur" (ibid. 791). Wagner's greatness was to have done precisely this.

Deeply embedded in Baudelaire's analysis of Wagner's work, and at the root of much of his earlier critical writing, is a wide-reaching exploration of what F. W. Leakey, in a reference to the poet's discussion of the *Lohengrin* prelude, calls "the self-evident 'necessity' of inter-sensorial analogy (or synaesthesia)" (175). At the same time, Baudelaire's decision to write about music heralds the renewal of an ancient musico-poetic polemic on the one hand and, on the other, the emergence in France of a highly influential and creative interest in the art of music that had burgeoned among writers and philosophers in Germany earlier in the century. The philosophical importance attributed to music by Schopenhauer in *Die Welt als Wille und Vorstellung* (1819), for instance, is a landmark in the history of European thought. For him, as for Nietzsche, his disciple, music occupied a privileged position among the arts. What drew such thinkers to music was, essentially, its abstractness. Free from the constraints of representation, music seemed to them to possess a unique capacity to express human passion in the fullest possible way. Without exhibiting ideas, as architecture can do, or representing them, as the arts of painting, sculpture and literature (because of the referential nature of verbal language) inevitably do, music had the potential to offer unmediated access to an intuitive understanding of the nature of human existence and the relationship of humankind to the material world.

Undoubtedly one of the most famous pronouncements made in the nineteenth century about the relationship between music and the other arts was that made in 1877 by the English critic and aesthete, Walter Pater, in his essay "The School of Giorgione":

> *All art constantly aspires to the condition of music.* For while in all other kinds of art it is possible to distinguish the matter from the form, and the understanding can always make this distinction, yet it is the constant effort of art to obliterate it. (132)

---

[13] '[...] all that is excessive, immense, ambitious, in man as a spiritual and physical being.'

For Pater, then, and for many artists and aestheticians of the period, music exemplified a seamless unity between form and content and thus represented an ideal which all creators, whatever their chosen medium, strove to attain. Baudelaire's *Tannhäuser* essay can certainly be seen as a major step in the French literary scrutiny of that ideal. Symptomatic of a further development in the same process was the anxiety felt by his great successor, Stéphane Mallarmé, at what he perceived to be the threat posed by music, and particularly by Wagner, to the supremacy of poetry. When, in response to an invitation from Edouard Dujardin, founder and editor of the *Revue wagnérienne*, Mallarmé came to write about Wagner, Baudelaire's work on the composer's behalf had borne fruit: Wagner had become a cult figure and French *wagnérisme* was in full flood. But Mallarmé held himself aloof from the general enthusiasm. Confronted with Wagner's aesthetic, he, like Baudelaire, felt an urgent need to define his own. Unlike Baudelaire, however, his need was to pit his own artistic aims against those of the composer. He expressed his reservations in a characteristically cryptic article published in 1884 in Dujardin's journal and entitled "Richard Wagner: Rêverie d'un poëte français" (541-546). Yet, precisely because of the nature of his reservations, the writing of this article proved to be as momentous an event for Mallarmé as the 1860 concerts had been for Baudelaire. From 1884 until his death in 1898, in a quest to realise the ideal alluded to by Pater, Mallarmé strove unceasingly to write poetry that would be, in his words, "Musique, par excellence" (381). His ambition was to create nothing less than a new poetic language whose purity and suggestive power would rival and ultimately surpass that of conventional music.

A challenge to music and musicians, and one to which a composer of our own time, Pierre Boulez, responded in an extraordinarily creative way. In the mid 1950s, Boulez used poems by Mallarmé – works that owed their very existence to their creator's attempt to 'take back' from music an allusiveness and suggestive power that he considered to be the birthright of poetry – as the basis for his song cycle *Pli selon pli*. Elsewhere I have discussed the irony of Boulez's choice, but there can be little doubt that this composer's admiration for Mallarmé both as poet and theorist takes us to the heart of certain developments which we, at the beginning of the twenty-first century, have come to see as essential aspects of a modern aesthetic, an aesthetic underpinned by the conviction that crossfertilisation between different art forms is both possible and highly desirable. In a startling and novel way, *Pli selon pli* demonstrates how much contemporary music, as well as contemporary literature and literary theory, owe to Mallarmé's theorising about the relationship between music and literature and the practices he developed on the basis of it. It will not do to leave the matter there, however. We must return to Baudelaire. Poet, critic, above all Wagnerian, he is in many ways at the root of it all. His vision, his courage, the strength of his weakness, to paraphrase Eliot, continue to resonate. If his *Tannhäuser* essay had one overriding motive, it was this: to expose to public scrutiny in one grand sweep the inclusive coherence of an aesthetic that lay behind a poetic output which, in the words of Mallarmé's successor, Valéry, enabled French poetry to take its place as "la poésie même de la modernité"[14] (598).

References

Baudelaire, Charles. *Œuvres complètes.* Claude Pichois, ed. 2 vols. Paris: Gallimard, 1976.

—. *Correspondance.* Claude Pichois, ed. 2 vols. Paris: Gallimard, 1966.

Breatnach, Mary. *Boulez and Mallarmé: A Study in Poetic Influence.* Aldershot: Scolar Press, 1996.

—. "*Pli selon pli*: A Conflation of Theoretical Stances". Walter Bernhart, Steven Paul Scher, Werner Wolf, eds. *Word and Music Studies: Defining the Field. Proceedings of the First International Conference on Word and Music Studies at Graz, 1997.* Word and Music Studies 1. Amsterdam: Rodopi, 1999. 265-275.

Eliot, T. S. "Baudelaire". *Selected Prose pf T. S. Eliot.* Frank Kermode, ed. London: Faber and Faber, 1975. 231-236.

Lacoue-Labarthe, Philippe. *Musica Ficta (Figures of Wagner).* Trans. Felicia McCarren. Stanford: Stanford Univ. Press, 1994.

Leakey, F. W. *Baudelaire and Nature.* Manchester: Manchester Univ. Press, 1969.

Mallarmé, Stéphane. *Œuvres complètes.* Henri Mondor, G. Jean-Aubry, eds. Paris: Gallimard, 1951.

Miner, Margaret. *Resonant Gaps: Between Baudelaire and Wagner.* Athens, GA: Univ. of Georgia Press, 1995.

---

[14] '[…] the characteristic poetry of modernity'.

Pater, Walter. "The School of Giorgione". Walter Pater. *The Renaissance*. London: Jonathan Cape, 1928. 128-149.
Valéry, Paul. *Œuvres*. Vol. 1. Jean Hytier, ed. Paris: Gallimard, 1957.

Do Mallarmé's *Divagations* Tell Us Not to Write about Musical Works?

Peter Dayan, Edinburgh

Mallarmé writes at length about poets and poetic works; but he never writes about musicians or musical works. (Wagner may seem to be an exception to this, but in fact, Mallarmé defines Wagner's operas as poetic works, rather than musical ones.) This is an inevitable consequence of the Mallarmean definitions of music (as opposed to literature) and of critical discourse. Literature begins from facts, from concrete reference, gradually questions factuality and the referential function, and thus points to something beyond, which it can suggest, but not say; the critic's rôle is to follow this process, to start from the particular, the individual, the mimetic, and to examine how, in the text, these categories become problematic. But music, though it can evoke, does not function in the first place by reference; therefore, Mallarmé's critical technique cannot be applied to it. Music remains an essential concept within Mallarmean aesthetics, because it proves that art need not be conceived of as primarily referential; however, the individual musical work is unable to provide the raw material for critical analysis. The question remains: should we consider ourselves bound to emulate this Mallarmean refusal to discuss musical works? The answer would be: to the extent that our critical discourse is based on Mallarmean assumptions, yes; which would doubtless not include 'cultural studies' approaches, but would include those in the tradition of Barthes or Derrida.

The answer to the question in my title (if I may be permitted to give the verdict before the trial) is yes, it seems to me that Mallarmé's *Divagations* (1897) do indeed tell us not to write about musical works. And it is towards that conclusion that I aimed in the paper I gave at the WMA conference in Ann Arbor. Now, in the first place this is a conclusion concerning the theories of Mallarmé, and no one else. I had wondered, before I gave the paper, to what extent this 'Mallarmiste' argument would seem relevant, 101 years after Mallarmé's death. The gratifyingly lively debate that followed the paper demonstrated, fortunately, that it remains very relevant to current theoretical concerns; indeed, that, as literary theorists have so often found, Mallarmé retains an extraordinary ability to spur us to question the fundamental presuppositions of our thinking and writing, and the results of the questioning are always salutary – whether we end up agreeing with

Mallarmé or not. In the course of the discussion, I learnt a great deal from members of the Association who know far more than I do about the theoretical inclinations of contemporary musicology, concerning the ways in which the Mallarmean heritage has been adopted, adapted, or evaded; some pertinent questions were asked (concerning impersonality, for example) which led me to clarify certain parts of my argument. I would like to express my gratitude particularly to Walter Bernhart, Mary Breatnach, John Neubauer, Jean-Louis Pautrot, and Werner Wolf, and apologise in advance for not having followed up their suggestions as far as I would have liked, due to constraints of space and time; I hope to do so in the future.

The text from which I claim to derive the above conclusion is, then, *Divagations*, which is, I think it is fair to say, Mallarmé's aesthetic sum. It was published just a year before his death, and it contains revised versions of, or at least extracts from, all his major theoretical writings. One of the beauties of the book is that I have a concordance to it, of which I have taken full advantage.

In *Divagations*, Mallarmé talks a great deal about music. It is the principal theme of several essays (such as "Plaisir sacré"), and it also recurs constantly as a central concept in his investigation of the nature of all forms of art. The word "musique" occurs more often than "littérature" or "lettres" or "poésie" (though not, I admit, more often than all three together); "orchestre", "symphonie", "chant", "chœur" are all common words, too. But despite the ubiquity of the theme of music in general, there is no discussion of specific composers (with one apparent exception, which I shall deal with shortly); and at no point in the book (with the same apparent exception) does Mallarmé ever cite, name, mention, or even evoke a specific work of music. Music remains, in *Divagations*, a substance, rather than a set of concrete pieces written by individuals.

This is in complete contrast to his treatment of dance, literature and painting. When he is talking about these latter arts, Mallarmé does not hesitate to be specific. Indeed, he names forty poets and a good half dozen painters, as well as several dancers and ballets. The comparison with painting is particularly instructive: Mallarmé writes at length about three individual painters – Manet, Whistler and Berthe Morisot; but outside the essays on those individual cases, the visual arts hardly get a mention. Dance and mime are treated similarly. Music, on the other hand, is never discussed in terms of individual cases, but it crops up incessantly in general discussions on the nature of art. Why this special status of music, this refusal to name musical names? Nor can one explain this away by reference to the biographical fact that Mallarmé didn't know much about individual composers or their works: amateur status never stopped Mallarmé. He writes, as we shall see, about Wagner and *Lohengrin* (the aforementioned apparent exceptions) without ever having seen a Wagner opera; he writes quite happily about dance, about which he certainly knew even less than about music, and he is perfectly prepared to name both ballerinas and ballets.

No, the reason for Mallarmé's exclusion of music from the corpus of works to be discussed is intrinsic to his very definition of music, in opposition to the other arts; and it becomes more or less apparent every time he undertakes to describe the nature of literature. But before investigating that definition, it is incumbent upon me to deal with the apparent exception to the above generalisations: Wagner, on whom there is an essay entitled "Richard Wagner – rêverie d'un poète français", and whose opera *Lohengrin* Mallarmé mentions in order to express his disgust at the way performances of it in Paris were halted by germanophobes in 1887. This apparent exception is not difficult to explain away; all one has to do is to demonstrate that Wagner, for Mallarmé, is not a musician, and *Lohengrin* is not a musical work.

I shall begin this demonstration from the one sentence in the whole of *Divagations* in which composers other than Wagner are named. Here it is – or rather, part of it (the whole of almost any Mallarmean sentence is too much to digest in one go):

> Chez Wagner [...] je ne perçois, dans l'acception stricte, le théâtre [...]; ni sa partition du reste, comparée à du Beethoven ou du Bach, n'est, seulement, la musique. (237)

Which one might attempt to translate thus:

> I do not see in Wagner's work theatre in the strict sense; nor, one might add, is his score, compared to Beethoven or Bach, simply music.

Unfortunately, that translation obscures entirely the main point I want to make about the passage. "Comparée à **du** Beethoven ou **du** Bach", writes Mallarmé (my emphasis). I crassly translated this, as I expect anyone spontaneously would, "compared to Beethoven or Bach"; which gives no hint that in the word "du" we have that inimitably French article known as the partitive. The partitive, as one tells one's students in their grammar classes, designates an indeterminate quantity of an uncountable substance. Here, indeed, we have two partitives, separated by an "ou"; which implies that the two uncountable substances, Beethoven and Bach, are in fact, for present purposes, interchangeable. They are merely representative examples of that larger uncountable substance known as Music.

Now, Mallarmé never refers to literature, painting or dance in this way. I'm sticking my neck out a bit here – I confess I haven't scrutinised every proper name in his collected works – but I would be willing to bet that he never precedes the name of a poet or of a painter with a partitive. He never says "du Shakespeare", "du Baudelaire", "du Manet" or "du Whistler". And there is a simple reason for that. Mallarmé, and in this he is the clear fore-runner of Derrida, is obsessed by the proper name, by the logically impossi-ble but necessary uniqueness of the individual author and of each individual work. I shall return to this theme; suffice it to say here that at the very heart of his analysis of literary works is his emphasis on their singularity[1]. A poem is not simply part of a substance; it betrays aspiration towards that substance known as Art, but it is itself irremediably individual.

The implication, then, is that in this sense, music is essentially different from the other arts. Whereas music appears to Mallarmé as a substance, the other arts are a collection of works, organised under the names of individual creators. Wagner is the borderline case in this. Let us return to that sentence. Its central message is this: Wagner's operas are not exactly theatre, but nor are they exactly music. In the following sentence, as he does half a dozen times elsewhere in *Divagations*, Mallarmé gives a special status to the hybrid genre of music crowned, as it were, by words: he calls it "la Fiction" or, simply, "Poésie"[2]. In other words, once music becomes the ally of

---

[1]   Several recent critics, including Robb and Temple, have commented at length on this Mallarmean obsession with the proper name, and on its inscription into his poetry.

[2]   The sentence following the one quoted above, naming Beethoven and Bach, is this: "Quelque chose de spécial et complexe résulte: aux convergences des autres arts située, issue d'eux et les gouvernant, la Fiction ou Poésie." ('Something special and complex results: situated at the other arts' points of convergence, born of them and governing them, Fiction or Poetry.') Cf. also 237, 246, 270, 283.

words, the words define its genre; it enters the domain of literature, and therefore ceases to be mere substance; it becomes, like all literature, divisible into works. Since Wagner's operas belong to this genre, he is not, strictly speaking, a composer, but a writer; which explains why Mallarmé, who can't write about composers, can write about Wagner. In Wagner's operas, says Mallarmé, "son principe même, à la Musique, échappe" (173); which could, I think – the syntax is ambiguous -, mean either that the very principle of music is absent in Wagner's operas, or that the very principle of Wagnerian drama escapes music; but whichever you choose, the fact is that his work is only technically musical; his scores are "une musique qui n'a de cet art que l'observance des lois très complexes"[3]; aesthetically, they belong to the genre of literature, of fiction or poetry. Which does not mean that Wagner's art is not great art; it simply means that Wagner's art is not music, but poetry, and Wagner is consequently not a musician, but a poet[4].

The case of Wagner thus confirms the proposition that Mallarmé writes about individual poets and poetic works, but never about individual composers or individual musical works.

* * *

One of Mallarmé's favourite metaphors for the literary work is that of the incomplete building. In his preface to *Divagations*, he describes the book as a "cloître brisé", a "broken cloister"; in the essay "Théodore de Banville", poetry is described as a "cri de pierre", a "cry of stone", consisting of "piliers interrompus" (interrupted pillars taking up the image of the broken cloister). This metaphor has a double function. It indicates that the basic matter out of which the poetic effect is built is concrete, solid, and earthbound. Poetry is made up of words, and an inescapable function of words is that they appear to refer to what we call the real world. Mallarmé bemoans this fact (though only provisionally, as we shall see). "Nul n'échappe,

---

[3] 'A music which only has of this art the observance of very complex laws.'

[4] It is interesting to note that Baudelaire, through a different route that I hope to explore in another essay, also arrives at the conclusion that Wagner's music is really poetry: "En effet, sans poésie, la musique de Wagner serait encore une œuvre poétique [...]." ('And indeed, even without the poetry, Wagner's music would still be a poetic work'.); see "Richard Wagner et *Tannhäuser* à Paris" 715.

décidément au journalisme"[5], he complains in the preface to *Divagations*; more poetically, in "Théodore de Banville", he writes: "La Poésie [...] tient au sol, avec foi, à la poudre que tout demeure"[6]. Language must be read as reference to this world; poetry is made of language, and so must similarly be read as reference to this world. It cannot **say** anything other than what happens in this world. However, that does not mean that poetry cannot **suggest** something else; suggestion being what is provided, precisely, by the incompleteness of the poetic work. Unlike a piece of journalism, a poem does not present its function as simply synonymous with what it says. The incomplete building serves to suggest the possible use of an unoccupied space, or rather of a space occupied by thought, but not by things; in poetic terms, this is a space that demands reflection, but escapes precise definition. "Les Divagations apparentes", says Mallarmé in his preface, "traitent un sujet, de pensée, unique – si je les revois en étranger, comme un cloître quoique brisé, exhalerait au promeneur, sa doctrine"[7]. What, exactly, is that subject? Mallarmé does not say, of course, and that is the point; that is why his writing must continue to appear divagations, ramblings. The subject is not in what he has actually constructed – his words are merely the "cloître brisé"; rather, the subject is what is "exhalé" from the book; not said, not concrete, but barely breathed.

The metaphor of the broken building is one of the two main ways in which Mallarmé clearly insists on the status of the literary work as a fragment suggesting a larger, unwritable whole. The other is by evoking the virtual existence of an ideal, absolute, ultimate book, a single perfect work which all poets are eternally trying to write. No one has managed it, of course, but Mallarmé suggests that every poet has to maintain, like him, an insane belief in it. In his famous autobiographical letter to Verlaine, he acknowledges that even he will not actually manage to write it; but he hopes that

---

[5] 'No one escapes, indeed from journalism.'

[6] 'Poetry, such is its faith, is rooted in the ground, in the dust which all things remain.'

[7] 'These apparent Divagations, ramblings, treat a subject, of reflection, one or unique – if I look back on them from outside, as a cloister, though broken, would breathe out its doctrine to the wanderer.'

je réussirai [...] à en montrer un fragment d'exécuté, à en faire scintiller par une place l'authenticité glorieuse, en indiquant le reste tout entier auquel ne suffit pas une vie. Prouver par les portions faites que ce livre existe, et que j'ai connu ce que je n'aurai pu accomplir. (374)

I will succeed in showing one fragment constructed, one facet where its glorious authenticity can be made to sparkle, indicating the whole of the rest for which one life is not enough. Proving by the portions made that this book exists, and that I have known what I will not have been able to realize.

Once again we have here the characterisation of the written work as a fragment, designed to suggest that which goes beyond it. But what is clearer here than in the 'broken building' metaphor is the nature of what goes beyond. It is a single book; universal, therefore necessarily impersonal, impossible to pin down, extant yet invisible and unwritten.

* * *

To sum up: in the field of literature, we have the work, produced by an individual, connected to the soil by its inescapable reference, and fragmentary; opposed to that individual work we have the virtual book, produced by no one, complete, and beyond any set of referents. The aim of critical discourse must always be to start from the former, and direct the gaze of the reader towards the latter, of which it cannot say anything concrete. In other words, the objective of the critic is to follow a poet's language from its vulgar factual reference to its point of ideal dissemination. Hence Mallarmé, reputed the poet of the death of the author, never writes as though authors were dead before we reach them; he begins by taking them alive, names them, characterises them, and then slowly and carefully kills them off.

This process of character assassination leads, as we have seen, to the concept of an ideal and impersonal book. But it also leads, far more consistently, to music, for the simple reason that music is the element in which the poet dies, or rather dissolves.

The broken building and the ideal book serve to indicate that poetry, as written by humans, must always appear fragmentary. But this condition does not apply to music. Music is neither apparently fragmentary, nor apparently written by humans. And to explain the reason for that, I will return for a moment to a path reasonably well trodden by Mallarmistes over the past twenty years: the status of music in relation to signification or reference.

Mallarmé does not, of course, explain this in the post-Saussurian terms to which we are all accustomed; indeed, the terms he uses often seem to puzzle modern readers. But he returns to the theme so frequently and so consistently in *Divagations* that I think one can draw some clear conclusions from it. Music is not a sign, but, as Mallarmé puts it, an ambiance[8]; it does not refer, and if it can be said to evoke, it is not in the same way as poetry, or indeed painting or dance. It evokes a general state, rather than a specific circumstance; and these evocations are always presented by Mallarmé as not rooted in the ground. They are always already, to use Mallarmé's term, evaporated in music. In his essay on the poet Théodore de Banville, after an apparently gratuitous evocation of orchestral music, Mallarmé sums up thus the difference between the art of words and the art of music:

– Quoiqu'y confine une suprématie, ou déchirement de voile et lucidité, le Verbe reste, de sujets, de moyens, plus massivement lié à la nature. (156)

– Although bordering on a supremacy, or rending of the veil and lucidity, the Verb remains, in subject, in means, more massively tied to nature.

Now, one might have thought, from what I have said so far, that if music is less massively tied to nature, that must mean it is aesthetically superior to literature. After all, literature seems permanently to be trying to escape from the bonds of nature. And of course, that is true, in one sense. Poetry must indeed eternally reach towards the unnatural lightness of music. However, this immediate privilege of music is also its aesthetic weakness ("– Quoiqu'y confine une suprématie, ou déchirement de voile et lucidité"). The supremacy of words is precisely that they do not **begin** beyond nature; they **reach towards** the state beyond nature. They begin on the non-ideal, the non-absolute, the human side of the veil, and strive to tear it; therefore, they force us to be aware of the veil's existence. In so doing, they invite a lucid appreciation of the paradoxical nature of the artistic enterprise. Music does not do this.

---

[8]   See, for example, 172, 197, 200, 202, 218.

The next sentence in "Théodore de Banville" is one of Mallarmé's most famous[9]:

> *La divine transposition*, pour l'accomplissement de quoi existe l'homme, *va du fait à l'idéal*. (156)

> *The divine transposition*, for the accomplishment of which man exists, *goes from the fact to the ideal.*

Now, why does Mallarmé put this broad statement of the point of human existence immediately after that sentence on the relationship between word, music and nature? The answer is: in order to bring out the reason why the point of human existence can only be aimed for in words. The transposition goes from fact to ideal. But music contains no facts. It begins and ends in the realm of the ideal. Therefore, it cannot demonstrate the transposition. Words, on the other hand, start from fact, and by demonstrating the unsatis-factory nature of the facts they contain, by the architecture of their frag-mentariness, they can suggest something else. Hence the superiority of poetry over music.

The very function of music in what Mallarmé calls "Poésie" is, indeed, dependent on its referential incapacity. Mallarmé repeatedly states (219, for example) that music is the equal of silence, "égale des silences"; by which he means that it is the opposite of talk, of communication. It says nothing; it explains nothing. Its only "signifiances" are "idéales" (207); a composer of music has "cette facilité de suspendre jusqu'à la tentation de s'expliquer", he is not subject 'even to the temptation to explain himself', and the "sub-limité" of a concert is therefore "obscure" (250). Music certainly demon-strates that art goes beyond that which can be explained or understood, and its function in poetry is to serve as a permanent reminder of this. But that demonstration is not enough. Mallarmé's constant aim is not merely to experience the ecstasy of art, but also to achieve the greatest possible lucid-ity concerning its nature. In a word, Mallarmé demands honesty as well as ecstasy. And that honesty, that lucidity, that authenticity, as he calls it, can-not be achieved either through music, or through an analysis of music. It can only be achieved through a discourse that continually questions both its

---

[9]   And it would be even if I hadn't quoted it in the title of my book on Mallarmé.

relation to the real world, and its relation to art; a discourse that is at once particular in its reference, poetic, and critical. Such is the language of Mallarmé's *Divagations*, of the genre that he termed the "poème critique"; such, too, in a different way but no less clearly, is the language of his late verse, and of *Un Coup de dés*.

* * *

One might recast these conclusions in a more modern perspective as follows: Mallarmé aims for a certain lucidity, which can only be achieved by analysing the dysfunction of reference, the inadequation between what is said and what happens in the text, in a way that renders problematic the status of the signified. This dysfunction of reference is the central characteristic of the representative arts, the arts that consist of signs: literature, painting, and, to Mallarmé at least, ballet. Even if music can be said to consist of signs, however, their primary effect is not produced through a perceived reference to the outside world. A word is always read in relation to its reference; a note of music, though in context it can contribute to an evocation, need not be so perceived. Therefore, music does not have to trouble itself with the dysfunction of reference. One could go further: Mallarmé reserves the label 'music' for precisely that which does not require him to consider the dysfunction of reference (hence the exclusion of Wagner). It means that the average art-loving bourgeois, who does not want to know about dysfunction, is more comfortable with the aesthetics of music than with those of modern literature (and prefers Bach or Beethoven to Wagner). But it means, too, that the work of music is inaccessible to Mallarmean critical discourse. The theoretician of art can discuss the general characteristics of music in opposition to those of referential arts; he can also discuss the social effects, function, and history of music. What he cannot do is analyse a musical work in such a way as to bring out what he is, by definition, looking for in any kind of text; which is the mismatch between the text perceived as communication, and the text perceived as a unique way of indicating that which cannot be communicated.

To put the same argument another way: you will remember the Mallarmean distinction between the individual, written book, and the ideal univer-

sal virtual book. The musical work corresponds to neither. It is not necessarily, self-consciously, inadequate and fragmentary, like the former; nor is
it virtual, like the latter. It is simply outside the opposition between them,
and it therefore offers no point of purchase to the critical discourse based on
that opposition.

Or to put it a third way: the birth of the reader, says Barthes in "La Mort
de l'auteur", must be payed for by the death of the author; to be more precise, as I have suggested, the birth of the critical, lucid reader depends on
the process of assassination of the author, which is accomplished by questioning the illusion of real life created by his work. But the musician gives
no such realistic illusion. Music is experienced from the beginning as
beyond realism, as anonymous.

> Le miracle de la musique est cette pénétration, en réciprocité, du mythe et de la salle
> [...]: absence d'aucun, où s'écarte l'assistance et que ne franchit le personnage. (288)

> Music's miracle is this reciprocal penetration of myth and auditorium [...]: an absence
> of any individual, in which the public gives way and which no character can cross.

Thus the musical performer, to Mallarmé, unlike an actor or a ballerina,
does not have to engage in the task of eliminating his own personality, for
that personality is not an issue. Mallarmé's favourite image for this musical
anonymity is that of the conductor who turns his back on the audience,
having no need to show them his face, "en l'anonymat et le dos con-
venables"[10]. And the aim of the orchestra seems to be to express, not (like
the literary work) the struggle of the author against his condition, but, at a
level which defies conscious representation and therefore escapes language,
that which all, always already, have in common: "les délicatesses et les
magnificences, immortelles, innées, qui sont à l'insu de tous dans le con-
cours d'une muette assistance"[11]. At this level, composer and performer
almost cease to be persons distinct from the listener; music allows communication on a plane that transcends the subject, without needing to erase it.
That is why the subject of music does not appear alive in the same way as

---

[10] 'Anonymously showing his back, as is only proper', 326; see also 281.

[11] 'Those qualities, delicate, magnificent, immortal, innate, which are present, unknown to
all, in the contribution of a silent audience.'

the subject of poetry; therefore, the subject of poetry cannot be killed in the same way, and the reader of music cannot be born.

* * *

Now, whether all this has any relevance to us as modern practitioners of the critical art depends on whether our critical discourse is bound by the same conditions as Mallarmé's. One major modern theoretical approach, certainly, to some extent at least, is not bound by those conditions: that which is generally called cultural studies. Cultural studies seeks not to evaluate works in aesthetic terms, but to situate them in their cultural context. It assumes that there is no point looking for a generally valid answer to the question: what is art? or, *a fortiori*, what is good art? And without these questions, Mallarmé's divagations lose all their focus; for his distinction between music and the representative arts is entirely dependent on his definition of art in general, as distinct, say, from journalism, banal conversation, or noise.

But, although this opposition has, perhaps, been surprisingly little articulated, one of the main theoretical premisses of cultural studies, as indeed of sociology, psychology and the human sciences in general, has a powerful enemy in the post-structuralist tradition whose most famous representatives are Barthes and Derrida. (One might add, as an important link in the chain between Mallarmé's literary heritage and modern theoretical discourse, Lacan.) This tradition perpetuates the basic Mallarmean presupposition that the interest of a text is to be sought by analysis, first, of the ways in which it does not simply refer; second, of how that refusal to be reduced to reference is inscribed in the functioning of the text; and third, of what that inscription tells us about the character of human aspirations. This definition applies, it seems to me, just as well to Barthes's *S/Z* or to Derrida's *La Dissémination* as it does to *Divagations*. It is obvious that certain texts lend themselves to such reading better than others; that some works reward this approach with the perspective of an endless play, while others can simply be 'seen through'. In this tradition, the former category is plainly more highly valued, aesthetically, than the latter. One need only compare *Mythologies*, which is about the culturally transparent, with Barthes's writing on Mallarmé, Proust or Balzac to see the point; indeed, he makes no bones about it in *Le Bruissement de la langue*, nor does he hesitate to proclaim in *S/Z* (10) that "le scriptible est [...] notre valeur", and to elaborate on this theme in *Le Plaisir du texte*. As for Derrida, his very definition of writing makes it plain that some ways of producing and reading texts are of little interest other than historical[12], while others illuminate – and this, I would suggest, is Derrida's value – the implications of the act itself. Nowhere is this clearer than in his very first foray into the field of literary theory, "Force et signification"[13], where, taking his cue explicitly from Mallarmé and from the Mallarmean theory of the unattainable absolute book, he states:

> C'est parce qu'elle est *inaugurale*, au sens jeune de ce mot, que l'écriture est dangereuse et angoissante. Elle ne sait pas où elle va, aucune sagesse ne la garde de cette précipitation essentielle vers le sens qu'elle constitue et qui est d'abord son avenir. Elle n'est pourtant capricieuse que par lâcheté. Il n'y a donc pas d'assurance contre ce risque. L'écriture est pour l'écrivain, même s'il n'est pas athée, mais s'il est écrivain, une navigation première et sans grâce. (22)

> It is because it is *inaugural*, in the younger sense of this word, that writing is dangerous and agonizing. It does not know where it is going, no wisdom is there to save it from this essential precipitation towards the sense which it makes and which is in the first place its future. Yet it is not capricious, unless it be through lack of courage. There is, then, no way to insure against this risk. Writing is for the writer – even if he is not an atheist, provided only that he is a writer – a primary navigation, that knows no state of grace.

Provided only that he is a writer ... it is obvious that for the young Derrida just as for Mallarmé, not everyone who performs the physical act of inscribing words on paper is a real **writer**; writers are those who have the courage to confront the question of what it really means to write. And what does it mean to write? In the first place, to accept that writing is a journey whose destination is always in the future, and never settled or determined.

But does Derrida's crusade against those who try to pin writing down, to give it a goal that could ever become present, have resonance in academe today? I think it does, though of course my perspective is limited. The study of literature in our universities, as far as I can see, is still justified, as it has been for a long time, in two ways: partly on the basis of an appeal to literary

---

[12] And I say that in full awareness of the fact that this use of the word 'historical' contains a value judgement fundamentally at odds with cultural studies.

[13] First published in 1963, and thus pre-dating almost all the works of Barthes mentioned above.

texts as cultural artifacts that can give us a better understanding of the particular culture which they are taken to represent (whence cultural studies); but also partly through an investigation of their function as a special kind of writing, in an important sense *better* than others. Of course, over the course of the past century, our sense of how literary texts are valuable has evolved, and I would argue that it has evolved precisely in the direction suggested by Mallarmé and Derrida: away from the supposition that they could be analysed by reference to a model, and towards the realisation that to read well always involves questioning the sense of the enterprise. One result of this abandoning of the model is that we are no longer able simply to tell our students what constitutes 'good literature', and why. But that does not stop either us or our students from knowing full well that we value certain texts above others, and that we would like the students to understand why, even though that understanding, as Derrida suggests, can never be insured.

In other words, I think it is fair to say that, just like Mallarmé, we investigate value through the inadequacy of reference. But when I say 'we', it will have been plain that I mean teachers of literature. What about musicologists? I am, unfortunately, too ignorant about the field to judge in general terms. But one thing struck me about the papers on the song cycle given at the Ann Arbor conference, and about the discussion that followed them: there was a continued enquiry into the sense of the term 'song cycle', both in its historical context (as it emerged in the nineteenth century), and in its usefulness as a conceptual tool to scholars today; and in the course of this enquiry, questions of organic unity were frequently central. Now, it seems to me unlikely that at any literary conference today (unless it were peculiarly untouched by the last thirty years of theory), such a search for unity and overarching units would have such prominence; precisely because literary theory since Mallarmé (or rather, since Mallarmé was rediscovered in the 1960s) values above all gaps, uncertain futures, the fear of castration, the impossibility of models, the space suggested by the broken cloister. I hasten to emphasize that I am by no means suggesting that the discussion on the song cycle was somehow theoretically backward. On the contrary: my point is that it suggests precisely the difference that Mallarmean theory would predict between musicology and literary criticism. The latter pursues, as I have said, the inadequacy of reference in writing; in that sense one might call it, in spite of all the abuses heaped on the word[14], deconstructive. Musicology cannot do this, because music does not appear primarily to refer; and for that reason, musicology has to be, not deconstructive, but constructive; it has to build a meaning from the musical text, whereas the literary critic is concerned, not with the building, but with its fragmentariness. Like Mallarmé, we can talk about the value and the nature of music as a substance, as an uncountable, in opposition to literature; but the central point of that opposition must remain the fact that literary criticism moves from the distinguishing features of the individual work towards the unsayable, whereas music criticism cannot. So there can be no equivalent in music criticism of works such as Mallarmé's essays on individual poets and literary works, nor of their modern successors such as *S/Z* or *La Dissémination*; and a Word and Music Association should be careful to avoid the fallacy that the techniques of post-Mallarmean literary criticism could be applied to music.

References

Barthes, Roland. "La Mort de l'auteur" (1968). Barthes. *Le Bruissement de la langue*. Paris: Seuil, 1984. 63-70.
—. *Mythologies*. Paris: Seuil, 1957.
—. *Le Plaisir du texte*. Paris: Seuil, 1973.
—. *S/Z*. Paris: Seuil, 1970.
Baudelaire, Charles. "Richard Wagner et *Tannhäuser* à Paris". *Curiosités esthétiques – L'Art romantique*. Ed. H. Lemaitre. Paris: Garnier, 1962.
Dayan, Peter. *Mallarmé's "Divine Transposition"*. Oxford: Oxford Univ. Press, 1986.
Derrida, Jacques. *La Dissémination*. Paris: Seuil, 1972.
—. "Force et signification". Derrida. *L'Écriture et la différence*. Paris: Seuil, 1967. 9-50.
Mallarmé, Stéphane. *Divagations*. Paris: Gallimard, 1976.
Matsumuro, S., N. Takeuchi, M. Kaneko, eds. *Mallarmé's Text Database. Divagations: Text and Word Index*. Tokyo: Taga Shuppan, 1991.

---

[14] Of which my favourite dates back to 1993, when I discovered that the politically correct term for 'car breaker' in French had become 'déconstructeur automobile', and one of the umbrella organisations for the profession had baptized itself GEDAF – Groupement pour l'écologie des déconstructeurs automobiles français.

Robb, Graham. *Unlocking Mallarmé*. New Haven: Yale Univ. Press, 1996.
Temple, Michael. *The Name of the Poet: Onomastics and Anonymity in the Works of Stéphane Mallarmé*. Exeter: Exeter Univ. Press, 1995.

When Is a Text Like Music?

Frédérique Arroyas, Guelph, Ont.

This essay explores interart analogies as they apply to readers' endeavors to deal with musical references in literary works. The effect of reference to music in a text is first examined. As a means of juxtaposing distinct art forms in the mind of the reader, reference may lead to an integration of certain features of a musical object within a literary text. The establishment of similarities and the challenges of difference when comparing musical and narrative forms are considered. Using the particular case of *Fugue*, a novel by Roger Laporte, we see how a 'blended' space which inherits features from both the textual and the musical domains may be constructed and lead a reader to conceptualize a 'literary fugue'.

Introduction : A reader-based approach

Though studying references to music and their relevance in works of literature is a major component of musico-literary studies, little attention has been paid to the cognitive processes involved when readers are confronted with metaphors and analogies that evoke the musical domain[1]. Operations that require the transgression of traditional aesthetic boundaries and the creative work in the elaboration of musico-literary relations need to be recognized in order to attain a fuller understanding and appreciation of interart metaphors and analogies.

This paper explores three meaningful stages in a reader's elaboration of a text-music interface. The occurrence of reference itself is first examined. It is in this preliminary phase that readers may engage in an investigation of the relationships between text and music. The role of reference as a motivational force in the perception of music in literary texts is one that must not

---

[1] Jean-Louis Cupers in his *Euterpe et Harpocrate ou le défi littéraire de la musique* (83) and Werner Wolf in *The Musicalization of Fiction* (72) both indicate, however, that this approach is necessary to account for the complex processes involved in the establishment of music-text metaphors and analogies.

be overlooked, as it is crucial to the mental processes that occur in metaphors and analogies. This leads to the analysis of a second phase involving
the establishment of similarities between distinct art forms. Here cognitive
theories of metaphor and analogy are used to expound on the creative and
constructive components of their integrative processes. I introduce the
concept of a "blended space" (Turner/Fauconnier 183), a locus that allows
for the domains of music and language to intermingle. It is through my own
reading experience of Roger Laporte's 1970 novel, *Fugue*, and the construction of a music-text analogy that I propose tangible examples of this possible
'blended space'. *Fugue* thus serves to illustrate the theoretical foundations
of musico-literary analogy. Lastly, I consider the effects of a text-music
analogy, the extent to which the construction of a 'blended space' affects
perception of the text, how, in other words, it structures its interpretation
and creates new meaning.

1. Factors that contribute to establishing
a reference to music in a text

The first step in establishing a text-music relation depends on a reader's
motivation to do so. Readers may consider that music has a role to play in a
certain literary work. They will rely on a variety of cues that motivate their
investigation of the musical domain and its possible relevance to the literary
work. Establishing reference can simply be a question of relying on explicit
cues in the text, on paratextual indices (outside knowledge gleaned, for
example, from reading an interview with the author where the author
acknowledges being influenced by music) or on the other hand it may
depend on a reader's particular aural perceptions.

An explicit reference to music will inevitably incite readers to seek out
how music may be relevant to a text's interpretation. Consider novels with
references to a generic type of composition in their title: *Fugue, Ricercare,*

Passacaille, Canone Inverso[2]. Just as we expect a musical piece with a title like *Passacaille* to present a specific and characteristic structure, a literary text with such a title will prompt its readers to investigate how the distinguishing features of the *passacaglia* may have been translated in the literary work. Furthermore, novels that contain references to specific works of music, for example Nancy Huston's 1981 *Goldberg Variations*, also bring into play not only the structural traits of the work but also potentially significant extramusical components such as historical or culturally relevant information. A reference to a composer, a musical instrument, or the insertion of a musical quotation (the 'Es muss sein' in Kundera's *The Unbearable Lightness of Being*[3]) will trigger us to question our musical knowledge and how such knowledge may be brought to the service of the text.

Explicit references to music in a text, however, are not a necessary condition for a reader's investigation of the musical domain and its relevance to the text. This investigation can come about simply when an *air de famille* (a family resemblance) is perceived between text and music. Two such instances come to mind. This family resemblance may be found when:

1) the acoustic qualities of language are perceived as being an important aspect of the text. Because language's intrinsic aural and rhythmic qualities are very often overlooked, reading a text where sound takes precedence as a mode of expression often sensitizes readers to a text's 'musicality'. It is in symbolist poetry that this link was most obviously cultivated[4]. The symbolists' expressed desire to write hermetic poetry had as its goal to liberate language from the conventions of meaning and bring out language's inher-

---

[2]   Cf. Roger Laporte, *Fugue* (1970, cf. parts 3 and 4 of this article); Geneviève Serreau, *Ricercare* (1973); Robert Pinget, *Passacaille* (1969) and Paolo Maurensig, *Canone Inverso* (1996).

[3]   Between the lines of his novel, Kundera inserts a musical quotation illustrating two motifs from the last movement of Beethoven's last quartet (cf. 32).

[4]   In his essay "Existence du symbolisme", a description and defense of the writing practices of Symbolist poets, Paul Valéry writes: "Certains écrivent avec le souci d'emprunter à la musique ce qu'ils peuvent en débaucher par voie d'analogies; ils essaient parfois de donner à leurs ouvrages le dispositif d'une partition d'orchestre." (693; 'Some among them write with the aim to borrow from music what they can extract by way of analogies; they sometimes try to impart to their works the modes of expression of an orchestral score.' [My translation])

ent musicality. Mallarmé's famous statement to a friend upon leaving a concert – that poets should reclaim (from music) what is rightfully theirs[5] – was indicative of his mission to venture into the realm of the unsayable where meaning is derived from connotation and feeling rather than from denotation[6]. As Kristeva wrote in her 1974 analysis of Mallarméan technique:

> Division du sens, de la proposition, du mot; perte de leur identité au profit d'un rythme, d'une musique, d'une mélodie – ainsi se dégage, des écrits théoriques de Mallarmé, le principe conducteur de sa pratique. Qu'un tel travail découvre les lois inhérentes au fonctionnement de tout langage, Mallarmé le suppose et le souligne à maintes reprises. Il insiste sur le fait que cette "science des lois linguistiques" est immanente au vers depuis toujours, mais qu'elle se manifeste plus encore, après Hugo, à travers la "crise de vers".
> (*Révolution du langage poétique* 212)[7]

Kristeva rightly points out that Mallarmé's transgressions of poetic conventions were inspired by music. His exploitation of formal signifiers in language and the pulverization of propositional meaning were in his mind intricately linked to the power of the musical medium. In my mind, Mallarmé exemplifies the reactions of many readers who are motivated to look to music as a medium of reference whenever meaning in a text is derived from sound, structure and from connotation instead of denotation.

2) A second instance of an unsolicited (uncued) appeal to the musical domain occurs when innovation in narrative structure incites readers to look to models outside the field of literature. Evocations of theme and variation

---

[5] "[...] nous en sommes à rechercher [...] un art de la transposition, au Livre, de la symphonie ou uniment de reprendre notre bien [...]." (368; '[...] our aim is to find [...] a way of transposing the symphony into the Book or simply to reclaim what is ours [...].' [My translation])

[6] See also Mary Breatnach's discussion of Mallarmé's theoretical principles and his relationship to music in this volume and in "*Pli selon Pli*. A Conflation of Theoretical Stances".

[7] 'Division of meaning, of the proposition, of the word; loss of their identity to benefit rhythm, a music, a melody – thus comes to light, from Mallarmé's theoretical writings, the conducting principle of his poetic practice. That such a practice should uncover the inherent laws governing language, Mallarmé presupposes it and emphasizes it many times. He insists on the fact that this 'science of the laws of linguistics' has always been present in verse, but that it is even more prevalent, after Hugo, in the 'crisis of verse'.' (My translation)

form, *leitmotif* or counterpoint are regular occurrences in literary criticism, as critics attempt to render respectively the presentation of multiple points of view, the recurrence of a figure associated to a particular theme or idea and the juxtaposition of independent narrative elements. Although the musical meanings of these terms cannot be strictly applied to a textual narrative, their use indicates that sensations similar to those brought out by aural exposure to musical theme and variations, *leitmotif* or counterpoint have been elicited in a reader[8]. Using the musical domain to explain literary technique in these cases indicates a way to explain something by what is more familiar in music than in literature. This reaction is motivated not by an explicit cue or reference but by a reader's or critic's attempt to describe sensations elicited upon reading the text. The ear would seem, then, to have its role to play in the act of reading as it receives and acknowledges sounds, allowing the identification of such things as patterns, dissonances, and structures.

Whether there is an explicit reference to music in the text or whether it is the textual features themselves that prompt readers to invoke music, my point is that one ends up with a similar result: cued or uncued references initiate the investigation of the music-text relationship. Such references also legitimate the reader's attempts to do so. Thus, a reader taking into account or mentally establishing references to music directs the text toward another sphere. References then can be considered as arrows that point outside the text, to a new context. We must remember, however, just as Kristeva explains in her work on intertextuality, that reference is not unidirectional. References must be thought of as double-headed arrows with the referent not only being indicated but also being brought back to work within textual parameters[9]. Reference to the musical domain brings a reader to incorporate, in his or her reading, new perspectives or new knowledge. Following the paths of certain references may then strategically orient a reading.

---

[8] See C. S. Brown's discussion of the use of terms such as harmony, leitmotiv and counterpoint in literary criticism in his *Music and Literature: A Comparison of the Arts*.

[9] Kristeva writes: "[…] déracinées de leurs contextes, [les références] renvoient à leur lieu non pas pour s'y identifier, mais pour l'indiquer et l'ajouter à cette infinité travailleuse dont elles sont les scansions." (*Semeiotikè* 333)

Yet, when a text is put against the backdrop of music and the intent is to establish similarities, specific and particularly daunting challenges are put to the reader. An indication of these challenges manifests itself in literary criticism. Too often, critical texts present analogies with a musical technique or form where the links are at best vague or tenuous. Often, we are left to determine for ourselves the basis upon which the analogy has been made. It is obvious that critics who present these similarities fail to recognize the differential space they have just leaped over. Given the fact that music and literature are two distinct media, it is imperative that we recognize the gap that exists between these two art forms and how it is that readers may come to terms with the distinctness of each mode of aesthetic expression and establish links between them. The following section is an attempt to elaborate on how analogies between music and literature may be made.

2. Interart analogies and 'blended spaces'

In order to take into account the mental processes that allow for the projection of a musical object onto a text, it is necessary at this point to briefly retrace the major trends that have marked the study of metaphor in the fields of linguistics, philosophy and the cognitive sciences.

In light of research done in the past few decades, metaphor has gone from being considered a rhetorical figure (where a figurative meaning is simply projected onto a literal meaning) to a creative process where meaning is produced through the interaction of two logically incompatible terms. Let us retain first that metaphor includes an interactive component in which each term contributes to the construction of meaning. In his influential book of 1962, Max Black provided the example of "Man is a wolf", in which he showed that the wolf metaphor as applied to 'man' suppresses certain human traits while accentuating others (cf. *Models and Metaphors*, 109). Thus meaning is structured by the interaction of these two terms and not just by imposing the distinguishing features of the wolf onto the man. Paul Ricœur, in 1974, went further in saying that "newly invented metaphors" (*The Rule of Metaphor* 62) – those whose meanings have not been set by convention – engage interpreters in a creative process whereby an icon, schema or figure is constructed[10]. This icon is a mental image consisting of similarities established by the interpreter and which allows for the reconciliation of logical incompatibility between the two terms. Ricœur emphasized the fact that this, of course, must be achieved by an active and creative mental process, that of the interpreter.

More recently, Mark Turner and Gilles Fauconnier have developed a theory of conceptual blending whereby "structure from two or more input mental spaces is projected onto a separate 'blended' space, which inherits partial structure from the inputs, and has emergent structure of its own" (183)[11]. This view is an elaboration of Ricœur's statement that there is creation of an 'icon, schema or figure' in the metaphorical process. It goes further however in that it stresses the independent nature of the 'blended space'. The blend has its own independent structure because it integrates only partial elements from each input domain but as well, because there is a mental juxtaposition of two mental spaces and an ensuing interaction.

To illustrate the formation of this blended space, let us look at one of the examples provided by Turner and Fauconnier. A catamaran in 1993 is racing

---

[10] C'est au travail de la ressemblance que doit, en effet, être rapportée l'innovation sémantique par laquelle une 'proximité' inédite entre deux idées est aperçue en dépit de leur distance logique. [...] Cette analyse de la ressemblance entraîne à son tour la réinterprétation des notions 'd'imagination productive' et de 'fonction iconique'. Il faut en effet cesser de voir l'image au sens quasi sensoriel du mot; elle consiste plutôt à 'voir comme...', pour reprendre une expression de Wittgenstein; et ce pouvoir est un aspect de l'opération proprement sémantique qui consiste à apercevoir le semblable dans le dissemblable. (*La Métaphore vive* 10; '[...] resemblance is no less required in a tension theory, for the semantic innovation through which a previously unnoticed 'proximity' of two ideas is perceived despite their logical distance must in fact be related to the work of resemblance. [...] This analysis of the work of resemblance suggests in turn that the notions of 'productive imagination' and 'iconic function' must be reinterpreted. Indeed, imagination must cease being seen as a function of the image, in the quasi-sensorial sense of the word; it consists rather as 'seeing as ...' according to a Wittgensteinian expression – a power that is an aspect of the properly semantic operation consisting in seeing the similar in the dissimilar.' [*The Rule of Metaphor* 6])

[11] We see here that Turner and Fauconnier replace the standard 'two domain model' where meaning is carried from a 'source' (the wolf in Black's example), to the target (man) with a model constituted by two or more 'input mental spaces' being projected and contributing to establish meaning. The consequence is that the customary view of projecting meaning from a source to a target is replaced by a more interactive model.

to beat the record sailing time between San Francisco and Boston set by a clipper in 1853. As it went to press a newspaper reports the catamaran was "barely maintaining a 4.5 day lead" over the clipper. This formulation, according to the authors, shows that the idea of maintaining a lead over the clipper requires the crew and observers to produce a blended space in which the boats are sailing simultaneously. Since in each of the actual runs there was only one boat present, the blend allows a comparison of their positions in the voyage. Thus the blended space is said to be "structured by a frame that was absent from the two input spaces and is not a logical consequence of their composition – a match race between contestants over a single course with a winner and a loser" (185)[12].

3. 'Blended spaces' and Roger Laporte's *Fugue*

In order to illustrate these theories more concretely and to tie them to the investigation of the reader's role in establishing a music-text interface, it would be useful at this point to consider a specific example. *Fugue*, a novel by Roger Laporte, was published in France in 1970. It belongs to the literary movement of the Nouveau Roman that spanned from the late 1950s to the early 1970s, a movement characterized by the exploration and extension of the semiotic possibilities of narrative form. *Fugue,* like other novels of the period[13], also reflects an interest in musical forms and techniques as a means of transcending the conventional uses of language and structure in literature.

---

[12] This particular example is not a metaphorical but rather a counterfactual projection. Counterfactuals set up, alongside a presupposed real situation, an imagined situation. Like metaphors and analogies, they also produce a blended space. I have chosen this example because it facilitates the visual representation of a blended space (the runs of the two boats instead of one). In their work, Turner and Fauconnier have studied conceptual blending in a wide array of linguistic and cognitive occurrences. The authors write:

> Blending is a general cognitive operation over categorization, the making of hypotheses, inference, and the origin and combining of grammatical constructions. Blending can be detected in everyday language, idioms, creative thought in mathematics, evolution of sociocultural models, jokes, advertising, and other aspects of linguisic and nonlinguistic behavior. (186)

[13] Other notable examples are: Michel Butor's *Description de San Marco* (1963, dedication to Stravinski); Alain Badiou's *Almagestes* (1964), in which the notes of a Wagnerian

The novel's title is representative of the type of reference to music alluded to earlier: the fugue's generic structure (its defining characteristics) serves as a field of exploration to establish the relevance of a title. The title thus opens up a metaphorical space. It functions as a **cue** or **generator** to set up two input mental spaces, the concept of the musical fugue and the idea of a novel. When a reader asks: how is the novel I'm reading a fugue? then both input spaces must be explored for the possibility of identifying counterparts in each domain and, as we saw in the catamaran example, establishing the effect of their interaction.

3.1. Literary and musical themes

Fugue is a long monologue in which a narrator proposes to write a novel that would expose his experience of writing in its immediacy, that is, as he sets his hand down to write on the blank page. The narrator states that his purpose is "to write a book that would itself be its own content, a book that would produce and register its own elaboration" (26). His project is dictated, he says, by his intention to "reveal the inner workings of the thought process" (26)[14]. The metafictional theme of writing is maintained throughout the novel. It is in fact its fundamental organizing principle.

In the fugal structure and in the novel, a single theme is present as a unifying element. In both, it is a base element that is 'searched out'[15]. In the case of the fugue, it is the multiple entries of, and variations on, the theme that expose its musical potential. In the novel, the narrator proposes various models that he hopes will shed light on the question "What is writing?".

---

theme serve as an organizing structure for the novel's last chapter; Jean-Pierre Faye's *Analogues* (1964), whose narrative techniques parallel historical developments in music from the Gregorian modes to atonal music, and Robert Pinget's *Passacaille* (1969) with its exploration of the *basso continuo* technique.

[14] Quotes from the novel are my translations. The French original reads: "[...] écrire un livre qui soit à lui-même son contenu, qui produise et inscrive sa propre formation, projet dicté par le souci de mettre à jour le fonctionnement réel de la pensée." (26)

[15] The term *ricercare*, a precursor form of the fugue, literally means 'to search out'. While the term does not appear in the novel, it is implied in the verbs the narrator uses to describe his activity: "découvrir", "déchiffrer", "interroger".

Thus the fugal theme or subject, as it is also called, and the novel's theme
can be projected onto each other as counterparts. Particular features – both
are monothematic compositions whose themes have a unifying function and
provide the potential for exploration and development – are recruited to
participate in the construct of a blended space.

The difference, the fact that the musical theme is a specific set of notes,
whereas the literary theme has no predetermined material but rather is
gleaned from the narrative content, simply does not enter the analogical
space. The blend that is produced thus incorporates particular (and partial)
features of both input spaces: a unifying function and a method of exploration. Through the act of comparison, we can see that this blended space has
become an independent entity that is, as Turner and Fauconnier write, "both
less and more than the two input spaces" (186). The blend incorporates the
features of a unique and unifying theme but it also highlights its function as
a rhetorical figure. The fugal and literary themes can be seen as a question or
subject that is proposed and is to be developed. This function links both the
novel and the fugue to rhetorical traditions of the sixteenth and seventeenth
centuries, an era in which literary and musical compositions were often
perceived in rhetorical terms[16].

3.2. Variation and the process of discovery

In order to advance in the writing process and the elucidation of this process,
the narrator of *Fugue* proposes various models or analogies to represent his
mental activity. These models appear in the form of questions and answers.

---

[16] Gregory Butler in his article "Fugue and Rhetoric" cites a large number of theoreticians
who considered the rhetorical power of the fugue. He writes:

In the later sixteenth century in northern European countries of Germany, France, and
England, the trend toward the application of rhetorical precepts to music manifests itself
in a particular predilection on the part of theorists to refer to certain musical structures
and compositional techniques in terms of specific rhetorical figures. From the very
beginning of this movement, fugue is conspicuous as the most frequently mentioned of
these techniques. (49-50)

For example, at the beginning of the novel, the narrator examines the self-reflexive nature of his enterprise:

> Qu'en serait-il donc de ce livre s'il s'agissait d'un Traité de physique? La formule de Newton ne serait pas seulement une formule, mais elle-même, ou mieux encore, elle seule serait pesante: la pesanteur s'exercerait dans la formule, par la formulation de la loi, et nulle part ailleurs. – Et si j'étais explorateur? Je ne pourrais découvrir mon lieu qu'au moment où j'en ferais la cartographie; [...] – Si j'étais historien, je ne rapporterais pas un fait révolu, mais je deviendrais le contemporain d'un événement par lequel je serais intimement concerné : la narration même l'aurait provoqué à tel point que le livre serait le seul champ de l'histoire. (12-13)[17]

The question/answer format not only allows the narrator to advance in what he calls, with Nouveau Roman theorist and novelist Jean Ricardou, the 'adventure of writing' ("*l'aventure d'une écriture*" [Problèmes 111])[18] but because this process entails proposing models to determine the specificity of writing, these models engage reflections on the similarities and differences between the proposed models and the writing process.

The question/answer procedure in the novel parallels the alternating, contrapuntal subject/answer format of the fugue, whereby a melodic line exposing the theme is followed by another melodic line or voice repeating the theme after a determined time lapse and most often in a different pitch or key (usually at an interval of a fifth). The fugue, as well, was originally a form that explored, through its work with the monothematic material, the 'grammar' of a musical language, namely counterpoint within the frame of the tonal system. The narrator's attempt to extricate the laws that govern the writing process as he embarks on a self-reflexive fiction is an analogue of

---

[17] 'What would this book be were it a treatise on physics? Then Newton's law would not only be a formula, but would itself be gravity. [...] – And what if I were an explorer? In that case I could only discover the terrain at the very moment of producing its map. [...] – If I were a historian, I would not be relating an event of the past, but I would become its contemporary and would be intimately affected by it: the narration of the event would have produced it to the point where the book was the only historical field.' (My translation)

[18] "Écrire m'est inconnu, et ainsi la réponse se borne à redoubler la question: ce serait seulement dans le livre que se produirait, et, en partie, pourrait se lire l'aventure d'une écriture inconnue." (15; 'Writing is for me the unknown, and thus the reply can only repeat the question: it is only by means of the book that one might produce and, in part, read the adventure of this unknown writing.' [My translation])

the musical fugue's underlying principles. Both in fact can be read as a reflection on the principles of a musical or linguistic system.

Moreover, the alternating questions and answers in *Fugue* suggest a never-ending process. As the narrator advances different models for the writing process, and is able to reflect on them, he also acknowledges that the laws he proposes can never quite capture the essence of writing. The writer-narrator realizes that all attempts to define writing must fail, as his descriptions can only be mere imitations or representations of his writing process. Thus, *Fugue* is a novel about a desperate attempt to grasp the elusive answer to the question "Qu'est-ce qu'écrire?"/'What is writing?' (12, 25, 30, 35 and passim). In the musical fugue, it is the time lapse between theme and reply as well as the answer's appearance on another interval that gives one the feeling that voices (or melodic lines) are chasing each another. The question and answer process thus becomes tied to the notion of difference and representation. Through the narrator's emphasis of the difference inherent in the process of 'imitation', the fugue's imitations or variations become linked to postmodern notions of difference and representation.

3.3. Derridean 'trace' and the elusiveness of closure and truth in *Fugue*

Another factor that contributes to the notion of a never ending chase in *Fugue* is derived from the implied problematization of the interpretation of signs. *Fugue*'s narrator finds that his writing is dictated not only by his own imagination but also by what he has already written. He insists that his text becomes detached from him once it has been written but that it continues to affect his future writing. The text then is an agent of the narrator's writing, acting independently of his own will. This alludes to the Derridean notion of 'trace', whereby text/writing is seen as a compilation of signs, a fixed material if you will, that allows for continuous and ever fluctuating interpretation.

Further, the notion of 'trace' implies that truth and closure are beyond reach. In the novel, the question 'What is writing?' can never be answered because writing is forever being influenced by what precedes it and is ever subject to change. This metaphysical issue is not prevalent when considering the structure of the musical fugue. Yet, through the process of comparison with the novel, the fugue, too, can be seen as exemplifying a chase for an elusive (and illusory) term of closure and stability. In the fugue, variations on the theme and thematic entries can go on indefinitely. Closure is not arrived at by exhausting the theme's musical potential but only comes when the composer/musician arbitrarily decides to enter into a stretto and return to the tonic key.

3.4. Countersubject and counterwriting

One of the most obvious counterparts to the fugue in this novel is the presence of a negative force exerted on the narrator while he writes and to which he assigns the term "contre-écriture" (counterwriting)[19]. This term of course would seem to be an adaptation of the countersubject in the fugue. In *Fugue*, the narrator discovers that "la contre-écriture" is both a destructive and a constructive force. While it sometimes brings out a fear in him that undermines his ability to write, it also creates the tension and opposition that force him to take on his task with more lucidity[20].

Just as we encountered in our discussion of musical and literary themes, counterwriting and the countersubject have no material similarities either, one is a set of notes, the other an acting force on the narrator's consciousness. It is thus in the respective roles each plays that one can draw parallels.

---

[19] S'opposant en effet à ce que provisoirement, et faute de mieux, j'appellerai mon écriture, puisque posée noir sur blanc par celui qui dit 'je', il y a en effet je ne sais quelle blancheur ennemie qui évide mon écriture, la disjoint d'elle-même, un blanchiment qui efface par avance ce que j'aurais pu écrire, me déloge sans cesse de ce que je ne suis pas en droit d'appeler mon écriture: cette rayure, cette éclaircie, ce sillon, je l'appellerai contre-écriture [...]. (18)

[20] Tout se passe comme si l'ouvrage était le lieu de l'affrontement entre un dedans et un dehors, entre l'écriture et la contre-écriture, adversaire qu'il serait pourtant injuste de considérer comme ennemi de l'ouvrage, puisque sans elle l'ouvrage se géométriserait, se cristalliserait en un Traité qui, pour être parfait, n'en signifierait pas moins, pour l'ouvrage, sublimé en l'Œuvre, une immobilité mortelle. La contre-écriture, inséparable de la douleur, est donc porteuse de vie: elle seule permet le renouvellement qui, en dépit du temps qui passe et de la variété des événements, maintient la proposition: écrire m'est inconnu, et c'est pourquoi on peut bien dire que le texte effectif est l'œuvre conjointe de l'écriture et de la contre-écriture. (38-39)

A fugue's countersubject consists of a melodic line that is chosen so as to offer a contrast to the melodic line of the theme. The role of contrast taken on by the countersubject can be seen as 'constructive' as well as 'destructive' since contrast can both stand as opposition through difference and yet allow the theme's specificity to stand out. Regarding the role of opposition between subject and countersubject, Gregory Butler, in his "Fugue and Rhetoric", translates a passage from Johann Adolph Scheibe's *Der critische Musikus* (Hamburg, 1745), in which this role is emphasized:

> The 8th figure is opposition (*antithesis*). When one places subjects against one another in order to make the principal subject that much clearer. This occurs especially in fugues, where one constantly sets the principal subject in opposition to still other subjects in order to better clarify it and render it all the more prominent. (89)

The blended space constructed from the input of the countersubject and "contre-écriture" is composed of the functional correspondence between the two. We see also that in the blended space the fugal countersubject is attributed a rhetorical function, that of opposition and giving clarity through contrast. As for the "contre-écriture", it is portrayed as a "sillon" (a furrow, track or trench) or a "rayure" (a stripe or groove) that reflects the visual presentation of fugal voices in the musical score (18). In the blend, countersubject and "contre-écriture" take on functional and visual characteristics that emphasize their corrosive yet positive function.

3.5. Single and double counterpoint and the interrelationship of ideas

Finally, the complexity of listening to a contrapuntal composition is also present in this literary fugue. In counterpoint, not only does a listener hear a horizontal progression as he/she follows the melodic lines, there is also a vertical dimension as the ear registers intervals formed by the superimposed voices. The superposition of voices is suggested in *Fugue* in a presentation of the writing process as a series of superimposed layers. The narrator considers the models he has proposed as a series of threads on a loom. He imagines himself in the role of a weaver who ties the threads to constitute the textual fabric. The text's complexity thus increases, as the narrator examines the varying relationships that emerge from interactions between various models. The relationships created through a simultaneous presentation of notes in musical counterpoint can be projected onto the mental activities of memory and comparison undertaken by the narrator (and the reader) as they consciously or unconsciously hold the threads of the text.

There is, moreover, an allusion to the technical prowess of double counterpoint in this novel. In a fugue, it is possible to invert the original vertical order of the upper and lower voices to create a new series of invervals. This inversion is known as double counterpoint. As we saw in the above paragraph, *Fugue*'s narrator metaphorically organizes the threads of his fabric into upper and lower strata. In doing so, he investigates their relationships in that configuration. Because he has assigned to the upper strata a 'leading' role, he realizes at a given moment that it is the lower strata that may be exerting its domination on his thinking. To account for this new development, he mentally flips the two 'layers' on a vertical axis and considers their inverted relationship. At this point, the narrator compares his text to a "palimpseste inversé", an 'inverted palimpseste' (124).

Considering the techniques of counterpoint and double counterpoint in the context of the narrative instances described above has contributed to the presentation of the writing process in the form of the superposition and interplay of ideas. The temporal simultaneity of melodic lines which can be achieved in music cannot be applied literally to a narrative. Thus, from the input space of the fugue, it is the idea of simultaneity that comes to highlight the work of memory and the investigation of relationships as they are portrayed in the narrative.

There are further counterparts that can be established between the fugue and *Fugue*. Just as an unusual vocabulary in the novel ("contre-écriture"/ 'counterwriting' [18 and passim], "rétrograde"/'retrograde forms' [30, 98], "une marche de l'écrevisse" [152, an evocation of the 'crab canon'], "renversement" [18, alluding to the inversion of counterpoint]) calls to mind technical terms used in fugal composition, an ambiguous semantic field that includes such notions as lines, layers, intervals, augmentations, contractions and sequences takes on a double meaning, as a reader considers the novel in terms of fugal technique. All these terms, in the context of the novel, refer to various stages of the narrator's writing experience and reflect the meanderings of the writing process. They also contribute to reinforcing the links between *Fugue* and the fugue, between the process of writing and the fugal treatment of a theme. The fugue, referred to in the novel's title, has introduced a musical context that makes these terms polysemic, and this distinct musical space offers new semantic possibilities for a reader to explore.

4. Effects of blended spaces in the interpretation of *Fugue*

I have touched upon a few of the possible correspondences which Laporte's novel offers readers ready to embark on a journey of text-music analogy. In establishing similarities between the fugue and *Fugue*, we saw that this process involved, in the first instance, a reliance on textual indices (the novel's title and a technical or polysemic vocabulary) to guide and motivate the reader to seek out musical correspondences. Through the act of comparison, similarities can be established which lead to the creation of a blended space. Independent of both input spaces, the blended space integrates a selection of features seen as relevant to both input spaces. Yet, although this third space is the result of a combination of the two input spaces, it does not hold all of their characteristics and it has an emergent structure of its own.

As we have seen, it is not simply a case of projecting one entity onto the other. When considering the fugue as a metaphor for the novel we could conceive it simply as projecting its characteristic features and structure onto that of the novel – exposition and development of a theme, the various imitations or variations in the form of models for the writing process, the existence of a countersubject in the force referred to as 'counterwriting' etc. However, in the blended space, only partial features of each input space are incorporated. In its distinctness, the blend highlights specific features of the fugue and of the novel and in doing so structures their perception and interpretation.

Further, as these features are brought into coexistence, their interaction produces a supplement of meaning and conceptualization. The novel, in this space, can be conceived as bringing into play a series of intertwining layers that influence each other. The horizontal succession of words and propositions is reorganized to take on vertical dimensions like the intervals formed in contrapuntal technique. As well, the materiality of writing in the Derridean sense is given a concrete counterpart in the example of the development of a fugal theme. Finally, the time and pitch differences which characterize the various entries of voices (a theme, its reply and further variations being delayed by a few measures and by transpositions into various keys) provide the narrator's quest with a visual and aural representation of his quest to answer the question 'What is writing?'. Overall, the novel is infused with the fugue's frenzied game of chase.

On the other hand, through a comparison with the novel, the fugue's rhetorical qualities are highlighted. The various techniques (countersubject, variation through inversion, augmentation etc.) can be linked with the rhetorical figures used by an orator in the exposition and development of a subject. The fugue can thus be conceived as a process of logical reasoning that includes refutations, confirmation, and exploration of a given topic. As well, the fugue becomes imbued with a philosophical dimension. The paradoxical nature of self-reflexivity and autogeneration or autopoiesis inherent in the narrator's quest – the novel is like M. C. Escher's hand drawing a hand – also brings out in the fugue the unlimited possibilities of variation. Variation in itself is self-referential, and the game of permutations fuels the idea of perpetual motion and thus links the fugue to the novel's underlying generative theme of an infinite process.

In the end, we see that the idea of the fugue in *Fugue* is enriched by the blending together of two very distinct entities, a novel and a generic musical form. The blend allows readers to transgress traditional categorization of artistic media. It also structures perception of both to create an entity that combines some of music's and language's or fiction's specificity. This literary fugue is one that encompasses notions of identity and difference, self-reflexivity, the impossibility of apprehending and representing reality and, via the concept of trace and the material nature of the musical theme, the never-ending process of variation in interpretation. In essence, the fugue being portrayed here exemplifies the postmodern principle of the illusory status of truth and origin.

5. Conclusion

To conclude, one has to concede that not all musico-literary analogies or metaphors will yield interesting results. Factors, such as a reader's lack of sensitivity to music, lack of technical knowledge and the sheer work involved in attempting interart analogies, are some of the conditions that may result in a musico-literary analogy being left unexplored. When it is explored, it may happen that the mapping is unsubstantial, too general or simply superficial and uninteresting. Nevertheless, the process is the same as when a mapping is successful and fruitful.

Answering the question then, 'when is a text **like** music?', I would emphasize that a text is like music when a reader is able to establish correspondences between the musical and the literary domains. This is by no means a simple task. To embark on such an enterprise, readers need to engage in musical and literary analysis and interpretation – thus making use of a double competence. Further, they must investigate a multitude of potentially significant leads, distinguishing and recruiting similarities to form an intermediary space in which two distinct art forms can coexist. This intermediary space, as we have seen, while it encompasses similarities, has its own emerging structure. This structure in effect directs the reader's perception of the text.

To privilege a cognitive approach in the investigation of musical metaphors and analogies in literature allows us to recognize the reader's investment in the interpretation process. When a reader perceives the presence of music in a text or when readers take authors to task when they suggest that their work is influenced by music, it is also in the reader's mind that we must look for an ontology of music, not only in the text. It is then that we can say that the text's virtual musicality becomes reality.

References

Black, Max. *Models and Metaphors*. Ithaca: Cornell Univ. Press, 1962.

Breatnach, Mary M. *"Pli selon pli*. A Conflation of Theoretical Stances". Walter Bernhart, Steven Paul Scher, Werner Wolf, eds. *Word and Music Studies: Defining the Field*. Amsterdam: Rodopi, 1999. 265-275.

Brown, C. S. *Music and Literature: A Comparison of the Arts*. Athens, Georgia: The Univ. of Georgia Press, 1948.

Butler, Gregory G. "Fugue and Rhetoric". *Journal of Music Theory* 21.1 (1977): 49-109.

Cupers, Jean-Louis. *Euterpe et Harpocrate ou le défi littéraire de la musique*. Bruxelles: Publications des Facultés universitaires Saint-Louis, 1988.

Fauconnier, Gilles. *Mappings in Thought and Language*. Cambridge: Cambridge Univ. Press, 1997.

Indurkhya, Bipin. *Metaphor and Cognition: An Interactionist Approach. Studies in Cognitive Systems*. Dordrecht: Kluwer Academic Publishers, 1992.

Kristeva, Julia. *Révolution du langage poétique*. Paris: Seuil, 1974.

—. *Semeiotikè: Recherches pour une sémanalyse*. Paris: Seuil, 1969.

Kundera, Milan. *The Unbearable Lightness of Being*. Transl. Michael Henry Heim. New York: Harper and Row, 1984.

Laporte, Roger. *Fugue*, Paris: Seuil, 1970.

Mallarmé, Stéphane. "Crise de vers". Mallarmé. *Œuvres complètes*. Paris: NRF, 1941. 360-368.

Ricardou, Jean. *Problèmes du nouveau roman*. Collection 'Tel Quel'. Paris: Seuil, 1967.

—. *Pour une théorie du nouveau roman*. Paris: Seuil, 1971.

Ricœur, Paul. *La Métaphore vive*. Paris: Seuil, 1975.

—. *The Rule of Metaphor*. Transl. Robert Czerny et al. Toronto: Univ. of Toronto Press, 1977.

Turner, Mark, Gilles Fauconnier. "Conceptual Integration and Formal Expression". *Journal of Metaphor and Symbolic Activity* 10.3 (1995): 183-204.

Valéry, Paul. "Existence du symbolisme". Valéry. *Œuvres complètes*. Vol. 1. Paris: Gallimard, 1957. 686-706.

Wolf, Werner. *The Musicalization of Fiction: A Study in the Theory and History of Intermediality*. Amsterdam: Rodopi, 1999.

The Song Cycle

Problems in Song Cycle Analysis
and the Case of *Mädchenblumen*

Suzanne M. Lodato, New York, NY

This paper assesses the work of two commentators – Patrick McCreless and David Neumeyer – who attempt to establish a methodology for lieder cycle analysis. Both assume that the group of songs that comprises a lieder cycle is organically unified by a large-scale tonal scheme that is either functional or associative and is reflective of poetic semantic meanings and inter-relationships. However, when their analyses of Schumann's *Liederkreis*, op. 39, and *Dichterliebe*, respectively, fail to conform to their expectations of musical and poetic unity, they invoke biographical information in order to explain the musical inconsistencies and complete the picture of a unified work. Such an approach, taken as a model and used across the board, can present methodological difficulties, particularly in situations in which the text and music of a song group do contain cyclic elements, but hermeneutic factors actually undermine the cyclicity of the group. The pitfalls that are encountered in this type of song cycle analysis will be illustrated by a brief discussion of Richard Strauss's song cycle *Mädchenblumen* (poetry by Felix Dahn).

Introduction

In my previous WMA conference paper, I discussed an organicist approach taken by song analysts who assume, *a priori*, that the text of a song serves as the basis for its musical setting. They seek direct correspondences between textual semantic meaning and musical elements such as harmony, figuration, or motivic relationships, or they seek to reveal structural homologies between poems and their musical settings. Most of this work falls under the category of Kofi Agawu's "pyramidal model" of song analysis, "in which words, lying at the top, provide access to meaning, while the music lies at the base and supports the signification of the text" (Agawu 6-7; cf. Lodato 99). While analysis based upon such presuppositions has remained influential in the field, commentary based upon other methods that assume a lack of correspondence between text and music in song (e. g., Lawrence Kramer's

work with structural dissonance and structural tropes) has recently prolifer-
ated (cf. *Music and Poetry* 146, 150; *Cultural Practice* 10).

Song cycle analysts, however, have almost exclusively employed methods that assume not only that direct correspondences between textual
meaning and music within individual songs exist, but also that relationships
among the poems in a song cycle are reflected in analogous relationships
among their musical settings[1]. If Agawu's categorizations were extended to
song cycle analysis, the bulk of these approaches could be said to proceed
according to his pyramidal model, falling into two subcategories of assumptions made in the pyramidal approach that I have discussed previously: 1)
music as related to semantic textual meaning, and 2) deep structural and
procedural homologies in music and text (cf. Lodato 103-105).

Two oft-cited articles written in the 1980s by Patrick McCreless and
David Neumeyer have manifested this orientation in their commentary on
Schumann's *Liederkreis*, Op. 39, and *Dichterliebe*, Op. 48, respectively, but
with an interesting departure from typical practice. Their methods focus first
on two steps common in current song cycle analysis, steps that are formalist
in approach: 1) establishing a narrative or, if one does not exist, a progression or arrangement of poems in the cycle in terms of affect or imagery; and
2) ascertaining the reflection of this plot or pattern in the musical setting,
either in terms of tonal plans (functional or associative) or motivic connections. It is when these two steps fail to reveal a large-scale musical plan that
would enable the group to be designated as a 'song cycle' that they turn to a
third step, that of invoking hermeneutic elements such as biographical or
other contextual information in order to explain the musical inconsistencies
and complete the picture of a unified work, 'unity' being their primary criterion for determining that a group of songs is a cycle.

As I have noted (cf. 107-108), most hermeneutically-oriented song
analysis, based on Kramer's approach, proceeds on the assumption that
poetic and musical meanings in a song do not correspond (cf. ibid. 99).

---

[1]   The assumptions regarding musico-poetic unity in the song cycle that tend to be made
by musicologists have been challenged at the 1997 and 1999 WMA conferences by both
Cyrus Hamlin and Walter Bernhart, who view the song cycle primarily as a literary genre
(cf. Hamlin, "The Romantic Song Cycle", and Bernhart's contribution to the present
volume).

Kramer's "structural tropes", which are located within the cultural context of the time in which a song was composed, mediate between different poetic and musical meanings (*Cultural Practice* 10). Indeed, some commentators, such as Hayden White, prefer a hermeneutic orientation in melopoetic investigations because such an approach enables commentators to avoid assuming that "the verbal text [is] a fairly easily discernible literalist statement which the musical matter 'translates' in one way or another" (292). McCreless and Neumeyer, on the other hand, turn to biographical information to aid in establishing direct poetic/musical correspondences and intrinsic inter-song musical connections that are assumed in the formalist approach but cannot be explicated by it.

While on the surface this new model of song cycle analysis seems to solve problems presented by both of the Schumann cycles, it can prove problematic when investigating song cycles by other composers. This discussion will summarize and assess song cycle analyses and interpretations, and the underlying assumptions that fuel them, by McCreless and Neumeyer. The limitations inherent in such presuppositions will be illustrated by means of their application to the analysis and interpretation of Richard Strauss's 1891 song cycle, *Mädchenblumen*.

McCreless's and Neumeyer's Analyses

From textual, musical, and hermeneutic standpoints, the most wide-ranging recent song cycle analysis is McCreless's discussion of Schumann's *Liederkreis*, Op. 39. McCreless seeks to unpack problems inherent in determining whether song groupings are collections or cycles by defining inter-song relationships as "unordered" or "ordered" (6). According to McCreless, song cycles tend to be thought of not merely as groups of related songs, which would be more aptly classified as collections, but more specifically, of ordered songs in which each is crucial to the integrity of the group as a whole. Re-ordering or removal of songs would undermine the cycle's completeness. These "unordered" and "ordered" relationship categorizations are applied to seven criteria set down in an earlier analysis of Schumann's

Dichterliebe, Op. 48, by Arthur Komar. Komar's list (cf. 63-66) comprises a graded set of pre-conditions, entirely musical, for determining whether a group of songs constitutes a collection or a cycle. Lower numbered items on the list represent more generalized relationships typical of collections, while items with higher numbers describe more specific inter-song connections found in song cycles. In McCreless's scheme, Komar's first three conditions are classified as "unordered" relationships and numbers 4 to 7 as "ordered" ones (cf. McCreless 8-9) (see Figure 1).

McCreless's "unordered" relationships	1. General similarity among the songs in musical style and length, poetry style, structure and subject matter. This factor alone would make this group a collection, rather than a cycle.
	2. More specific correspondences among the songs exist (for example, themes, harmonic progressions, rhythmic figures) than exist among randomly selected songs from the same time period.
	3. In addition to the relationships in #2, some of the motivic or thematic groups recur from one song to another untransposed.
McCreless's "ordered" relationships	4. Some songs are paired, as indicated by "elements of local continuity" (64) seen in adjacent songs.
	5. In addition to numbers 2-4, the keys of songs in their compositional order make up a "coherent" (65) key scheme.
	6. There is a global ordering scheme or compositional plan that accommodates the ordering of non-paired songs and structures the conclusion of the cycle.
	7. Coupled with #6, an entire cycle is essentially "governed" (65) by one key.

Fig. 1: Arthur Komar's Criteria for Evaluating Song Collections and Cycles

In unordered relationships, according to McCreless, similarities among movements can be identified, but there is no obvious reason why they occur in specific locations aside from possible associations with the text. Ordered

relationships actually generate or form a global scheme from a purely musical standpoint in which reasons can be determined for occurrences or recurrences of musical events at specific times (cf. 7). He defines three major
types of ordering in nineteenth-century multi-movement works, including
song cycles: 1) text-music relationships, in which musical motives are
consistently associated with particular textual motives throughout the cycle;
2) the keys of the songs comprise a tonal scheme that is "quasi-narrative" (8)
in and of itself; or 3) the movements form "abstract pattern[s]" (ibid.) that
constitute a design, for example, a symmetrical or binary division fashioned
by keys, motives, rhythms, other musical elements, or affect. These elements
are also used to connect pairs or other subgroups of songs (cf. ibid.). In
regard to the second and third items, McCreless does not deal with one
problem presented by the supposed ordering function of a tonal scheme or
an abstract pattern: namely, the tonal scheme or abstract musical design
might not necessarily reflect the particular narrative or abstract design in the
poetic arrangement.

These criteria, to which McCreless adds considerations of Schumann's
ordering of the Eichendorff poems (which were not originally part of a
poetry cycle or group) and biographical information regarding Schumann's
upcoming marriage, are used to compare the compositional and published
orderings of Schumann's *Liederkreis.*

Both orderings reflect Schumann's arrangement of the poems not in
accordance with a plot, but with what Jürgen Thym has described as a binary
design in which the *Stimmungen* of the first six poems depict, overall, "happiness", while the second six depict, overall, "grief and affliction", and
songs with more specific affective shadings occur in symmetrical analogous
locations in the two halves (Thym 223, qtd. in McCreless 12-13). Ordered
tonal and motivic relationships that support these two affective groupings in
both cycle orderings are identified by McCreless. The published order
reflects shifts in the song sequence within each of the halves from that of the
order of composition. McCreless finds that the compositional order emphasizes an ironic, embittered view of love, while the published order portrays a
more optimistic view, in keeping with Schumann's upcoming marriage to

Clara Wieck[2]. He concludes that it was this desire to project a happier view of marriage that explains the slightly looser musical structure and less compelling tonal plan of the compositional order that result from the re-ordering of songs according to their *Stimmungen*.

While McCreless turns to hermeneutic techniques after he sees discrepancies in the unifying musical scheme of the *Liederkreis*, Neumeyer denies that the tonal scheme is the primary determinant of cyclicity and flatly rejects the idea, promulgated by Komar, that the tonal scheme is the only factor worth considering. By use of Schenkerian analysis, Komar claims to demonstrate that *Dichterliebe* consists of "interdependent 'movements' governed by a single key [C♯]" (66), but Neumeyer finds not only that *Dichterliebe* lacks a unified tonal scheme, but also that the cycle's tonal progression (in thirds, fourths, and fifths) is no different from tonal progressions in Schumann's non-cyclic dance collections such as *Carnaval*. Therefore, these key relationships will not serve an 'ordering' function peculiar to this cycle. In addition, he finds the narrative structure of the poems to be too loose to serve as the sole basis for a unified work. Although Neumeyer's stated aim is analysis by means of "the 'equalizing' of text and music" (97), he too turns to a third element outside of both the textual and musical realms – Schumann's relationship with his wife Clara – to prompt a reinterpretation of the first two poems that leads to a reconception of the first two brief songs as one musically unified prologue/statement structure. "Im wunderschönen Monat Mai" becomes Schumann's prologue, an announcement of a confession of love to Clara, to the second song, "Aus meinen Thränen spriessen", which serves as the actual confession. Viewing the two songs as one, Neumeyer interprets the C♯ dominant seventh in "Im wunderschönen Monat Mai" as resolving in "Aus meinen Thränen spriessen" to F♯ minor, which is the submediant of the A major tonic. Neumeyer asserts the necessity of seeking to reveal that the cycle is "organically unified on a higher plane" (97), but nevertheless makes unity of

---

[2]   In his contribution to the present volume, Thym shows that in Schumann's Berlin autograph the Eichendorff settings are interspersed with settings of works by other poets, thereby undermining McCreless's hypothesis that Schumann originally intended to set the Eichendorff poems in the compositional order that he cites in his article (see "A Cycle in Flux: Schumann's Eichendorff *Liederkreis*").

key in the two songs the end-point of his analysis. Unfortunately, his article only deals with the first two songs. It would be interesting to see whether a musico-textual-hermeneutic analysis of the full cycle along these lines would support the concept of a large-scale tonal plan.

The significance of these approaches lies far more in their commonality than in their divergences. Both commentators assume *a priori* that organic unity determines the status of a multi-song work as a song cycle. When neither the key scheme nor the poetry collection themselves constitute an organically unified entity, both analysts invoke biographical information. But this approach does not fully provide answers in all cases. For example, what if the opposite situation from that seen in the two Schumann cycles occurs – that is, what if the poetic and/or musical elements in a multi-song work are cyclic, but biographical information or compositional history actually undermines the work's cyclical status?

One case in point is Strauss's 1888 setting of Felix Dahn's (1834-1912) poetry cycle *Mädchenblumen*, published in 1891, chosen for this paper because virtually no discussion of the cycle exists, and therefore a brief investigation involving musical and textual analyses and hermeneutic considerations can be employed afresh without the coloring of previous commentary. Strauss set all four of the *Mädchenblumen* poems intact; several inter-poetic relationships in Dahn's *Mädchenblumen* point to the designation of this work as a poetry cycle; and the tonal lay-out of the music setting is characterized by ordered inter-song relationships. An examination of how Strauss's post-compositional activities compromised the cyclical elements of *Mädchenblumen* will follow the discussion of cyclicity in both the poetry cycle and the musical setting below.

Mädchenblumen

In each of the *Mädchenblumen* poems, a flower personifies a different female type – a typical nineteenth-century poetic conceit (see Figure 2). The fact that no narrative exists in the cycle prompts the analyst to seek other unifying factors within this common theme, such as, perhaps, different aspects of one

overarching situation or emotional state, or, as was common in the early nineteenth century, gradual intensification of emotional expression (cf. Turchin
221, 279). Indeed, in this group of poems, progressions within various
parameters can be discerned. The number of lines in each of the one-stanza
poems increases throughout (twelve, eighteen, twenty and twenty-four lines,
respectively). Physical descriptions of the girls gradually increase in number
and specificity of characteristics as the cycle progresses, leaving the impression of a female image gradually coming into focus. Indeed, in "Wasserrose",
the final song, a veritable riot of impressions bursts forth, with words and
phrases such as "colorless", "transparent", "silver glow", the dark moth, the
girl's dark hair, her alabaster cheeks, and her grey eyes. The concept of a fully
developed picture in the final poem is further reinforced by the fact that
neither the word *Mädchen* nor *Maid* appears at all in the first two poems,
"Kornblumen" and "Mohnblumen", where metonymies are used ("die Gestalten, / Die milden" in the first poem, and "die [...] gesunden [...] Seelen" in the
second). Because "Blumen" forms both part of the title and the first word of
each of the first two poems, its delay to the last line of the third poem,
"Epheu", becomes significant. The word *Mädchen* also appears for the first
time in the cycle in the second line of "Epheu". "Wasserrose" combines the
devices of the first three songs by stating the word *Blume* immediately in the
first line, succeeded by a lengthy description of the flower itself, and then
using the word *Maid* in line 14 in the second half of the poem, in which a
detailed description of the girl is rendered. For the first time, the girl takes on
an identity separate from that of the personifying flower.

1. Kornblumen

Kornblumen nenn' ich die Gestalten,
    Die milden, mit den blauen Augen,
Die, anspruchslos, in stillem Walten,
    Den Thau des Friedens, den sie saugen
Aus ihren eignen klaren Seelen,
    Mittheilen allem, dem sie nah'n,
Bewußtlos der Gefühlsjuwelen,
    Die sie von Himmelshand empfahn:
Dir wird so wohl in ihrer Nähe,
    Als gingst Du durch ein Saatgefilde,
Durch das der Hauch des Abends wehe
    Voll frommen Friedens und voll Milde.

2. Mohnblumen

Mohnblumen sind die runden,
Rothblutigen, gesunden,
   Die sommersproß-gebraunten,
   Die immer froh gelaunten,
Kreuzbraven, kreuzfidelen,
Tanz-nimmermüden Seelen,
   Die unterm Lachen weinen,
   Und nur geboren scheinen,
Die Kornblumen zu necken,
Und dennoch oft verstecken
   Die weichsten, besten Herzen
   Im Schlinggewächs von Scherzen,
Die man, weiß Gott! mit Küssen
Ersticken würde müssen,
   Wär' man nicht immer bange,
   Umarmest du die Range,
Sie springt, ein voller Brander,
Aufflammend auseinander!

3. Epheu

Aber Epheu nenn' ich jene
   Mädchen, mit den sanften Worten,
Mit dem Haar, dem schlichten, hellen,
   Um den leis gewölbten Brauen,
Mit den braunen, seelenvollen
   Rehenaugen, die in Thränen
Stehn so oft, in ihren Thränen
   Grade sind unwiderstehlich;
Ohne Kraft und Selbstgefühl und
   Schmucklos, mit verborgner Blüthe,
Doch mit unerschöpflich tiefer,
   Treuer, inniger Empfindung
Können sie mit eigner Triebkraft
   Nie sich heben aus den Wurzeln,
Sind geboren, sich zu ranken
   Liebend um ein ander Leben: -
An der ersten Liebumrankung
   Hängt ihr ganzes Lebensschicksal,
Denn sie zählen zu den seltnen
   Blumen, die nur einmal blühen.

4. Wasserrose

Kennst du die Blume, die märchenhafte
   Sagen-gefeierte Wasserrose?
Sie wiegt auf ätherischem, schlanken Schafte
   Das durchsichtige Haupt, das farbenlose,
Sie blüht auf schilfigem Teich im Haine,
   Gehütet vom Schwan, der umkreiset sie einsam,

Sie erschließet sich nur dem Mondenscheine,
    Mit dem ihr der silberne Schimmer gemeinsam.
So blüht sie, die zaubrische Schwester der Sterne,
    Umschwärmt von der träumerisch dunkeln Phaläne,
Die am Rande des Teiches sich sehnet von ferne,
    Und sie nimmer erreicht, wie sehr sie sich sehne. -
Wasserrose, so nenn' ich die schlanke,
    Nachtlockige Maid, alabastern von Wangen,
In dem Auge der ahnende, tiefe Gedanke,
    Als sei sie ein Geist und auf Erden gefangen.
Wenn sie spricht, ist's wie silbernes Wogenrauschen,
    Wenn sie schweigt, ist's die ahnende Stille der Mondnacht,
Sie scheint mit den Sternen Blicke zu tauschen,
    Deren Sprache die gleiche Natur sie gewohnt macht.
Du kannst nicht ermüden, ins Aug' ihr zu schauen,
    Das die seidene lange Wimper umsäumt hat
Und du glaubst, wie bezaubert von seligem Grauen,
    Was je die Romantik von Elfen geträumt hat.

Fig. 2: Mädchenblumen *by Felix Dahn (1834-1912)*

The implied pairing of "Kornblumen" and "Mohnblumen" by their titles is also borne out in lines 8 and 9 of "Mohnblumen", which directly refer to the first song ("Und nur geboren scheinen, / Die Kornblumen zu necken"; 'And only appear to be born / To provoke the cornflowers'). "Epheu" is directly linked to the previous poem by its first word, the conjunction "Aber". The first and second, and then third and fourth songs are also affectively paired in terms of intensity of the *Stimmung* expressed. The peace, ease, comfort and gentility of "Kornblumen" and the liveliness, playfulness, and open sexuality of "Mohnblumen" project a lighter tone than the deep feelings and heightened sensitivity of "Epheu" and the mysterious and ethereal qualities of "Wasserrose".

Based on the analytical techniques employed by McCreless and Neumeyer, one might expect to find ordering characteristics in Strauss's setting, such as a linear, functional tonal scheme, that reinforce progressive aspects of the text, or textual and motivic associations that reflect the song pairings. If there are departures from ordering techniques, one would then seek answers in textual material, biographical information, and/or compositional history.

Some similarities in style among the songs constitute 'unordered' relationships. A melodic contour made up of a large ascending leap (usually a sixth, seventh or octave) and a stepwise descent reappears throughout the cycle but is not associated with specific textual motives. In addition, the melodic lines of the first, third, and fourth songs are characterized by unusually long, asymmetrical phrases, with the disjunct outbursts of the second song, "Mohnblumen", presenting a sharp contrast. Both these elements lend the cycle a certain color but are not ordering factors.

Some functionality and key association can be discerned in the tonal layout, and these elements fulfill ordering functions with varying degrees of success. The original key scheme of the four songs (D♭ major, G major, E♭ major, and F♯ minor and major) appears on the surface to follow no tonal functional logic (see Figure 3). However, the D♭ of "Kornblumen" is enharmonically equivalent to C♯, which as the dominant of F♯, the key of "Wasserrose", and serves as a link between the first and final songs. A further connection between "Kornblumen" and "Wasserrose" becomes evident in the final song's brief B♭-major section (mm. 54-57), which sets lines 19-20 ("Sie scheint mit den Sternen Blicke zu tauschen, / Deren Sprache die gleiche Natur sie gewohnt macht") and recalls the first song briefly in a vocal line cadence on D♭ (m. 58). The fact that the D♭ cadence occurs over C♯7 harmony, the dominant of the F♯ tonic, further strengthens the connection between the first and last songs of the cycle by emphasizing the enharmonic equivalence of D♭ and C♯. A relationship can be seen between this passage and one similar in musical function and textual content in "Kornblumen". In "Kornblumen", a cadence on the dominant (A♭) occurs in m. 15 at the end of the setting of lines 7-8 ("Bewußtlos der Gefühlsjuwelen, / Die sie von Himmelshand empfahn"). Both of these pairs of lines express communication between the flower/girl and natural forces (heaven in "Kornblumen", the stars in "Wasserrose").

This arrangement begs the question of why Strauss would not have simply set "Kornblumen" in C♯ major. The answer, it seems, lies both in Dahn's poetry pairings and in Strauss's assertion about the 'experimental' nature of this cycle in a letter to his publisher Eugen Spitzweg (7 June 1889). As can be seen in the tonal plan, the keys alternate between those on the flat and sharp sides of the circle of fifths (see Figure 3), a technique that will become a hallmark of Strauss's song style later on. The first two poems, paired by their 'lighter' affect, comprise a flat-sharp song pair, as do the third and fourth poems, which are paired by their more intense affect. At the same time, this flat/sharp scheme creates two other pairs: the first song and final song, part II of which is in F♯ (with seven sharps), contain the most flats and the most sharps, respectively, and form the more 'traditional' pair from a compositional stylistic standpoint; the second and third songs – a sharp/flat pair with fewer sharps and fewer flats – comprise the stylistically 'experimental' pair.

The more traditional approach to the first and last songs is evident in their harmonic schemes and accompanimental patterns. Both "Kornblumen" and "Wasserrose" focus strongly on one key and are basically uneventful harmonically. The tonal scheme of "Kornblumen", which is almost entirely in D♭ major, is less complex than that of "Wasserrose" (F♯ minor-F♯ major-B minor-F♯ minor-F♯ major-B♭ major-F♯ minor), which moves from its F♯ tonic to B minor and B♭ major (mm. 54-57), the latter of which is a remote key. Otherwise, its focus on the F♯ tonic recalls the single tonic of "Kornblumen". Both the syncopated block chords in the accompaniment of "Kornblumen" and the undulating sixteenth-note chords in part II of "Wasserrose" (from m. 49) that highlight the lyrical vocal line are in keeping with earlier nineteenth-century lieder compositional practice.

The middle two songs, "Mohnblumen" and "Epheu", showcase a number of modernist techniques that will appear in Strauss's songs later in the 1890s. Although the first two songs are paired in terms of their lighter affect, "Mohnblumen" represents a sharp affective contrast to "Kornblumen" in a different sense, with its highly disjunct, declamatory vocal line, discontinuous accompanimental textures, chromaticized harmonizations, and frequent modulations, often through distantly-related keys (mm. 14-20), that characterize Strauss's modernist song technique. This sharp contrast in compositional style, as well as the difference of a tritone between the keys of the two songs (D♭ major and G major) reflects the difference in *Stimmung* between the two poems, in which the personae of the poppies and the cornflowers are set in sharp opposition to one another.

"Epheu", the third song, represents a deeper foray into modernist practices. This song passes through several more keys[3], many of them distantly
related, than does "Mohnblumen". It is more metrically complex than the
second song, with triplet figurations in the accompaniment that are set
against the dually-organized vocal line melody, as well as frequent metric
shifts between 4/4, 3/2 and 3/4 that accommodate the semantic sense of the
text rather than poetic line units. The phrases in "Epheu" are highly asymmetrical, partially as a result of the constant shifts in meter, that, along with
frequent syncopations, create an almost conversational, spontaneous
melodic line. Such a flexible line is not so strongly present in "Kornblumen", which is also characterized by asymmetrical phrases.

Part I of "Wasserrose" (mm. 1-48) is linked to the two experimental
songs by modernist techniques exemplified by polymeter (the vocal line in
6/8 and the accompaniment in 2/4) and an asymmetrical accompanimental
pattern consisting of alternating sixteenth-note quadruplets and eighth-note
triplets.

If this commentary were to end here, it could be concluded that *Mädchenblumen* is a coherent song cycle, with a poetry cycle organized in
accordance with both semantic and structural progressions; an enharmonic
dominant/tonic relationship between the first and last songs in keeping with
the poetry cycle's progressive nature; and the flat-side/sharp-side alternation
of keys reflecting the affective pairings (in terms of intensity) of the first two
and the second two poems. The alternate, more compelling flat/sharp pairings of the outer, 'classic' songs versus the inner, 'experimentalist' songs
would become more problematic in determining a key plan that reflects
poetic relationships, since this pairing does not parallel the structure of the
poetry cycle. If, however, I invoke the song cycle's compositional history,
the integrity of the tonal plan of *Mädchenblumen* becomes seriously compromised. At the same, though, examining the compositional history reveals
Strauss's preoccupation with experimentation, serving as a possible explanation for the classic/experimentalist dichotomy that is evident in the outer
and inner song pairs.

---

[3]   The key scheme of "Epheu" is E♭ major-A major-A minor-B♭ major-E♭ major-G♭ major-
E♭ major-F♯ minor-G major-E♭ major).

In letters to Spitzweg, he describes the *Mädchenblumen* songs not only as very complex, but as 'wholly original experiments' ("ganz eigentümliche Experimente") and 'very unrewarding' ("sehr undankbare") (7 June 1889, 23 October 1890). Other correspondence to Spitzweg, Adolf Fürstner, who eventually published the cycle, and his parents indicates that *Mädchenblumen* was not only a musical experiment, but, possibly more important to Strauss, a financial one as well. Strauss was determined to obtain the unusually high fee of 800 marks for the four songs. After he offered the cycle to Fürstner on 20 October 1890 (cf. Fürstner 7[4]), his letters show him holding fast against the publisher, who did not expect this 'unrewarding' cycle to sell well (cf. 30 October 1890, 4 November 1890). When the deal was consummated for 800 M (cf. 7 November 1890), Strauss gleefully wrote to Spitzweg, "das ist doch toll" (13 November 1890).

This preoccupation with the fee for the cycle turned out to have interesting ramifications for the cycle's tonal cohesiveness. During the negotiations, Strauss offered (and subsequently produced) a transposition of *Mädchenblumen* for low voice in order to insure enough sales to justify the enormous fee that he was demanding. The key scheme of the low-voice edition does not maintain the intervallic pattern of the original composition: the high-voice tonal plan is D♭ major-G major-E♭ major-F♯ minor/major, while the low-voice tonal scheme is A major-D major-C major-C♯ minor/major (see Figure 3). Secondly, in the same letter, Strauss actually requested that the songs be sold separately because he felt that sales of the entire cycle would generate less profit (cf. 4 November 1890).

As shown on the cover of the 1891 *Mädchenblumen* edition, Fürstner indeed published the songs both as a cycle and separately, in both high- and low-voice editions, in both the original German and an English translation[5]. Not long after initial publication, consumers could purchase *Mädchen-*

---

[4]   Ursula Fürstner reproduces in facsimile Strauss's card offering *Mädchenblumen* to Adolph Fürstner.

[5]   Strauss's letter of 8 April 1891, thanking Fürstner for the handsome *Mädchenblumen* edition, indicates that the original high-voice edition was published as of that date, and his letter to Fürstner of 4 July 1891, enclosing corrections to the proofs of the low-voice transpositions, indicate that the edition for low voice probably appeared fairly soon after that time.

blumen as a whole work, or they could purchase any or all of the songs separately, in any combination of keys, to be sung in German and/or English.
More often than not, song cycles are published in transpositions in order to
increase sales. But it is the issuance of non-intervallic transpositions and the
sale of the separate components of the cycle in the first year of publication,
both at Strauss's instigation that call into question whether *Mädchenblumen*
is truly a 'song cycle' (according to McCreless's and Neumeyer's implied
definitions of the term) or merely a poetry cycle set to music.

Edition	"Kornblumen"	"Mohnblumen"	"Epheu"	"Wasserrose"
High Voice (original key)	Db major 5 flats	G major 1 sharp	Eb major 3 flats	F# minor/major 3 sharps/6 sharps
Low Voice (transposition)	A major	D major	C major	C# minor/major

Fig. 3: Richard Strauss's Mädchenblumen: *Tonal Lay-Outs of Original and Transposed Editions*

On the other hand, Strauss's musical experiments, which highlight the
clash between his classicist background and his modernist tendencies at this
point in his career, are still evident in the transposed version for low voice.
The clarity of the stylistic contrast between the inner and outer songs precludes the need for key associations to act as markers. In other words, even
when the cycle is stripped of its original key scheme, musical style still fulfills an ordering function. Yet it is still uncertain that *Mädchenblumen*
would be a song cycle without this tonal plan, since the outer 'classic' and
inner 'experimentalist' song pairs reflect neither the progressive structure
nor the affective pairings of the Dahn cycle. Nor does the classi-
cist/modernist trope articulated by this scheme have any relation to either the
semantic content or the context of Dahn's *Mädchenblumen*, which typifies
the style of the sentimental and steadfastly conservative *Münchener Dichter-
schule* patronized by King Maximilian II of Bavaria (1811-64).

Conclusion

Characteristics found in *Mädchenblumen* that enable it to be deemed a song
cycle, including 'ordered' elements, are certainly present in both the four
poems and Strauss's original musical setting for high voice. An analyst
whose criterion for defining a song group as a cycle consists primarily of
large-scale poetic/musical unity need not move into the hermeneutic realm
to determine that *Mädchenblumen* is a cycle; indeed, doing so seriously
undermines its song cycle status. The results of my discussion of *Mädchenblumen* bring me to the question of whether the approach employed by
McCreless and Neumeyer should be taken as a model for all song cycle
analyses, or only investigations of song groups in which cyclic organization
is not explicated by analyzing intrinsic musical properties. Proceeding along
the latter line of action, that is, only making use of hermeneutic elements in
song analysis when they can help to fulfill previously conceived expectations, would consist of *ad hoc* reasoning, an approach whose problems
Agawu has discussed (cf. 8-9). Yet as seen in my *Mädchenblumen* analysis,
employing the first approach could easily compromise a work's song cycle
status, assuming that the analyst's definition of a song cycle is in accordance
the assumptions made by McCreless and Neumeyer.

Since poetic/musical unity, even when informed by hermeneutic factors,
proves to be so elusive in song cycle analysis, perhaps the solution lies in
seeking a different means of defining the song cycle, a topic that has been
the focus of recent WMA papers by Cyrus Hamlin and Walter Bernhart,
who see the song cycle as a literary genre. Another possible avenue of
inquiry, which is seldom pursued, is investigation of the possible roles of
performance and audience reception in defining groups of songs as 'cyclic'[6].
At any rate, moving beyond assumptions of poetic and musical unity in our
ways of defining the song cycle might be the only means of establishing the
meaning and significance of this genre over the past two centuries and into
the next.

---

[6]   A starting point for such an inquiry could be Lawrence Kramer's 1994 article, "Performance and Social Meaning in the Lied".

References

Agawu, Kofi. "Theory and Practice in the Analysis of the Nineteenth-Century *Lied*". *Music Analysis* 11/1 (1992): 3-36.

Bernhart, Walter, Steven Paul Scher, Werner Wolf, eds. *Word and Music Studies: Defining the Field*. Amsterdam: Rodopi, 1999.

Dahn, Felix. "Mädchenblumen". Dahn. *Gedichte*. Berlin: F. A. Herbig, 1857. 16-20.

Fürstner, Ursula. "Richard Strauss und der Fürstner-Verlag". *Internationale Richard-Strauss-Gesellschaft. Mitteilungen* 50 (Sept 1966): 7, 9-10.

Hamlin, Cyrus. "The Romantic Song Cycle as Literary Genre". Bernhart et al., eds. 113-134.

Komar, Arthur, ed. *Schumann*, Dichterliebe: *An Authoritative Score*. New York: Norton, 1971.

Kramer, Lawrence. *Music and Poetry: The Nineteenth Century and After*. Berkeley: Univ. of California Press, 1984.

—. *Music as Cultural Practice, 1800-1900*. Berkeley: Univ. of California Press, 1990.

—. "Performance and Social Meaning in the Lied: Schubert's 'Erster Verlust'". *Current Musicology* 56 (1994): 5-23.

Lodato, Suzanne M. "Recent Approaches to Text/Music Analysis in the Lied: A Musicological Perspective". Bernhart et al., eds. 95-112.

McCreless, Patrick. "Song Order in the Song Cycle: Schumann's *Liederkreis*, Op. 39". *Music Analysis* 5/1 (1986): 8-11.

Neumeyer, David. "Organic Structure and The Song Cycle: Another Look at Schumann's *Dichterliebe*". *Music Theory Spectrum* 4 (1982): 92-105.

Ott, Alfons. "Richard Strauss und sein Verlegerfreund Eugen Spitzweg". *Musik und Verlag: Karl Vötterle zum 65. Geburtstag am 12. April 1968*. Ed. R. Baum and W. Rehm. Kassel: Bärenreiter, 1968. 466-475.

Strauss, Richard. Letter to Eugen Spitzweg. 7 December 1889. Weimar, #30. Z. 1950/298. Strauss, Richard, Sammelstücke. Handschriften-Abteilung, Münchner Staatsbibliothek.

—. Letter to Adolph Fürstner. 20 October 1890. Weimar, #3. Strauss correspondence. Ana 330; I, Fürstner [1890-1949]. Handschriftenabteilung, Bayerische Staatsbibliothek.

—. Letter to Eugen Spitzweg. 23 October 1890. Ott, 470.

—. Letter to Adolph Fürstner. 30 October 1890. Strauss, Richard. Weimar, #4. Strauss correspondence. Ana 330; I, Fürstner [1890-1949]. Handschriftenabteilung, Bayerische Staatsbibliothek.

—. Letter to Adolph Fürstner. 4 November 1890. Strauss, Richard. Weimar, #6. Strauss correspondence. Ana 330; I, Fürstner [1890-1949]. Handschriftenabteilung, Bayerische Staatsbibliothek.

—. Letter to Adolph Fürstner. 7 November 1890. Strauss, Richard. Weimar, #7. Strauss correspondence. Ana 330; I, Fürstner [1890-1949]. Handschriftenabteilung, Bayerische Staatsbibliothek.

—. Letter to Eugen Spitzweg. 13 November 1890. Ott, 470.

—. Letter to Adolph Fürstner. 8 April 1891. Strauss, Richard. Weimar, #12. Strauss correspondence. Ana 330; I, Fürstner [1890-1949]. Handschriftenabteilung. Bayerische Staatsbibliothek.

—. Letter to Adolph Fürstner. 4 July 1891. Strauss, Richard. Bayreuth, #15. Strauss correspondence. Ana 330; I, Fürstner [1890-1949]. Handschriftenabteilung. Bayerische Staatsbibliothek.

Thym, Jürgen. "The Solo Song Settings of Eichendorff's Poetry by Schumann and Wolf". Diss. Case Western Reserve Univ. 1974.

White, Hayden. "*Commentary*: Form, Reference, and Ideology in Musical Discourse". Steven Paul Scher, ed. *Music and Text: Critical Inquiries*. Cambridge: Cambridge Univ. Press, 1992. 288-319.

"Willst zu meinen Liedern deine Leier drehn?"
Intermedial Metatextuality in Schubert's "Der Leiermann" as a Motivation for Song and Accompaniment and a Contribution to the Unity of *Die Winterreise*

Werner Wolf, Graz

Owing to the emergence, over the past few centuries, of 'aesthetic' art, the motivations for, and functions of, individual works of art in Western culture are commonly no longer defined by specific, pragmatic contexts or situations. In some cases the work of art itself compensates for its pragmatic uncertainty by means of meta-aesthetic or meta-textual elements. However, in music only forms which involve text, such as songs and song cycles, can do so. This essay shows that in this respect Schubert's *Die Winterreise* is an especially interesting example, as the concluding "Der Leiermann" does not only motivate the text of Müller's poem cycle metapoetically at its very end but also the fact that in Schubert's *Die Winterreise* a singer is accompanied by a musician. Thus the implied answer 'yes' to the final question in "Der Leiermann" cited in the title of this essay has an intermedial relevance, for on a meta-level this self-reflexive question refers both to the text of the song cycle and to the second medium present in Schubert's work: music. The intermedial metatextuality of the last song also opens up a possibility of reading *Die Winterreise* on a fictional level as a 'duodrama' of wanderer and hurdy-gurdy man and at the same time creates a special, cyclical unity: by retrospectively suggesting a fictional origin of the performance of singer and piano player the last song reveals the self-begetting structure of *Die Winterreise* and invites a re-reading of the entire cycle as a re-enactment staged by both wanderer and hurdy-gurdy player.

1. The questionable cyclicity of song cycles, and the special case of *Die Winterreise* due to the concluding song "Der Leiermann"

What renders a song cycle a song **cycle** has often been discussed[1], and various criteria have been proposed to account for the supposed or genuine unity of this musico-literary form. Yet, from an etymological point of view,

---

[1] Lately, e.g., by Cyrus Hamlin; see also the contributions to this volume by Walter Bernhart, Suzanne Lodato and Leon Plantinga.

the term 'song cycle', though time-hallowed and sanctioned by composers themselves, seems often to be a misnomer: for instance, if applied to Franz Schubert's *Die schöne Müllerin* and even to Robert Schumann's *Liederkreis*. For 'cycle', in a temporal art, should imply a cyclic movement, in which unity is created by an ending that points back to a beginning. In contrast to this, there is no such pointing back at all in many so-called 'song cycles', and there is often not even a hermeneutic motivation to see a connection between ending and beginning so that the persistent critical quest for unity in a song cycle has come under attack, as can also be seen in several contributions to this volume, notably in the essays by Leon Plantinga and Jürgen Thym[2]. So, strictly speaking, instead of 'song cycles', we had perhaps better speak in these cases of 'song collections'.

However, there **are** examples where either the music of the last song takes up the first song, as in Schumann's *Frauenliebe und Leben*[3] and in Richard Strauss' *Mädchenblumen*[4], or where the text somehow refers to the beginning or to the entire series of songs, as in Schumann's *Myrten* with its concluding mention of a "Kranz", a 'garland'[5]. There are also cases in which both music **and** text of the framing songs create the impression of cyclicity, one of the most obvious examples being Ludwig van Beethoven's *An die ferne Geliebte*[6].

---

[2]   For the looseness of many nineteenth-century song cycles cf. also Hamlin.

[3]   Compare especially the opening bars of the first song, "Seit ich ihn gesehen" (Schumann, p. 84), with the concluding *Adagio*, "Tempo wie das erste Lied" (Schumann, p. 105), of the last song, "Nun hast du mir den ersten Schmerz gethan".

[4]   For more details see Lodato's interpretation in this volume. Lodato, however, also emphasizes the fact that in particular the gestation of *Mädchenblumen* relativizes the unity of this song cycle.

[5]   In the last song, "Zum Schluss", a "Kranz" in honour of the beloved woman is mentioned: the speaker has weaved it as an imperfect substitute for the perfect 'garland' which love will confer on her in eternity (Schumann, p. 57). Clearly, this 'imperfect garland' is a veiled meta-poetic reference to the song cycle, the "Liederkranz" itself, which is the representational substitute for the perfect union of love hoped for after the speaker's death.

[6]   This cyclicity is due to conspicuous word and music recurrences in the first song, "Auf dem Hügel sitz ich spähend", and the last, "Nimm sie hin denn, diese Lieder" (Beethoven, pp. 42 f. and 54): both songs contain similar text passages ("Denn vor Liedesklang entweichet jeder Raum und jede Zeit, und ein liebend Herz erreichet, was ein liebend Herz geweiht" – "[...] dann vor diesen Liedern weichet, was geschieden uns so weit, und ein liebend Herz erreichet, was ein liebend Herz geweiht"), and these passages are set to identical melodies. Both songs are also remarkable for their metapoetic quality (see below, note 23).

A particularly interesting, though less obvious case in point is Schubert's setting to music of Wilhelm Müller's poem cycle *Die Winterreise*. In Schubert's work the cyclic structure is not directly evident, as in the framing songs of *An die ferne Geliebte*, by a recurrence of musical and textual elements[7]. It is rather suggested indirectly in the concluding song, "Der Leiermann", arguably the most intriguing element of the entire cycle, by both the music and the text of the last metapoetic question, "Willst zu meinen Liedern/Deine Leier drehn?" (Müller 123, ll. 19-20). "Der Leiermann" is also the song which among all the texts of *Die Winterreise* has triggered most comments. Of course, its metatextual implications have not gone unnoticed, as can be seen, for instance, in the anticipation of parts of my own title in the title of Wolfgang Hufschmidt's monograph (*Willst zu meinen Liedern deine Leier drehn? Zur Semantik der musikalischen Sprache in Schuberts "Winterreise" und Eislers "Hollywood-Liederbuch"*). Hufschmidt read the wanderer's last unanswered question as a means of Müller's to trigger a composer's response. According to Hufschmidt, Schubert answered this appeal by reducing his musical means in "Der Leiermann" to the level of a *musica pauperum*, indicating thereby his solidarity with the outcast hurdy-gurdy man (cf. 42). In contrast to this reading, I do not want to focus on the social issues underlying Schubert's song but rather on two related aesthetic issues which, to my knowledge, have not yet been highlighted in criticism. I will concentrate on the functions of the last song with respect to a possible pragmatic motivation for *Die Winterreise* and also with reference to the vexed question of the unity of this work[8] as an intermedial combination of word and music, of song and accompaniment, forming a genuine song cycle.

---

[7] Hamlin has tried to establish a musical connection between the end of "Der Leiermann" and the beginning of the first song, "Gute Nacht", but the connection is not obvious so that he himself feels obliged to caution that "such a return to the beginning of the cycle [...] should not be taken literally" (132).

[8] Cf., as one of the most recent discussions of this question, Hamlin and the research mentioned in his essay.

2. Art's lack of pragmatic motivation: fictional substitutes
in literature, and the problematic pragmatics of music

It is a truth universally acknowledged that human activities must have motivations and that such motivations influence both their structure and possible
functions. This is also true of aesthetic activities, including literature and
music. However, owing to the Western conception, developed over the past
few centuries, of art as something not immediately 'useful', the identification of motivations, in particular those that go beyond biographical or
critical concerns of the artist or author, has become difficult. This difficulty
is linked to what Wolfgang Iser, with an eye to fictional literature, has called
the 'lack of a pragmatic situation' (cf. "Die Wirklichkeit der Fiktion" 290
and 294). Before the emergence of 'aesthetic' art, the motivations and functions of texts and artworks were commonly defined by specific, pragmatic
contexts or situations for which these works were produced. These 'extra-
compositional' frames were on the whole sufficient for the identification of
functions, and optional 'intracompositional' indications of motivation
typically only served to reinforce these functions. With the rise of art as a
predominantly non-pragmatic phenomenon the relation between function,
motivation and frame has, however, changed. In many cases different
frames can now attribute varying functions to individual works, functions
which have also become relatively independent of their original motivations. In some cases, however, the work of art itself attempts to compensate
for its pragmatic uncertainty or lack of pragmatic function by providing an
intracompositional, often fictional motivation.

Generally, intracompositional motivations are established through self-
reflexive, 'metatextual' or 'meta-aesthetic' elements within the work of art.
Obviously, literature, whose semiotic nature does not only privilege referential meaning but also allows explicit self-reflexivity, has the special
advantage of conveying its own motivation by such intracompositional
means. Novels, such as Daniel Defoe's *Moll Flanders* or Samuel Richard-
son's *Pamela*, simulate a pragmatic motivation by means of characters who
self-reflexively profess an urge to confess or to communicate extraordinary
or distressing events and states of minds. Poems, such as William Wordsworth's famous "Daffodils", can be motivated by the metatextual device of

presenting the speaker as a poet, who, as it were, has a professional interest in conveying his experience in written form. And William Shakespeare's plays, at their endings or at other memorable moments, frequently contain explicit metatextual passages explaining their existence and even their performance, a famous example being Cassius's comment made after Julius Caesar's assassination:

> [...] How many ages hence
> Shall this our lofty scene be acted over,
> In states unborn, and accents yet unknown!
> (*Julius Caesar*, 3.1.111-113)

The performance of music, even of 'pragmatic' music composed for a certain occasion or for certain uses, is here markedly different. This is particularly true of 'pure', non-intermedial music: instrumental music. Due to its lack of semantic precision it cannot provide fictional intracompositional motativations but must entirely rely on a framing situation: a church service, a concert, a dancing entertainment or the joyfulness of a situation in which people express their feelings by making music.

In song, however, a metatextual motivation comparable to fictional literature is possible, owing to the combination of music and words that may carry a clearly self-reflexive semantic message. Such a motivation may be remembered from folk songs containing invitations to sing, and it also exists in choral texts such as "Nun singt dem Herrn ein neues Lied" ('Now sing a new song unto the Lord'). Usually, what is thus pragmatically justified is the music making or the singing, but hardly ever, if it exists in the first place, the accompaniment[9].

In 'pragmatic' music, intracompositional motivations for song provided by metatextuality mostly occur as a confirmation of an obvious reference to a framing situation. In non-pragmatic music, such as artsongs (*Kunstlieder*), similar references would be less obvious, but the combination of music and poetic text here opens other and more elaborate possibilities, including a

---

[9]   This is also true of the verse "Psalter und Harfe, wacht auf" ('psalter and harp, awake') from the famous German choral "Lobe den Herren", for here the 'awakening' of musical instruments called for is only a metonymy for the music making in general, but it is no covert reference, for instance, to the actual organ accompanying the voices of the congregation.

(fictional) motivation for the accompaniment. An excellent example of such a double motivation for song **and** accompaniment can be found in Schubert's "Der Leiermann". As I will argue, this twofold motivation is a significant contribution to the unity of *Die Winterreise* and is actually the reason why this work is truly a song **cycle**, that is, a series of songs with a cyclic form.

3. The wanderer as 'singer': the metatextual motivation for, and the contribution to, the unity of the poem cycle in Müller's "Der Leiermann"

A first and in fact decisive step towards a pragmatic motivation for *Die Winterreise* as a song **cycle** is already made on the verbal level of Müller's text, with which I will start. Susan Youens, in her 1991 book *Retracing a Winter's Journey*, has proposed an interesting though, I think, simplifying reading of Müller's work. For her, the entire text is a "Monodrama" (51), a sort of monologue by the wanderer, in which "Müller [...] deliberately excludes [...] the implied presence of an auditor" (53). Since there are "no implied or actual listeners from within the poem to hear his tale" the reader becomes a sort of "eavesdropper" of a text, psychologically motivated by the wanderer's "inner compulsion, a directive from within to forge his own path alone in the snow" (ibid.). According to Youens, "Müller wanted his poetry to speak directly to the heart, without the intervening obstacle[...] of [...] apparent poetic artifice [...]" (ibid.)[10]. In this quasi modernist psychological reading, *Die Winterreise* becomes an "Inward Voyage" (55), and the hurdy-gurdy man in the last poem turns into "a *Doppelgänger* phantom, a projection of the wanderer's mind" (297)[11].

---

[10] Cf. also ibid.: "Throughout the cycle, the wanderer talks to himself as if entirely alone, inducting the reader-spy directly into his mental processes with no narrator, no intermediary present."

[11] Cf. also 299 f.: "The wanderer's creation of a *Doppelgänger* from within his wounded soul [...]". In a comparable way Lawrence Kramer conceives of the singer and the hurdy-gurdy player as "the halves of a divided self" (218). Both interpretations jump too quickly to psychological, if not psychoanalytical, conclusions and in their emphasis on a metaphorical dimension underrate the more downright 'mimetic' reading which underlies my

While I would not totally rule out this reading, which focuses on **one** romantic convention, namely on the 'introverted' poem, it is at least problematic in its one-sidedness, as has recently been pointed out by Cyrus Hamlin. One need not even refer, as Hamlin has done, to another romantic convention, namely "the [...] need of an audience for the poetic expression of seemingly naive effusions" (118); Youens's interpretation disregards elementary conventions of poetry in general. Lyric poetry is usually written in the present tense and may be read as a transcript of the thoughts of a lyric persona, whether these remain in the state of an interior monologue or soliloquy or attain the form of uttered communication. Yet this does **not** mean that, in the poetic world, all contents of these thoughts must automatically be imagined as mere "projections". Such an interpretation as a "projection" is especially questionable if there are no clear indications pointing in this direction and if there are, on the contrary, deictic elements referring to a fictional outer reality. In "Der Leiermann", such a deictic element already occurs in the first line, "Drüben hinter'm Dorfe", and there are no indications rendering the hurdy-gurdy man less real than, for instance, the crow accompanying the wanderer[12].

Drüben hinter'm Dorfe
Steht ein Leiermann,
Und mit starren Fingern
Dreht er was er kann.

    Barfuß auf dem Eise
Schwankt er hin und her;
Und sein kleiner Teller
Bleibt ihm immer leer.

    Keiner mag ihn hören,
Keiner sieht ihn an;

---

interpretation, a reading of the wanderer and the hurdy-gurdy man as two distinct characters present in the fictional world.

[12] Neither is this reality brought into question by the fact that, at the outset of the last poem, the hurdy-gurdy player is still perceived as stationed 'over there' ("drüben"), that is, at a certain distance from the wanderer, while in the last stanza he must be within hearing range. We simply have to imagine that between the first and the last stanzas the wanderer has approached the old man: such *Leerstellen*, as Wolfgang Iser has called similar 'gaps of meaning' with reference to fiction (cf. "Die Appellstruktur der Texte" 235), do not only occur in fiction (or drama for that matter), but are especially frequent in poetry as a genre challenging readerly imagination to an especially high degree.

Und die Hunde brummen
Um den alten Mann.

Und er läßt es gehen,
Alles, wie es will,
Dreht, und seine Leier
Steht ihm nimmer still.

Wunderlicher Alter,
Soll ich mit dir gehn?
Willst zu meinen Liedern
Deine Leier drehn?
(Müller 123)

This is not to say that the hurdy-gurdy man cannot **also** be read as a symbol
or allegory, for instance, of a certain kind of music[13]. Yet, on a literal level,
he is simply a character met by the wanderer, and this meeting, as I will
show, has a decisive metatextual and – in Schubert's work – also an intermedial relevance. In an earlier essay Youens herself had viewed the hurdy-
gurdy player more plausibly in such a literal way as a real presence in the
fictional world (cf. "Retracing a Winter Journey" 132 f.). He is in fact the
only human being whom the wanderer encounters during his journey and
the only person to whom he speaks, or more precisely, to whom he
addresses questions (see the last stanza, ll. 17-20). Although, according to
Richard Kramer, "[w]e are not given to know the answers" (182), there is no
problem about finding them, and most critics agree that the answers are
'yes' (cf., e.g., Eggebrecht 41, and Baumann/Luetgert 50): "the old man and
the wanderer leave the cycle together", as Youens has remarked in her essay
("Retracing a Winter Journey" 132).

  If this is so, it has important reverberations on the reading of Müller's
sequence of poems, their internal motivation and structure. Up to the last
poem before "Der Leiermann" we might concede that Youens's interpretation in *Retracing a Winter's Journey* is at least right in so far as the wanderer seems to soliloquize. Yet with "Der Leiermann" there is a possibility
to readjust this view. It now appears that the text does not remain in the state
of a soliloquy which we follow as an expression of the wanderer's synchro-

---

[13]   For further interpretations as "Charon", the wanderer's "*Doppelgänger*" or "artist" cf.
Baumann/Luetgert (49), who have tried to liken the entire *Winterreise* to the rendering of a
near-death-experience.

nous experience, and that not only parts of "Der Leiermann", but in fact the entire poem cycle is uttered in the company of, if not to, the hurdy-gurdy man. How is this possible? Literally, "Der Leiermann", and with it Müller's poem cycle, stops after the last question "Willst zu meinen Liedern/Deine Leier drehn?" (ll. 19-20), and R. Kramer, in a literal-minded way, has indeed asked: "What kinds of song are we to imagine might still be left to sing?" (183). Yet the explicitly metatextual, or to be more precise, meta-poetic term used here, namely "Lieder", suggests a self-reflexive reference to the poems we just have read, since "Lied", in accordance with a romantic convention often used by Müller himself (cf. Baumann/Luetgert 50), not only refers to 'song' but also to a lyric poem.

This opens two further possible readings of Müller's *Die Winterreise* which both go beyond the standard reading (reading a), i.e. the mere impression of following the transcript of the wanderer's journey as a present experience that comes to an end after the last song: according to the first alternative (reading b), we would for once be entitled to do something which has been proscribed ever since L. C. Knight's famous ironic question "How many children had Lady Macbeth?", namely to imagine a continuation of the life of a fictional character beyond the textual boundaries in the strict sense. However, in this case the continuation is suggested by Müller's text itself and consists in the idea that the wanderer will sing songs in the company of the hurdy-gurdy player which are similar to, or identical with, those we have just read. This prospective reading would, however, entail an unwelcome redundance on the content level or, as it has been termed in lyric theory, on the level of the 'enounced', and this would indeed be unneces-sary[14], as there is a second alternative (reading c): it consists in switching our focus from the level of the 'enounced' and its hypothetical continuation to the discursive reality of the level of the textual transmission or 'enuncia-tion'[15]. If we consider this level and connect it with the metapoetic sugges-tion in "Der Leiermann", the series of poems we are about to finish reading retrospectively **is** the very text which is uttered to the hurdy-gurdy man (cf.

---

[14]   As Hamlin has pointed out: "No one would want the cycle, long and complex as it is, to start all over again after reaching the end." (132)

[15]   For this theoretical distinction between 'enounced' (the content) and 'enunciation' (the discursivation of a poem and everything linked with it) cf. Hühn (vol. 1, 9-20).

also Hamlin 133). In this view, *Die Winterreise* is no longer the transcript of present experience filtered through the mind of the wanderer but a re-enactment of past events and feelings[16].

Whatever possibility we prefer, two results come into focus: the first refers to the structure of the sequence of poems and the position of "Der Leiermann" in it. If we consider the level of the enounced as the verbalization of an experience with a continuation in the future, the events preceding "Der Leiermann" can also be conceived of as the pre-history leading up to the meeting of the two men; and if we consider the enunciation of the text as a consequence of this meeting, *Die Winterreise* becomes the re-enactment of an experience, a re-enactment triggered by this decisive meeting. In any case, the series of poems pivots on "Der Leiermann": it could as well start with this text as end with it. This interchangeability of ending and beginning points to a structure which distinguishes *Die Winterreise* from other sequences of poems and gives it a formal quality and a unity which go beyond the impression of a series of naive and simple expressions of subjective feelings: it renders *Die Winterreise* a true **cycle** of poems[17].

What is more, "Der Leiermann" is not just an ending of a poem cycle pointing back to the beginning. The concluding poem thus points back, because, according to our readings (b) and (c), it self-reflexively displays the fictional **origin** of the entire *Winterreise*. Owing to this feature, Müller's *Die Winterreise* perfectly fits into a pattern which, in fiction, is epitomized by Marcel Proust's *A la recherche du temps perdu* and was named by Steven Kellman the "self-begetting novel"[18]. In analogy to this, *Die Winterreise* can be called a '**self-begetting poem cycle**'.

---

[16] It has repeatedly been noticed (cf. Georgiades, and Hamlin) that *Die Winterreise* does not follow the usual logic of narratives in all respects. However, although I think that *Die Winterreise* does show elements of narrativity (see below, note 32), there is no need for presupposing a narrative logic for any of the readings proposed by me, since the events underlying the cycle of poems are in any case transmitted by the wanderer's thoughts or his psyche (to this extent the psychic reading of Youens would be acceptable if, on the fictional level, one does not deduce from the fact that we read a transcript of thoughts that the thinker must necessarily be alone).

[17] Cf. also Youens ("Retracing a Winter Journey"), who has convincingly argued against the view of Müller as a "'simple and naive'" (128) poet.

[18] Georgiades (cf. 389) and Feil (cf. 147) try to account for this special function of "Der Leiermann" by expelling this song, as it were, from the 'story' proper and likening it to a paratextual epilogue. Yet there are no textual indications according to which "Der Leier-

The self-reflexive ending of Müller's poem cycle has yet another consequence. Its enunciation does not merely rest on accidental and incalculable
external motivating factors; in addition it obtains an intracompositional
justification: by transforming the wanderer, on the fictional level, from a
subject whose experience, as in so many poems, is only formulated in
thought, into a '**singer**'[19] who, in the company of the hurdy-gurdy man,
sings his songs aloud to an audience. In the old man, who is socially at the
margins of society, the wanderer has found a congenial soul[20] to go with
him, as he himself feels an outcast, too, owing to his disappointed love[21].

Of course, in a recital of Müller's text as mere poems this 'singing',
derived from the self-reflexive term "Lieder", remains metaphorical, and
must be put in inverted commas, since there is no real song. The self-
reflexivity of "Der Leiermann" thus seems somewhat limited. This limitation is even more evident with reference to the hurdy-gurdy man. If the person reciting Müller's text, can be considered to impersonate the wanderer
staging his 'songs' as a result of his meeting the old man, there is no-one
present who could impersonate this man, unless the audience took his place.
It is one of Schubert's achievements to have expanded these limits, as will
be seen in the following.

4. The *Leiermann* as musician: metatextual and metamedial motivation for the accompaniment and the unity of Schubert's song cycle

So far, I have actually only discussed Müller's cycle of poems, that is, the
text, its motivation and the unity resulting from this motivation: I have not

---

mann" should be read on another fictional level than the rest of *Die Winterreise*; hence the
idea of a self-begetting structure seems to be more appropriate.

[19] A first hint in the text pointing in this direction is to be found in the first stanza of
"Mut": "Wenn mein Herz im Busen spricht,/Sing' ich hell und munter." (Müller 123)

[20] Cf. also Youens ("Retracing a Winter Journey" 132) and Smeed (110).

[21] This similarity, however, does not necessarily mean that the hurdy-gurdy man is a
Doppelgänger, as has been claimed (see above, note 13), nor that he is an imaginary
double, as L. Kramer and Youens (cf. *Retracing a Winter's Journey*) suggest.

yet referred to the **music** and **its** motivation, that is, to the fact that Schubert took Müller's text as the basis of a **song** cycle. In Schubert's setting this text to music in precisely the way he has done, that is, for a male singer and, perhaps, a male pianist, an additional internal motivation emerges in the last song, a motivation which fills a decisive gap left by Müller in his merely verbal text. In a performance as vocal music, "Der Leiermann" not only contains a *raison d'être* for the text uttered by the wanderer, but also for the very act of involving music in the form of an **accompaniment**: if the implied answer to the wanderer's questions as to whether the old man will go with him and accompany his songs is 'yes', and if this can be read as a self-reflexive clue for interpreting *Die Winterreise* as the songs being performed by these two, it follows that there is not only a correlation between the wanderer, the vocal part and the singer, but also between the hurdy-gurdy man, the piano part and the piano player[22]. In performance, *Die Winterreise* thus is not a "monodrama", as Youens has claimed (*Retracing a Winter's Journey* 51), but at its end turns out, in a retrospective reading, to be a musical 'duodrama' with the singer figuring as the wanderer and the piano player representing the hurdy-gurdy man in the act of their 'going' or performing together, the very act prepared and motivated by the last two questions in "Der Leiermann"[23]. There does not seem to be any explicit 'dramatic' interaction between the characters of the 'duodrama' on the fictional level, it is true, yet interaction does take place on the musical level, namely in the relation between voice and accompaniment, and the responses of the accompaniment to the singing voice can in turn be imagined to illustrate the hurdy-gurdy man's responses towards the wanderer.

---

[22] Hamlin (cf. 133) restricts the self-reflexivity of "Der Leiermann" to the singer alone without accounting for the hurdy-gurdy man; Youens, by calling the wanderer a "Musician" ("Retracing a Winter Journey" 133), also blurs these correspondences.

[23] Thus Schubert can be said to go one step further than Beethoven did in *An die ferne Geliebte*: in setting Jeitteles' *Liederkreis* to music, Beethoven, like Schubert, actually carried out what in *An die ferne Geliebte* is already suggested in the metapoetic question and answer contained in the first song, "Will denn nichts mehr zu dir dringen, nichts der Liebe Bote sein? **Singen will ich, Lieder singen**, die dir klagen meine Pein" (Beethoven 42, emphasis added); this is similar to what Schubert did with reference to Müller's metapoetic text; yet the parallel stops here: contrary to what I argue as happening in the concluding song of *Die Winterreise*, there is no motivation for the **accompaniment** in any of the songs of Beethoven's song cycle.

The impression that singer and piano player will 'go together' (reading b) or have already joined each other (reading c), is in fact anticipated or expressed by Schubert in the musical affinities between vocal and piano parts, which are especially clear in "Der Leiermann". These affinities have often been commented on by musicologists[24] and need not be explained here once again in all details. Let it suffice to recall some essential features. What is most frequently mentioned in comparisons between the two parts is the seeming response taking place between both in the last few bars. In bar 56 the vocal part, singing the decisive question "Willst zu meinen Liedern [...]?" imitates, though in another rhythm, the hurdy-gurdy motif of the preceding bar and then is answered, as it were, by the only *forte* outbreak in the piano part in bar 58 (see Figure 1):

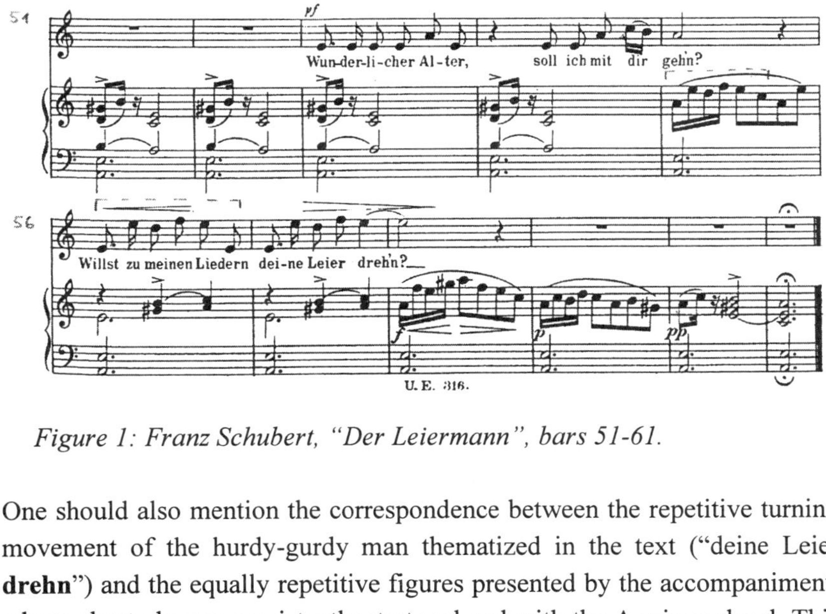

Figure 1: Franz Schubert, "Der Leiermann", bars 51-61.

One should also mention the correspondence between the repetitive turning movement of the hurdy-gurdy man thematized in the text ("deine Leier **drehn**") and the equally repetitive figures presented by the accompaniment, whose short phrases persistently start and end with the A minor chord. This is an acoustic evocation of cyclicity in word and music, and one is tempted to read it not only as a 'mimetic' re-presentation of hurdy-gurdy music with

---

[24] Cf. Eggebrecht (41 f.); Youens ("Retracing a Winter Journey" 132 f.), Smeed (112), Hufschmidt (138), and R. Kramer (183), who even speaks of an "intimate response to the wanderer" on the part of the hurdy-gurdy man.

its persistent droning basses and repeated open fifths but also, on a meta-aesthetic level, as a mirroring of the cyclicity implied in the song cycle as a whole. At any rate one can say that the intermedial 'going together' of text/song and accompaniment which is semantically pre-figured in the answer 'yes' to the concluding questions of Müller's poem is here taken seriously by Schubert and is illustrated in an audible unity of the two constituent parts of his *Kunstlied*[25]. Müller's **metapoetic** motivation for the poem cycle is thus expanded by Schubert into a **metamedial** *raison d'être* for the union of word and music in a song cycle, and at the same time the self-reflexivity in Müller's "Der Leiermann" becomes 'intermedial metatextuality', since it refers no longer to the textual medium alone but also to the second medium present: music.

With an eye to the relation between song and accompaniment in "Der Leiermann" one could even argue that Schubert here did not only illustrate the interaction or affinity between singer and hurdy-gurdy man, but also dramatized the paradox implied in all self-begetting texts, namely that such a text is at the same time an ongoing present or a pre-history, and the re-enactment of this pre-history. On the one hand the striking similarity between the harmonic, tonal and melodic simplicity of the vocal and the piano parts could be explained in a 'mimetic way' by considering the accompaniment as the representation of the hurdy-gurdy the wanderer hears when he approaches the village and to which he unconsciously sets his own tune. Conceived of in this way the similarity between vocal part and accompaniment would point toward a reading of *Die Winterreise* as a dramatization of a present or of a pre-history leading up to the moment of origin which motivates the existence of the work of art the receiver experiences.

On the other hand the reference to "Drüben hinter'm Dorfe" suggests a distance which would render such an attention on the part of the wanderer not very probable. It is in fact remarkable that the imitation of the hurdy-gurdy in the accompaniment seems to determine the vocal part from the very beginning of the song and that the harmony between the vocal and the piano parts exists even **before** the meeting between wanderer and hurdy-

---

[25] The intimate relation between word and music confirms Georgiades' remark that, in *Die Winterreise,* the piano part is generally much more than a mere accompaniment, a "Spiel-begleitung" (360).

gurdy player is thematized, before the decisive final questions are asked, and perhaps even before the wanderer can hear and respond to the hurdy-gurdy music. All this suggests that the wanderer is already singing to the old man's accompaniment at the outset of the song and even previous to it[26]. The musical anticipation of the correspondence between wanderer and old man points to the possible alternative reception of *Die Winterreise* as a re-enactment in which both already 'harmonize' in their common performance.

Whatever reading one chooses, the result, as I have already pointed out, is a sort of musical 'duodrama', in which the *Miteinandergehen* of wanderer and hurdy-gurdy man fulfills several functions. On the intrafictional level it has a social and a therapeutic function: it provides solace to both. The old man need no longer be lonely and has finally found someone to listen to him, and the wanderer, similar to the wedding guest in Coleridge's "Rime of the Ancient Mariner", yet without his implication of guilt, has found a means to vent his grief: by repeating, refining and sublimating it in art[27].

As Youens has said, this social and therapeutic function also has meta-aesthetic implications which transcend the intrafictional level and affect the relation between art and society: from what can be deduced from "Der Leiermann", singing and music, "no matter how humble", appear as "means of survival in a hostile world" ("Retracing a Winter Journey" 132). This has particular relevance in the context of romanticism, where the artist and his work have lost their anchoring in patronage and the traditional institutions, throne and altar, and have to redefine their *raison d'être*[28].

One could even go one step further: interestingly, the last questions are addressed to the hurdy-gurdy man, the representative, if one likes, of instrumental music, and in the fictional world it is **his** 'yes' which, in the above readings b) and c), triggers *Die Winterreise* as a cycle of songs with

---

[26]   This retrospective view, which focuses on the enunciation, is taken up by Eggebrecht: "Die Frage am Ende des Gedichts ist im Lied zum Geschehnis geworden: der Sänger *geht* bereits mit dem Leiermann, und dieser *dreht* schon jetzt seine Leier zu dessen Lied." (42)

[27]   Smeed takes a somewhat too bleak outlook on this re-enactment by claiming that the wanderer "must endlessly repeat and relive his sufferings in song" (109).

[28]   Cf. Feil (148), who refers to Dietrich Fischer-Dieskau's interpretation (cf. 292) of "Der Leiermann" as an 'ironic self-portrait' of Schubert, without, however, specifying whether he means the 'self-portrait' to be embodied by the wanderer or the hurdy-gurdy man. Baumann/Luetgert (49) are here more precise in mentioning the possibility of viewing the hurdy-gurdy man as as a representative of "the artist".

accompaniment. On a metamedial level, this can be read as a covert celebration of instrumental music, even of a humble kind, as an equal and in fact
decisive partner in the union of the two arts of poetry and music[29]. It might
even be that the "minimalist aesthetic" on which the music of the last song
seems to be based (L. Kramer 218)[30] is not only to be conceived of, indexi-
cally, as an illustration of how low the wanderer has sunk owing to his
broken heart, but also meta-aesthetically as a modest irony on Schubert's
part pointing self-reflexively to the contrasting, far more sophisticated
musical aesthetics informing the other songs of *Die Winterreise*.

Finally, as has already become clear, the implicitly affirmative answers
to the final questions and the suggested illustration of their consequences in
the existence and nature of Schubert's song cycle can also be read as one of
the rare cases in which non-pragmatic vocal music internally motivates its
existence, performance and texture. This has an effect not often encountered
in song cycles: it gives retrospective plausibility to the activity of both the
singer **and** the piano player beyond the external frame of a recital. It offers
them roles to play and thereby could even be said to contribute to the emergence of a rudimentary aesthetic illusion[31]. It is true, imagining the wanderer's 'story'[32] as a repetition or a re-enactment dramatized by two charac-

---

[29] The implicit importance which Schubert here seems to attribute to (instrumental) music
renders Hamlin's contention doubtful according to which the genre 'song cycle' is "essentially literary" (114). At least with respect to *Die Winterreise*, but also with a view to *An die
ferne Geliebte*, this claim is not entirely convincing.

[30] For the "'gigantic simplicity'" of "Der Leiermann" cf. also Youens (*Retracing a Winter's Journey* 297-301, quotation p. 300).

[31] For the possibility of aesthetic illusion in lyric poetry in general cf. Wolf ("Aesthetic
illusion in lyric poetry?"). In the case of "Der Leiermann" the aesthetic illusion can only be
rudimentary, since the identification of singer and piano player as roles in a 'duodrama' are
too fleeting: as soon as this impression emerges, the cycle has come to an end. So what remains is rather the idea that here, contrary to Youens's alleged absence of "apparent poetic
artifice" (*Retracing a Winter's Journey* 53), a work of art self-reflexively points to itself as
an artefact. This aspect has been emphasized by Baumann/Luetgert, who aptly describe the
"startling effect" of the metatextual ending of the cycle as "wrenching the audience out of
the music and back to the awareness that they are listening to a singer [...]" (50).

[32] Taking into account Hamlin's convincing criticism, according to which the story-quality
of *Die Winterreise* is doubtful (cf. esp. 116), I am here using the term 'story' with due caution, yet want to insist on the fact that *Die Winterreise* does contain essential elements of
'narrativity', in particular a series of temporally distinct experiences which are causally
connected to the wanderer's initial, heart-breaking disappointment in love, and a telos: the

ters is only possible in a retrospective reading and thus exists only in theory. Yet this theoretical repetition is realized in the reception history of *Die Winterreise* on the external communication level each time this song cycle is actually re-enacted in a performance.

The self-begetting auto-reflexivity of *Die Winterreise* with its consequences for the possibility of a pragmatic motivation thus creates a curious ambivalence. On the one hand, owing to the imagined cyclic repetition built into the very nature of a self-begetting work of art, it gestures towards a transgression of the textual limits and thus contains an element of openness. On the other hand, it also contains an element of closure similar to the self-reflexive thematization of the story as a re-enacted text which we encounter, for instance, at the end of *Hamlet*, where Shakespeare has Horatio say "[...] let me speak to th'yet unknowing world/How these things came about" (*Hamlet* 5.2.380-381). As in this instance, the metatextual thematization in "Der Leiermann" functions as an end signal, marking the point where the fictional experience underlying the song cycle becomes artefact. This ambivalence of openness and closure is doubled in a curious detail in the history of the gestation of Schubert's "Der Leiermann", as discussed by Richard Kramer. Originally, the song was set in B minor, with the effect, that, according to Kramer, "[t]he cycle ends not with any tonal resolve" (184). Yet Schubert "acquiesced to a transposition of the song away from B minor" to A minor and thereby established a link with the identical tonality of the preceding "Nebensonnen", which came to neighbour "Der Leiermann" in Schubert's arrangement[33]. This creates, in Kramer's view, "a false sense of closure" and amounts to a "tampering with the [...] essence of the cycle" (184), which for him "is effectively without end" (187). However, rather than a "tampering with" the "essence" of Schubert's work, this allegedly "false sense of closure" on the level of the tonalities chosen by Schubert perhaps best corresponds to the ambivalence of closure **and** openness suggested by the self-begetting structure of *Die Winterreise.*

---

aestheticization of the wanderer's experience in a cycle of poems/songs, as thematized in "Der Leiermann".

[33] For the history of Schubert's setting Müller's *Die Winterreise* to music and the changes occurring in the process cf. Georgiades (357 f.), Youens ("*Winterreise*: In the Right Order") and Plantinga's essay in this volume (141-163).

5. Conclusion: intermediality and aesthetic self-reflexivity

The self-reflexive motivation for the song cycle at the end of *Die Winter-reise* appears to be an exception in the seemingly innocent and natural intermedial enterprise of composing song cycles. Yet, as Hans Heinrich Eggebrecht has emphasized (cf. "Vertontes Gedicht"), setting poetic texts to music is never an innocent activity, for it always presupposes a reading of a work of art, hence an act of interpretation. There is, of course, no compulsion that such interpretive activities lead to an intermedial artefact with a meta-aesthetic self-reflexivity which thematizes and even justifies its very intermedial status. However, as Ulla-Britta Lagerroth has shown in her contribution to the First International Conference on Word and Music Studies, a contribution which focuses on musicalizing tendencies in literature, and as I myself have since shown in the field of musicalized fiction (cf. *The Musicalization of Fiction*), there **is** in fact a certain affinity between intermediality and aesthetic self-reflexivity. To be sure, this affinity is stronger in more unusual cases of intermediality such as musicalized fiction. However, as the case of Schubert's *Winterreise* illustrates, it can also be spotted in more conventional and indeed institutionalized variants of intermediality, such as the song cycle. It testifies to Schubert's greatness as an interpreter and composer that he answered the self-reflexive challenge already built into Müller's seemingly naive sequence of poems, that, in responding to the concluding questions in Müller's text by his music, he added a pragmatic motivation for the accompaniment and the singing to the already existing motivation for the wanderer as a reciter of poems, and that he thus created a work of art which, owing to its self-begetting structure, reveals a compelling aesthetic unity and truly merits the generic term '**song cycle**'.

References

Baumann, Cecilia C., M. J. Luetgert. "*Die Winterreise*: The Secret of the Cycle's Appeal". *Mosaic* 15/1 (1982) *Death and Dying*: 41-52.
Beethoven, Ludwig van. *Ausgewählte Lieder für eine Singstimme mit Klavierbegleitung. Ausgabe für tiefere Stimme*. Leipzig: Peters, n.d.

Bernhart, Walter, Steven P. Scher, Werner Wolf, eds. *Word and Music Studies: Defining the Field. Proceedings of the First International Conference on Word and Music Studies at Graz, 1997*. Amsterdam: Rodopi, 1999.

Eggebrecht, Hans Heinrich. "Vertontes Gedicht: Über das Verstehen von Kunst durch Kunst". Günter Schnitzler, ed. *Dichtung und Musik: Kaleidoskop ihrer Beziehungen*. Stuttgart: Klett-Cotta, 1979. 36-69.

Feil, Arnold. *Franz Schubert: "Die schöne Müllerin", "Winterreise"*. Stuttgart: Reclam, 1975 (2nd ed. 1996).

Fischer-Dieskau, Dietrich. *Auf den Spuren der Schubert-Lieder: Werden – Wesen – Wirkung*. Wiesbaden: Brockhaus, 1971.

Georgiades, Thrasybulos G. *Schubert: Musik und Lyrik*. Göttingen: Vandenhoeck & Ruprecht, 1967.

Hamlin, Cyrus. "The Romantic Song Cycle as Literary Genre". Bernhart et al., eds. 113-134.

Hufschmidt, Wolfgang. *Willst zu meinen Liedern deine Leier drehn? Zur Semantik der musikalischen Sprache in Schuberts "Winterreise" und Eislers "Hollywood-Liederbuch"*. Saarbrücken: Pfau, 1993.

Hühn, Peter. *Geschichte der englischen Lyrik*. 2 vols. Tübingen: Francke, 1995.

Iser, Wolfgang. "Die Appellstruktur der Texte: Unbestimmtheit als Wirkungsbedingung literarischer Prosa". Rainer Warning, ed. *Rezeptionsästhetik: Theorie und Praxis*. Munich: Fink, 1975. 228-252.

—. "Die Wirklichkeit der Fiktion: Elemente eines funktionsgeschichtlichen Textmodells der Literatur". Rainer Warning, ed. *Rezeptionsästhetik: Theorie und Praxis*. Munich: Fink, 1975. 277-324.

Kellman, Steven G. *The Self-Begetting Novel*. London: Macmillan, 1980.

Knights, L. C. "How Many Children Had Lady Macbeth?". L. C. Knights. *'Hamlet' and Other Shakespearean Essays*. Cambridge: Cambridge Univ. Press, 1979 ([1]1933). 270-308.

Kramer, Lawrence. "The Schubert Lied: Romantic Form and Romantic Consciousness". Walter Frisch, ed. *Schubert: Critical and Analytical Studies*. Lincoln: Univ. of Nebraska Press, 1986. 200-236.

Kramer, Richard. *Distant Cycles: Schubert and the Conceiving of Song*. Chicago: Univ. of Chicago Press, 1994.

Lagerroth, Ulla-Britta. "Reading Musicalized Texts as Self-Reflexive Texts: Some Aspects of Interart Discourse". Bernhart et al., eds. 205-220.

Müller, Wilhelm. *Gedichte. Vollständige kritische Ausgabe*. Ed. James Taft Hatfield. Berlin: B. Behrs, 1906.

Schumann, Robert. *Sämmtliche Lieder für eine Singstimme mit Klavierbegleitung*. Vol 1. Ed. Anton Rückauf. Vienna: Universal Edition, n.d.

Smeed, J. W. "'Strange Old Man': Thoughts on the Closing Lines of *Winterreise*". *German Life and Letters* 45/2 (1992): 109-113.

Wolf, Werner. "Aesthetic illusion in lyric poetry?". *Poetica* 30 (1998): 18-56.

—. *The Musicalization of Fiction: A Study in the Theory and History of Intermediality*. Amsterdam: Rodopi, 1999.

Youens, Susan. "Retracing a Winter Journey: Reflections on Schubert's *Winterreise*". *Nineteenth-Century Music* 9/2 (1985): 128-135.

—. "*Winterreise*: In the Right Order". *Soundings* 13 (1985): 41-50.

—. *Retracing a Winter's Journey: Schubert's "Winterreise"*. Ithaca: Cornell Univ. Press, 1991.

Design and Unity in Schumann's *Liederkreis*, Op. 39?

Leon Plantinga, New Haven, CN

Musical scholars have praised Schumann's Eichendorff *Liederkreis*, Op. 39, as strongly unified by devices such as melodic correspondence and systematic succession of tonalities. Co-ordination of such factors with the poetic texts of the songs usually plays a very minor role in such analyses. The assumption is that the name *Kreis* or 'cycle' designates a single, elaborately integrated work whose parts occur in an inviolate order. This idea has little historical justification. In the nineteenth century titles of song collections were applied rather casually, and criticism of the time shows great interest in co-ordination of poetic and musical expression in individual songs, but almost none in a thorough-going musical unification of cycles. The background of Schumann's Op. 39 and the nature and succession of the songs themselves seem more in accord with the nineteenth-century view than with that of modern-day music theory. Such a realization need not detract from our admiration of this splendid collection.

Artists who create diminutive self-contained works and propose to send them out into the world have certain decisions to make. To issue such things singly would be commercially unsatisfactory, and perhaps aesthetically also; thus we tend to encounter them in groups. And the individual items in these groups need to appear in some particular succession, whether or not that succession reflects a larger plan or points to a significance transcending that of its constituent parts. Lyrical poems, however disparate their subject matter, often come in collections whose ordering shows evidence of some general plan. Wordsworth's and Coleridge's *Lyrical Ballads* began, according to Coleridge, with a proposed organization around two sorts of poems, those with supernatural subjects and those with "subjects [...] chosen from ordinary life" (Butler/Green, eds. xi). Some approximation of his plan was realized in the publication of 1798; but Wordsworth, pursuing a different scheme, later distributed his poetry from the *Lyrical Ballads* among the various topical sections of his collected editions (cf. ibid. 3-15). Heine's celebrated *Buch der Lieder* of 1827 is arranged in large sections that follow the chronological order of their composition. The first of these, "Junge Leiden", is further divided, along rough topical and generic lines, into groups called "Traumbilder", "Lieder", "Romanzen", and "Sonette". In nineteenth-century Paris lithographers exhibited series of travel scenes, several of them often framed together, at the Salon of the Académie. These miniature works, grouped by region, they then sold as sets by subscription (cf. White/White 80).

Composers have long done much the same. In France of the later seventeenth century short stylized dance pieces were published in groups or suites, as in J. C. Chambonniers's *Pièces de clavessin* [...] *livre premier* (Paris 1670), in which the individual allemandes, courantes, and sarabandes (evidently composed at very different times) are arranged in suites unified by key. But as many as three or four appearances of the same dance type (especially among the courantes) probably constitutes an invitation for the player to pick and choose, thus to construct, in effect, a new suite at each performance. In the following century J. S. Bach and his contemporaries seemed to prescribe more in the way of order, offering suites for soloists or ensembles in which the succession of movements was largely prescribed. Still, a clear distinction between the standard dances – the allemande, courante, sarabande, and gigue that appear in virtually all the suites – and the optional dances (gavotte, bourée, anglaise, and others) suggests the survival of an element of choice for the player as well. And in the earlier nineteenth century, as a European middle class with a taste for printed music grew apace, music publishers, particularly in Germany and Austria, responded with torrents of collections of little pieces; these were often arranged in rough generic groupings – *Nocturnes, Romanzen, Impromptus* – and sometimes purveyed under fanciful titles like *Tonblumen* (Heinrich Dorn), *Pensées fugitives* (Adolph Henselt), or *Papillons* (R. Schumann). There is no reason to believe that musicians were expected to play the collections straight through from beginning to end. In fact, when Liszt programmed Schumann's *Carnaval* in Leipzig in 1840, the reviewer for the *Allgemeine musikalische Zeitung* criticized him for playing "so many [of the individual numbers] at once, and in immediate succession" (228)[1].

---

[1]   The appearance of such music on a concert program was something of an exception: a more usual venue for the playing of published piano music of any sort, with the exception of piano concertos, was *Hausmusik* performed by amateur musicians; here expectations as to full and orderly performance were surely even less fixed.

In the earlier nineteenth century songs with German poetic texts, too, tended to appear in substantial collections that sometimes bore fashionable titles like *Liederkranz, Liederreihe,* and, occasionally, *Liedercyklus* or *Liederkreis*. In the composition and grouping of songs, of course, any plan for ordering the constituent parts is likely to reflect the collaborative nature of the enterprise (though in nineteenth-century Germany this was a collaboration about which one of the parties, the poet, was almost never consulted, notions of intellectual property being at the time somewhat less exacting than they are now). Composers went about collecting poems and ordering their settings of them in various ways. Sometimes the poet handed the composer a ready-made succession. In 1814 the Berlin composer Friedrich Himmel set Christoph August Tiedge's collection of poems *Das Echo oder Alexis und Ida. Ein Poetic Ciclus von Liedern* in its original order in his *Liederspiel, Alexis und Ida*. Similarly, in his *An die ferne Geliebte* of the following year – in the first publication specifically named a *Liederkreis* – Beethoven evidently retained the order of Alois Jeitteles's poems, though he may himself have written an added fifth stanza to the first poem. Schubert's *Die schöne Müllerin* of 1823 follows the order of the published cycle of Wilhelm Müller, but with the omission of a prologue and three of the poems.

But as a rule the composer played a more decisive role in choosing poems and settling upon their order of presentation within publications of songs. Schubert's collections of songs on poems from *Wilhelm Meister*, D. 478 and 877, observe the order of neither the edition of Goethe's *Gedichte*, which was his apparent source, nor of the novel where they first appeared. And we can see this among other representatives of the *Wanderlieder* tradition to which *Die schöne Müllerin* belongs (a tradition that really got its start with the Uhland/Konradin Kreutzer cycle of that name in 1816). The poetry for such collections typically presented a loose episodic narrative of the wanderer's adventures; the beauty of such an arrangement is that the number and order of its events, especially in the interior of the series, may be altered without distortion of the whole. Composers often took advantage of this freedom. The history of Schubert's other great wanderer cycle, *Winterreise*, is a good example. In February of 1827 Schubert composed the twelve poems of Müller's cycle just as he found them in the journal *Urania* from 1823, and regarded his cycle as finished. Later in the same year he discovered that Müller had in the meantime expanded the series to 24 poems (cf. Müller), some of which were now interspersed among the original 12. Schubert thereupon composed the new poems, simply putting them all together as a Part Two of the cycle. Whether the composer's reordering of the poetic episodes, and his clothing them with all that marvelous music, resulted in a distinctive new psychological progression, a higher and inviolable artistic unity, cannot be addressed here. The point to be made is only that composers of song collections often felt very little bound by the particular order in which they found a poet's work, even when the succession of poems at hand seemed to fit a preconceived plan.

Schumann's habits in gathering and ordering poems for his song collections of 1840 ran the gamut from strict adherence to a poet's examplar to quite individual assemblages of the work of multiple poets. At one end of the spectrum is the Heine *Liederkreis*, Op. 24, in which Schumann sets in order the nine poems of one section of the *Buch der Lieder* (this group of poems appears under the heading "Lieder" in the section of early poems entitled "Junge Leiden"). Schumann's following Opus, *Myrthen*, which he called a *Liederkreis*, lies at the opposite extreme. The texts of these 26 songs were taken from the works of ten different poets (now counting Marianne von Willemer separately from Goethe). The Eichendorff *Liederkreis*, Op. 39, lies between these extremes, but somewhat closer to the apparent ease and freedom of *Myrthen*: there is only one poet, but the individual poems come from all the disparate sections of Eichendorff's *Gesammelte Gedichte* of 1837, a collection representing the poet's accumulated work of several decades. Clara Wieck, likely with Schumann's help, had selected and copied the poems for the *Liederkreis*, in exactly the order in which they are scattered in the 1837 edition, into a notebook entitled "Abschriften verschiedener Gedichte zur Composition". Schumann then composed them in a very different order, and published them in 1842 (with Haslinger of Vienna) in yet a third order. Finally, for the second edition of 1849 (by Whistling of Leipzig), Schumann made one final adjustment, replacing the opening song, "Der frohe Wandersmann", with "In der Fremde" – so that, as the cycle already included a song with this title, the series as we now know it has two such.

Did Schumann's arrangement and re-arrangement of Eichendorff's poetry result in a new, coherent poetic unity? Did Schumann believe, for example – as some commentators have simply assumed[2] – that he was putting these twelve poems, and, by extension, their music, into the mouth of a single persona? The prehistory of some of the poetry he chose may have a bearing on this question. Six of these poems had made an earlier appearance in Eichendorff's prose works, four of them imbedded, *Wilhelm Meister*-like, in his novel *Ahnung und Gegenwart* of 1815. Here the poems seem rather explicitly related to their immediate context in the novel, most of them being recited or sung by its principal characters. "Waldesgespräch", for example, is introduced as a "Lied über ein am Rheine bekanntes Märchen". It is recited in alternating stanzas by the character Leontin and a pair of hunters in an open-air bar scene on the banks of the Rhine – in partial explanation of the otherwise mysterious appearance in the forest of that vindictive Rhine-nymph, Lorelei. And might the conviviality of this scene be reflected in the pervading distance and good cheer – perhaps a vaguely tongue-in-cheek air – of Schumann's music for this poetry? A piano prelude opens the song with a purposefully naive 'once-upon-a-time' theme that is carried over into the first stanza (Example 1). After the final stanza, where the Lorelei has pronounced her death sentence upon the protagonist ("kommst nimmermehr aus diesem Wald"), the piano swings directly back into that innocuous opening music; we are assured that this is but woodland lore, not human tragedy.

Waldesgespräch.

---

[2]   Among them, for example, is Ferris (cf. 149-150). Despite certain rather erratic conclusions this dissertation is in many respects an informative and useful treatment of the subject.

Example 1: Robert Schumann, "Waldesgespräch" (from Liederkreis, *Op. 39), measures 1-8.*

"Die Stille" and "Wehmut" are both ascribed in the novel to the erratic and disturbed youth Erwin. The leading character Friedrich overhears the eerie "Zwielicht" sung of an evening by an unknown person shortly after he (Friedrich) has witnessed a scene of apparent betrayal by his beloved with his friend. Stanzas 2 and 3 allude pointedly to that situation:

> Hast ein Reh du, lieb vor andern,
> lass es nicht alleine grasen [...].

And:

> Hast du einen Freund hienieden,
> trau' ihm nicht zu dieser Stunde [...].[3]

So these poems in their earlier context seem quite specific to certain characters and particular situations. We cannot be certain that the well-read Schumann was acquainted with *Ahnung und Gegenwart*. But among the great many poems scattered throughout the novel, these four appear in suspiciously close proximity: all within 25 pages of the 300-page edition consulted here, while in the Eichendorff *Gedichte* of 1837, Schumann's putative single source, they are widely dispersed among four different sections of the book. And in the *Liederkreis* these four poems turn out to be symmetrically placed in pairs within the two halves of the collection. Thus both the choice of poems and their ordering in the cycle suggest a depend-

---

[3] 'Should you have a fawn you love more than others / let it not graze alone.' 'Should you have a friend on earth / do not trust him at this hour.'

ence upon the novel, a dependence not at all evident in Eichendorff's edition of 1837. If Schumann did know these poems in their earlier surroundings, it would have required a remarkable feat of reinterpretation for him to imagine them as a coherent utterance – much less an intact narrative – attributed to a single persona. And even if he had no knowledge of the novel, surely he (and we as well) would be hard-pressed to attribute any such unifying principle to so heterogeneous an assemblage as this, with the ballad-like "Waldesgespräch", the supremely lyrical "Mondnacht", and the rather primitivist "Die Stille". If we insist upon finding unity and coherence here, about the best that can be done is to trace certain very general patterns of attitude and mood in this succession of poems, as Jürgen Thym did with commendable caution in his dissertation of 1974[4].

In recent years musical scholars, especially in the United States, have shown a lively new interest in Schumann's music. Music historians studying the autograph sources of the instrumental music, foremost among them Linda Roesner, have described a 'modular' process of composition in which segments of music of varying sizes, even within movements of sonatas, are repeatedly rearranged, pointing to a certain contingency or frailty in the final order. The music theorists have gone in exactly the opposite direction. There have been animated discussions of the C-major *Fantasie*, in which the piece is measured up against sonata form, with the lurking implication that herein its validation must ultimately lie. Following in the footsteps of Rudolph Reti's conclusions about the *Kinderszenen*, some recent theorists have turned their attention to Schumann's published sets of smaller pieces, seeking to distinguish among them the true 'cycles' from the mere 'collections'. Published sets of songs made a decisive entry into the discussion with Arthur Komar's commentary on *Dichterliebe* in the Norton Critical Score of 1971. Komar attempted to demonstrate an underlying musical structure encompassing all 16 songs of the series by positing something resembling a Schenkerian *Urlinie* fashioned from their successive tonalities

---

[4]   In his monograph on the *Liederkreis*, published in the year of Thym's dissertation, Herwig Knaus notes the origins of these four poems in *Ahnung und Gegenwart*, and makes a strenuous (and rather forced) effort to relate the surrounding events in the novel to situations in the lives of Schumann and Clara Wieck (cf. 14-15).

(cf. 77-81). Schenker, always chary of ascribing any such overall structure
to successions of pieces, would surely have been astonished. Komar's
Urlinie, in any case, is a very peculiar one: for one thing it goes up rather
than down, and, within the series of 16 songs, nos. 5-14 must be represented
as an 'interruption'. And many must feel something essential is missing
from such an analysis, where there is by design almost no consideration of
Heine's poetry.

Much more circumspect and sophisticated is Patrick McCreless's discussion, in an article of 1986, of the ordering of songs in the Eichendorff
Liederkreis. He focuses on two separate arrangements of the songs, that of
the (presumed) order in which Schumann composed them, and the order,
familiar to us, of the second edition of 1849. In both he recognizes a
division into two equal halves (therein agreeing with many recent commentators on the *Liederkreis*). In both of these orderings he detects elaborate
symmetries that unify each half of the series and also relate each of them,
with a kind of architectural uniformity, to the other half: the difference
between the two orderings being that in the earlier one those relationships
between halves are linear (i. e. song #1 relates to song #7, #2 to #8, etc.),
while in the final version the pattern of relationships describes a mirror
image (#1 is paired with #12, #2 with #11, etc.). The principal factor creating these symmetries is a network of motivic correspondences. To get an
idea of what these are like, let us take a look at McCreless's first two
examples.

One of the motivic relationships that unifies the first half of the set (in its
published order), he says, is heard between the beginnings of the first song,
"In der Fremde", and the sixth, "Schöne Fremde" (Examples 2a and 2b).

But the falling stepwise melodic figure comprising this motivic resemblance, we may feel, is not distinctive enough to be much of a factor in our
hearing of this cycle, particularly in view of the quite unrelated texts at
those two points, the difference in harmonic context – the one passage
directed toward the tonic, the other toward the dominant – and all at a
remove of five songs.

McCreless's second motivic correspondence, between the beginning of
the justly famous "Mondnacht", and the following song, "Schöne Fremde"
(again), may have a bit more to be said for it (Examples 3 and 2b).

In der Fremde.

Example 2a: Robert Schumann, "In der Fremde" (from Liederkreis, Op. *39), measures 1-5.*

Schöne Fremde.

Example 2b: Robert Schumann, "Schöne Fremde" (from Liederkreis, Op. 39), *measures 1-7.*

Example 3: Robert Schumann, "Mondnacht" (from Liederkreis, Op. 39), *measures 5-13.*

The initial melodic similarity and a common harmonic construction (both examples approaching the super tonic and tonic through their dominants) are noticeable enough. But again, the verbal and larger musical contexts seem too dissimilar for such a resemblance to rise to the level of anything more than a curiosity. And the same can be said, I think, for virtually all the motivic correspondences that McCreless and others have advanced as unifying factors in the cycle. A possible exception, to my ears, is the more explicit reuse of melodic shapes between the seventh song, "Auf einer

Burg", and the otherwise very different eighth song, the second "In der Fremde" (Examples 4a and 4b).

Auf einer Burg.

Example 4a: Robert Schumann, "Auf einer Burg" (from Liederkreis, *Op. 39), measures 1-8.*

Example 4b: Robert Schumann, "In der Fremde" (from Liederkreis, *Op. 39), measures 1-9.*

Perhaps the *Rauschen* in each poem prompted this whimsical repetition of melodic gesture on Schumann's part.

Schumann is capable, however, of repeating himself, in other contexts, in a much more striking fashion. Let us look, for a moment, at the remarkable tenth song, "Zwielicht". In the text, indistinct, menacing nocturnal nature imagery symbolizes human horror of unknown dangers, of betrayal and loss:

> Dämm'rung will die Flügel spreiten,
> schaurig rühren sich die Bäume [...].

And:

> Manches geht in Nacht verloren –
> hüte dich, sei wach und munter![5]

The piano introduction (Example 5) features a remarkable wandering, directionless figure in even eighth notes in which a single line almost imperceptibly spawns a second voice. The figure is arranged in sequences that persistently outline in alternation that harmonically most ambiguous sonority, the diminished triad, with descending sixths whose accidentals defeat any firm determination of key. During the first four measures of this informally imitative texture, that profound insecurity of tonality is also abetted by the absence of a bass line. We hear ambiguous suggestions of B

---

[5] 'Twilight wants to spread its wings, / the trees stir eerily.' 'Many a thing is lost in the night – / beware, stay awake and alert!'

minor and of E minor alternating with A minor until the newly-arrived bass guides the music purposefully to E minor in mm. 7-8. Thereupon the whole process begins anew as the same music, in all essentials, serves for the first stanza.

Zwielicht.

ritard.
laß es nicht al - lei - ne gra-sen, Jä - ger ziehn im Wald und bla-sen,
18
p
Stimmen hin und wie-der wan - dern. Hast du ei - nen Freund hienie - den,
p Im Tempo
22
pp
ritard.
Im Tempo
trau' ihm nicht zu die - ser Stun - de, freund - lich wohl mit Aug' und Mun - de,
26
sinnt er Krieg im tück' - schen Frie - den. Was heut' ge - het
30
pp
p
Ped.
mü - de un - ter, hebt sich mor - gen neu - ge - bo - ren. Man-ches geht in
34

Example 5: Robert Schumann, "Zwielicht" (from Liederkreis, Op. 39*).*

This song makes the nearest approach of any in the cycle to a strophic setting. So we get the same melody again for the second stanza (from m. 16); now the bass (which seems even more sorely needed in support of the voice) finally joins in, but with the insistent ambiguity of playing off beat. Such harmonic-rhythmic disjunction is compounded in the third stanza (from m. 24), where the bass is elaborated into something of a contrapuntal line that still remains obstinately off-beat, now at the quarter-note level.

The expressive effect Schumann seems to be aiming for is a maximum of indeterminacy. Tonal orientation is shrouded and evaded. The opening music makes a furtive promise of an imitative texture that is soon abandoned. The bass voice is persistently out of alignment with the other voices or absent altogether. Schumann responds to the insecurity and anxiety of Eichendorff's poem with music that raises uncertainty to a principle. And with all those diminished and minor sonorities, this is a melancholy uncertainty in which a favorable outcome is hardly to be expected. Then, too, we can perhaps sense a certain air of ennui and resignation in those ubiquitous drooping melodic shapes, as if the music were steadily attuned to the first line of the final stanza, "Was heut' gehet müde unter"[6].

We might take note of two other prominent techniques used in this song. For the first half of the final stanza, Schumann finally makes matters more explicit and emphatic as he transforms the even eighth notes of the accompaniment into insistent repeated chords, and provides an intact bass line, for the first time on-beat. But the harmony, though more explicit, remains unstable (passing through B minor and A minor en route to an ultimate E

---

[6] 'Whatever sinks down tired tonight [will rise again tomorrow, newly born].'

minor), and sounds at a consistently low dynamic level. This music still has
a repressed air about it; there is little impression that anything has really
been resolved. The other striking technique used in this song is the
recitative-like melodic writing that makes a tentative appearance at the
endings of the first three stanzas, and then, in much more emphatic fashion,
at the close of the song. Of the various types of eighteenth-century
recitative, the nineteenth century was strongly attached only to the most
dramatic variety, what Rousseau had called *récit obligé* (141-142). This is
what is heard upon the initial entry of the human voice in the finale of
Beethoven's Ninth Symphony, and it appears in countless nineteenth-
century ballads at moments of high gravity or alarm (the most familiar
example is the end of Schubert's "Erlkönig"). The tense warning at the close
of "Zwielicht" merges into this sort of recitative with a dramatic leap of a
diminished seventh in the voice, followed by a stern augmented sixth chord
and its attenuated resolution in the piano.

In July of 1840, two months after composing the Eichendorff
Liederkreis, and just after completing the *Frauen-Liebe und -Leben* cycle,
Schumann set five further poems from the volume of Chamisso's *Gedichte*
that he had used for *Frauen-Liebe*, and published them two years later as
Op. 40. These five poems are all translations by Chamisso, four of them
from the Danish of Hans Christian Andersen. The second of these, "Muttertraum", is a macabre meditation upon disillusionment and betrayal: the
mother gazes, enchanted, upon her child, who must seem to her like an
angel; her fond hopes for him stray to the future; thus do mothers dream in
their hearts. But the raven and his crew know better: "Your angel will be
ours; the robber will become our food." (The penultimate line of the Danish
text actually says, "Your angel will become a thief" – making more explicit
an implication that the son will be hanged for robbery and that the ravens
will feed on his body.)

The beginning and ending of Schumann's setting of this poem is shown
in Example 6a and 6b. Here, in the piano introduction, we see the same
wandering, even-note motion as in the opening of "Zwielicht", with similar
tonal ambiguity and a bass again persistently off-beat. Once more, this
introduction provides the music for the first stanza. And when in the last
stanza the raven croaks out his threat, he does so to a chordal
accompaniment much like that of the final stanza of "Zwielicht" – an

accompaniment that is again eerily soft. And, like the final warning of "Zwielicht", this threat is couched in recitative-like declamation.

Example 6a: Robert Schumann, "Muttertraum" (from Fünf Lieder, *Op. 40), measures 1-8.*

Example 6b: Robert Schumann, "Muttertraum" (from Fünf Lieder, *Op. 40), measures 27-40.*

Here we have between two songs not a few transient melodic correspondences, but a thorough-going reuse of musical motives and techniques that create a fundamental similarity of musical expression. What leads Schumann thus to revisit the manner of "Zwielicht" surely has to do with resemblances in subject matter and mood between the texts of these two poems, with their kindred themes of threat, insecurity, and the deceptiveness of appearance. It is in this relationship, in specific musical responses to specific poetic stimuli that the patterns of Schumann's art as a composer of songs can best be understood. His own practice as a critic would seem to offer confirmation: in his reviews of songs Schumann typically speaks first of the idea and tone of a poem, and then of the relationship – for him always a most delicate and to a degree a subjective one – between poetic and musical utterance (cf. Plantinga 164-171).

What lies behind all the efforts, mainly by American music theorists, to seek out, within all the expressive diversity of the Eichendorff *Liederkreis* – usually with scant reference to the poetry – elaborate unifying patterns of musical correspondence and symmetry? For one thing, it is called a *Liederkreis*, which evokes notions of 'cycle' and 'cyclic', that in discussions of music have acquired particular implications. McCreless is quite clear about this, when he says at the very beginning of his article:

> In the context of art song, we attribute to the word 'cycle' not only the implication of relatedness of members of a set, but also implications of order and interdependence; in a *bona fide* song cycle, the omission of any of the songs, or the rearrangement of their order, constitutes a threat to or negation of its cyclic character. (5)

But how do we come about such exacting standards for the cycle or *Kreis*? There is no reason to think that anyone in Schumann's day placed any such construction on these terms. In music criticism of the time, the words *Liederkreis*, *Liederreihe*, and *Liederkranz* were used informally and more-or-less interchangeably, and it seems impossible to find anyone advocating the kind of musical unity within such groupings that some commentators these days insist upon. Critics of the lied in Schumann's time more often emphasized instead a need for contrast and variety within song collections; another common theme is a desire for expressive intensification and climax in successive songs (cf. Turchin 24 and 204-206). Schumann's review, in 1836, of Carl Loewe's *Esther*, a *Liederkreis in Balladenform*, set to the poetry of Ludwig Giesebrecht, may illustrate his own view of the matter (cf. 143). He begins by saying, 'each of the songs has its special tone', and proceeds, song by song, to recount poetic impressions and their congruence with the expressive effects of Loewe's music. Schumann, while heartily approving of Loewe's *Liederkreis*, says very little about motivic correspondences among songs, and nothing whatever about any question of a larger musical unity in the cycle. The single instance of musical cross-reference to which he calls our attention occurs where a later poem recalls a scene from the first one; at that point, Schumann says, "[d]er Rückblick auf den Anfang des Ganzen hebt sich in der Musik zart hervor"[7]. The musical repetition is immediately bound to events in the text, and Schumann seems to see this gesture as a kind of poetic backward glance, not a device calculated to create formal unity.

One musical factor in Loewe's *Liederkreis* that Schumann notes with some consistency is the succession of tonalities of the songs. And in his own collections this is clearly not a matter of chance or indifference. In some

---

[7] 'The backward glance toward the very beginning emerges gracefully in the music.'

cases, as in the Heine *Liederkreis* and *Myrthen*, there is a hint of system or
closure: the final song in both cases is in the same key as the first. In the
Eichendorff *Liederkreis* – i. e. in its final ordering in the second edition –
the melancholic beginning and exultant ending share a tonic, F#; but the
first song is minor, the last major. And, curiously, the tonics of the first
three songs are repeated in reverse order in the last three. But a search for
comprehensive, systematic key relations within the Schumann song collections hardly repays the effort: all explanatory schemes tend to excessive
complication and still seem to require certain exceptions and approxima-
tions.

The single relatively consistent principle seems to be this: that the tonalities of adjacent songs be reasonably closely related. Thus the cycles tend to
hover about in one part of the tonal spectrum: the Heine and Eichendorff
Liederkreise both live on the sharp side, while *Dichterliebe* starts out there,
works its way gradually into the flats, and then back again. A desire for
smoothness in succession of tonalities is often reflected in music criticism of
the time. In a letter of March 1841 to Ignaz Moscheles, Mendelssohn
touches on this matter (while seemingly subordinating it to other considerations). After reporting that he has arranged for publication for a collection of
Moscheles's songs, Mendelssohn continues:

> "Die Tonarten folgen sich zwar aufs Allertollste: F dur und H dur und alles durcheinan-
> der; aber ich habe immer gefunden, daß Einem kein Mensch die schönste Tonartenfolge
> dankt, dagegen eine gewisse Abwechselung von langsam und schnell, ernst und heiter
> durchaus verlangt wird; daher verzeih das Tonartenfricassee."[8] (Mendelssohn-Bartholdy
> 208)

A succession of closely related keys was surely a desideratum, but not, it
seems, so as to confer upon the song cycle some comprehensive abstract
unity. Such a succession might suggest occasional cross-references and
pairings, but mainly it was intended to ease the way, for performers and
listeners, from one song to the next.

---

[8] 'The keys follow one another in the maddest fashion: F major and B major, all mixed
up. But I have always found that no one thanks you for the loveliest succession of
tonalities; rather, what is demanded is a certain alternation of fast and slow, serious and
cheerful; so please excuse the fricassee of keys.'

The search for elaborate large-scale integration in Schumann's song cycles – for which that tired old metaphor 'organic unity' is still often invoked – is undertaken with the best of intentions, i. e. for the theoretical validation of works of music that many among us already love and admire. There is abroad a widespread conviction, inspired by Schenker, but by no means limited to the Schenkerians, that the principal, and perhaps sole ultimate virtue in music is large-scale formal unity. But there was apparently no such understanding among musicians of the mid-nineteenth century, and it is hard to imagine a compelling reason for us to feel bound by such a view now.

More in accord with the attitude of Schumann and his contemporaries toward the experience of the song cycle – and, probably, more true to the nature of the works themselves – would be an analogy with a visit to an art gallery for an exhibition of paintings of the same genre by a single artist. The identity of genre suggests some uniformity of, say, the size of the paintings, and, in a general way, of their subject matter, while their being the work of a single painter would suggest some consistency of style. There might be, in an occasional painting, a striking return to an idea or motif that had appeared elsewhere in the series, and the artist (or the director of the gallery) may have taken care to place two such paintings side-by-side. But it would hardly occur to us to invent elaborate schemata designed to show a comprehensive and detailed integration of each painting within the exhibit as a whole, such that the slightest reordering within the series would destroy its integrity. Sometimes, to be sure, artists have offered us series of works governed by a single narrative or succession of events, as in Hogarth's *The Rake's Progress*, or Goya's "The Second of May in Madrid: The Charge of the Mamelukes" and "The Third of May in Madrid: The Execution of the Defenders". But in most circumstances under which we look at a group of paintings, neither an iron-clad ordering of its parts, nor, *a fortiori*, an all-embracing scheme insuring formal unity is to be expected.

So it is with song cycles. Some few, like *Frauen-Liebe und -Leben*, follow a specific narrative provided by the poet. Here, of course, the order of songs is immutable, and Schumann has enriched the progression by adding in the piano epilogue a poetic, and perhaps nostalgic backward glance toward the beginning. Some follow a much looser narrative pattern, such as *Die schöne Müllerin*, originally published in five separate volumes, where the opening and close – the protagonist's setting out into the world and his death – are prescribed, but where no rigid pattern to the poetic or musical events in between these points seems to be necessary. And in the Eichendorff *Liederkreis*, the exultation of the final song, "Frühlingsnacht", surely makes for a rousing close (though the celebration comes on with unexpected suddenness). It may add something for a few listeners that the isolation and dejection of the first number are heard attached to the same tonic as that final song. And some suggestions of an almost casual pairing of songs, particularly the use of similar melodies in the otherwise very divergent songs #6 and #7, "Auf einer Burg" and "In der Fremde", is diverting, if maybe puzzling. But to look for a great deal more in the way of integration, of structural unity in this series of songs, seems to me a mistake. Nor should this in any way blunt our enjoyment of the individual or additive effect of these songs, or of our esteem for Schumann's splendid artistic accomplishment.

References

Allgemeine musikalische Zeitung 42. Leipzig: Breitkopf & Härtel, 1840.

Butler, James, Karen Green, eds. *Lyrical Ballads and Other Poems, 1797-1800, by William Wordsworth*. Ithaca, NY: Cornell Univ. Press, 1992.

Eichendorff, Joseph von. *Ahnung und Gegenwart. Werke*, vol. 2. Frankfurt a. M.: Bibliothek deutscher Klassiker, 1985.

Ferris, David. *From Fragment to Cycle: Formal Organization in Schumann's Eichendorff Liederkreis*. Ann Arbor, MI: Univ. Microfilms, 1993.

Knaus, Herwig. *Musiksprache und Werkstruktur in Robert Schumanns Liederkreis*. Munich: Emil Katzbichler, 1974.

Komar, Arthur, ed. *Robert Schumann:* Dichterliebe. *An Authoritative Score*. Norton Critical Scores. New York, NY: Norton, 1971.

McCreless, Patrick. "Song Order in Schumann's *Liederkreis*, Op. 39". *Music Analysis* 5 (1986): 5-28.

Mendelssohn-Bartholdy, Felix. *Briefe von Felix Mendelssohn-Bartholdy an Ignaz und Charlotte Moscheles*. Ed. Ignaz Moscheles. Leipzig: Dunker & Humblot, 1888.

Müller, Wilhelm. *Gedichte aus den hinterlassenen Papieren eines reisenden Waldhornisten*. Dessau, 1824.

Plantinga, Leon. *Schumann as Critic*. New Haven, CN: Yale Univ. Press, 1967.

Reti, Rudolph. *The Thematic Process in Music*. New York, NY: Macmillan, 1951.

Roesner, Linda. "The Autograph of Schumann's Piano Sonata in F Minor". *The Musical Quarterly* 61 (1975): 98-130.

—. "Schumann's Revisions in the First Two Movements of the Piano Sonata in G Minor, Op. 22". *Nineteenth-Century Music* 1 (1977): 97-109.

Rousseau, Jean-Jacques. *Dictionnaire de musique*. Amsterdam, 1768.

Schumann, Robert, ed. *Neue Zeitschrift für Musik* 5. Leipzig, 1836.

Turchin, Barbara Pearl. *Robert Schumann's Song Cycles in the Context of the Early Nineteenth-Century Liederkreis*. Ann Arbor, MI: Univ. Microfilms, 1991.

Thym, Jürgen. *The Solo Song Settings of Eichendorff's Poems by Schumann and Wolf*. Ann Arbor, MI: Univ. Microfilms, 1974.

White, Harrison C., Cynthia A. White. *Canvases and Careers*. New York, NY: John Wiley and Sons, 1965.

A Cycle in Flux
Schumann's Eichendorff *Liederkreis*

Jürgen Thym, Rochester, NY

The essay reviews the compositional genesis of Schumann's Opus 39, from Schumann's selecting the Eichendorff poems to his setting them to music and, finally, his ordering the songs as a *Liederkreis* for the 1842 and 1849 editions. Schumann's song cycle begins in the two editions with two very different 'first' songs, each of which projects a vastly different emotional trajectory on the remaining eleven songs. While I argue that Schumann's ordering principles, both textual and musical, imbue the series of songs with cyclical features, the ambiguity about how to begin the cycle puts into question various assumptions about motivic recall and key-sequence usually identified, unproblematically, as contributing to cyclic coherence. Rather than forcing constructs of unity on Opus 39, it may be more appropriate to recognize (and find aesthetic pleasure in) the discontinuities and non-sequiturs of this cycle-in-flux and view these features as continuations of Romantic modes of narrative which various authors have seen in Schumann's piano cycles of the 1830s.

Schumann's *Liederkreis*, Opus 39, is generally considered one of the great song cycles in the history of the German lied. But what makes it a cycle is less than clear. In fact, some of the principal defining characteristics of song cycles such as Beethoven's *An die ferne Geliebte*, Schubert's *Die schöne Müllerin*, or even Schumann's *Dichterliebe* do not apply here. The poems of Opus 39 do not form a lyric cycle, they do not outline a story in the conventional sense, and, even if we assume some kind of teleological narrative in the sequence of emotional states displayed in the songs, Schumann complicated or thwarted that pat assumption by replacing, in the second edition of the *Liederkreis*, the opening song of the cycle with a different one, which, in turn, projects a vastly different emotional trajectory. And the ambivalence about how to begin the cycle opens up questions about motivic-thematic recall and key-sequence, two aspects that various authors, including myself in an earlier study, have identified as contributing to the cyclic coherence on the musical side. Questions upon questions and no easy answers.

Stage 1: Selecting the Poems

A review of the compositional genesis of the songs that later were gathered to become the *Liederkreis* may be of some help in our quest for answers. In the case of text settings such a review begins appropriately with the selection of the poetry to be set. In 1839 Robert Schumann and Clara Wieck started collecting poems by mostly contemporary poets and entering them into a book titled (in the handwriting of Robert Schumann) "Abschriften von Gedichten zur Composition". Many of these poems, including more than a dozen Eichendorff poems (see Table 1), would, at some later stage, serve as texts to be set to music. Even though both Schumanns added poems to the book well into the early 1850s, the Collection was begun as a joint project of two artists who, during their time of courtship, wanted to be linked by artistic and spiritual bonds when they were physically separated. Schumann set to music the lion's share of the poems gathered in the Collection, but Clara contributed with a number of Rückert songs, which, together with others by Robert, were published as *Liebesfrühling*, Opus 37 (cf. Hallmark), a few years after the couple were married.

Table 1: Excerpt from the Table of Contents of Abschriften von Gedichten zur Composition *[Source: Kaldewey, "Die* Gedichtabschriften *Robert und Clara Schumanns"]*

Eichendorff:
No.10   Der frohe Wandersmann ("Wem Gott will rechte Gunst erweisen") [Op. 39, no. 1; Op. 77, no. 1]
No.11   Im Walde ("Es zog eine Hochzeit den Berg entlang") [Op. 39, no. 11]
No.12   Zwielicht ("Dämmrung will die Flügel spreiten") [Op. 39, no. 10]
No.13   Auf einer Burg ("Eingeschlafen auf der Lauer") [Op. 39, no. 7]
No.14   In der Fremde [II] ("Ich hör' die Bächlein rauschen") [Op. 39, no. 8]
No.15   Schöne Fremde ("Es rauschen die Wipfel und schauern") [Op. 39, no. 6]
No.16   Wehmut ("Ich kann wohl manchmal singen") [Op. 39, no. 9]
No.17   Intermezzo ("Dein Bildnis wunderselig") [Op. 39, no. 2]
No.18   Liebesmut ("Was Lorbeerkranz und Lobesstand")
No.19   Die Stille ("Es weiß und rät es doch keiner") [Op. 39, no. 4]
No.20   Frühlingsnacht ("Über'n Garten durch die Lüfte") [Op. 39, no. 12]
No.21   In der Fremde [I] ("Aus der Heimat hinter den Blitzen rot") [Op. 39, no. 1]
No.22   Mondnacht ("Es war, als hätt' der Himmel") [Op. 39, no. 5]
No.23   Waldgespräch ("Es ist schon spät") [Op. 39, no. 3]
No.24   Der traurige Jäger ("Zur ew'gen Ruh sie sangen") [Op. 75, no. 3]

Note: The poems appear exactly in the order in which they appear in the 1837 edition of Eichendorff's collected poems; 14 of the 15 poems were set by Schumann either as piano-accompanied solo songs or, in one instance, as a choral setting.

The early months of 1840 were times of emotional turmoil because of Clara Wieck's father's stubborn refusal to give his consent to the marriage. The upheaval caused by suits and countersuits, legal delaying tactics and just plain procrastination turned the courtship of the two lovers into a court battle. We do not know exactly when the poems eventually used in Robert's Opus 39 were entered into the Collection in Clara's handwriting, but their selection clearly has something to do with the biographical circumstances in which the couple found themselves. Nearly all of the poems incorporate in some form the image of wedding, of togetherness and separation of lovers; yes, we may even go so far as identifying the relation between man and woman as one of the topics that runs like a red thread through almost all of the songs gathered later as *Liederkreis*. In addition, most poems (9 out of 12) feature a forest as backdrop for the lyrics, and many (7 out of 12) are set at night time or dusk. I do not want to make too much of these coincidences, conventions and clichés that mark the surface of Eichendorff's poetic language. Indeed, in many of Eichendorff's poems springs or brooks are murmuring, idyllic lakes are located in mysterious forests, treetops and leaves are rustling, horn calls can be heard echoing in the woods, and nightingales sing of love. These images recur in Eichendorff's poetry with an almost mannered frequency in ever new constellations, and whoever selects a group of his poems is bound to generate correspondences because of the formulaic nature of the poet's language. In any case, for Schumann and his bride, the Eichendorff poems were of one cloth. The poems belonged together and formed, on a very personal level, a poetic unit that the two lovers created together as part of their courtship in emotionally charged times.

Stage 2: Composing the Songs

In the second half of April 1840 Robert Schumann spent two weeks in Berlin with his bride (who was living at that time with her mother), reaffirming his determination and receiving Clara's promise to go through with the marriage plans no matter what. Upon his return to Leipzig, Schumann began immediately to work on text settings and, within a little more than three weeks, had composed most of the Eichendorff poems entered by Clara in the Collection. The four songs "Waldesgespräch", "In der Fremde" [I], "Die Stille", and "Mondnacht" were composed on three days: May 1, 4, and 9. "Intermezzo" probably was set before May 16; "Schöne Fremde", "Wehmut", "In der Fremde" [II], "Frühlingsnacht", "Zwielicht", and "Im Walde" were written between May 16 and 20. "Auf einer Burg" may have originated on May 20 or 22. "Der frohe Wandersmann", the opening song in the 1842 edition of the cycle, stands apart from the rest; it carries a date of June 22. This distinctive date of composition – a full month later than the rest – prefigures the problematic role of the song in the cycle, which we shall see in a moment. (See Table 2.)

Table 2: Schumann's Eichendorff Songs in the Berlin Autograph (with dates of composition) [Source: Knaus, Musiksprache und Werkstruktur*]*

No.43   Waldesgespräch (1 May 1840)
No.44   In der Fremde [I] (4 May 1840)
No.45   Mondnacht (9 May 1840)

No.48   Intermezzo (before 16 May 1840)

No.52   Schöne Fremde (16/17 May 1840)

No.54   In der Fremde [II] (18 May 1840)
No.55   Wehmut (17/18 May 1840)
No.56   Frühlingsnacht (18 May 1840)
No.57   Die Stille (4 May 1840)
No.58   Zwielicht (19 May 1840)
No.59   Im Walde (20 May 1840)
No.60   Auf einer Burg (20/22 May 1840)

No.??   Der frohe Wandersmann (22 June 1840)

Note that the Eichendorff Songs are interspersed with settings of poems by other poets. "Der Nussbaum" and "Widmung" – by Rückert and Mosen, respectively – stand between "Mondnacht" and "Intermezzo"; "Intermezzo" is followed by four non-Eichendorff settings including Heine's "Die beiden Grenadiere", and "Rotes Röslein" stands between "Schöne Fremde" and "In der Fremde" [II].

It is clear from Table 2 that the order in which the songs were composed and the order in which they occur as fair copies in the Berlin autograph have little to do with the orderings in which the songs were published in the 1842 and 1849 editions. Patrick McCreless (cf. 17-22) has argued that Schumann at one time may have contemplated ordering the individual settings for a cycle exactly as he had composed them. (He makes his case mainly by hypothesizing a succession of keys departing from and returning, several times, to the key of E in both major and minor.) He disregards, however, the fact that Eichendorff was not the only poet Schumann set in May of that year and that the Eichendorff songs are interspersed in the autograph with settings of non-Eichendorff texts. (See facsimile in Knaus, Appendix) There is little evidence for such an ordering; a more likely explanation is that Schumann at this stage of the compositional process was mainly concerned with setting the individual poems and that putting the songs into a sequence for publication, perhaps as a cycle, was a task to be taken up later. Schumann, of course, was aware of the cyclic potential of the songs he was setting during those weeks. (A few months earlier he had composed nine Heine poems, which we know as the Heine *Liederkreis*, Opus 24, and the publication of that group of songs proceeded quickly with Breitkopf und Härtel during the weeks he was working on his Eichendorff settings.)

　　Three letters from Robert to Clara are instructive for defining the stages of the emerging cyclic project. The first was written on May 2, shortly after his return from Berlin:

> Dir ist wohl ganz wie mir der Kopf ordentlich schwer von alle dem großen Glück, das wir zusammen genossen haben […] ich bin noch nicht ruhig […]. Und Musik habe ich in mir, daß ich den ganzen Tag nur singen möchte. Vor allem aber will [ich] die Lieder aufschreiben. (Boetticher 338)[1]

The second is from the middle of the month, May 15:

> Ich habe wieder so viel komponiert, daß mir's manchmal ganz unheimlich vorkömmt. Ach, ich kann nicht anders, ich möchte mich totsingen wie eine Nachtigall. Eichendorffsche [Lieder] sind es zwölf. Die hab' ich aber schon vergessen und etwas Neues angefangen. (Clara Schumann, ed. *Jugendbriefe* 314)[2]

---

[1] 'Like me, your head probably is still spinning from all the great happiness we experienced together […] I still have not calmed down […]. And I have music inside me that I would like to sing the whole day. But first of all I want to write down the songs.'

[2] 'I have composed so much that it seems to me uncanny at times. I cannot help it and would like to sing myself to death like a nightingale. There are twelve Eichendorff songs, but I have already forgotten those and begun something new.'

And on May 22:

> Der Eichendorffsche Zyklus ist wohl mein aller Romantischstes und steht viel von Dir darin […]. Dein Buch ist nun schon auskomponiert und Du müßtest duchaus neue Gedichte mitbringen […]. Heute […] war das Wetter abscheulich und ich sitze den ganzen Tag in meiner Klause […]. Gibt es denn noch Worte für die bestialische Frechheit [Wiecks]: In meinen Eichendorffschen Zyklus paßt das schlecht. Ich hatte den Skandal auch eine Weile vergessen, manchmal packt es mich aber auch zum Niederwerfen. (Boetticher 340)[3]

A few things are obvious from these statements: 1) What may have begun just as a setting of individual songs of texts by Eichendorff and other poets had by the middle of May, and certainly by May 22 at the latest, turned into a project on a different scale, which would gather the brief vocal miniatures into something larger, namely a song cycle, featuring twelve Eichendorff songs. As we have noted, Schumann had not composed "Der frohe Wandersmann", the opening song of the 1842 edition, at that time. We may surmise, therefore, that, by mentioning the number 12 in the second letter, he probably meant the dozen Eichendorff songs that had been completed or were close to completion by the middle of May 1840. (These are the songs that correspond to those included in the 1849 edition.) 2) Schumann's biographical circumstances continue to be close to the surface of the composition of the songs, both in a positive and negative way, with Clara, his beloved in the distance, on the one hand, representing a muse spurring him on to creative activity, and Friedrick Wieck, his (soon-to-be) father-in-law, on the other hand, acting as a foil and ogre, from whom the composer found refuge in the Romantic world of Eichendorff's poetry. We may not want to subscribe wholesale to the interpretation of a musical cryptographer like Eric Sams (cf. 22-26), who sees Clara, in the form of musical codes based on the letter names of melodic pitches, literally pervading much of Schumann's work during this time. Still, he may be on to something here (cf. ibid. 97-99): the textual change in "Mondnacht" ("nur" or 'only', an expression of exclusiveness appropriate for people on the verge of getting

---

[3] 'The Eichendorff cycle is perhaps my most Romantic work, and it contains much of you in it […]. Your book is now already composed, and you would have to bring new poems […]. Today the weather was ghastly, and I am sitting in my study the whole day. Are there any words for the beastly audacity [of Wieck]; it does not fit into my Eichendorff cycle. I had already forgotten the scandal for a while, but sometimes it still grabs me and gets me down.'

married, instead of the filler "nun" or 'now') is perhaps a Freudian slip of the pen and a reverberation of the loving couple's biographical circumstances. The same song contains one possible case of encoding – the musical notes E, B, and E in the bass spell in German the word E-H-E ('marriage').

Stages 3 and 4: Common Ground

Almost without exception, writers on Schumann's Opus 39 have used as the basis for their comments the order of the songs as published in the second edition of 1849, in which the first song "Der frohe Wandersmann" is replaced by the sombre "In der Fremde" [I]. The earlier version did not remain completely unnoticed, but the fact that it begins with a lighthearted song of wandering has caused it to be viewed as less authentic. "Der frohe Wandersmann" has been dismissed, for the most part, as inferior (cf. Sams 93), unrelated to the cycle, and a concession to a Viennese publisher catering to popular taste (cf. Knaus 17), as disturbing the tight tonal unity of the cycle (cf. Walsh 35), or as an afterthought that came to the composer much later (cf. Turchin 238). In addition, Kurt Hofmann (cf. 90-93) perhaps inadvertently confused the matter, erroneously listing the first edition as containing both of the 'first' songs, for a total of thirteen, not twelve. The bias toward the later edition may be attributed to the forces of inertia bred by habit or to the ideology surrounding the "Fassung letzter Hand" as definitive of an artwork's shape. Schumann's adage that first ideas are almost always preferable (even though he was quite a reviser and tinkerer) should have given pause, or slowed down, an overly enthusiastic embrace of the 1849 edition. It was not until a few years ago that Jon Finson (cf. "The Intentional Tourist") rattled our complacency by making a case for the 1842 version as a plausible alternative and for taking the possibility of beginning the cycle with "Der frohe Wandersmann" much more seriously. Even though I have problems with Finson's interpretation of Schumann's revision as a sign of the composer's growing conservativism, I would like to accept the premise, for the time being, and treat both versions as equally valid.

There is no doubt that the differences between the 1842 and 1849 versions are acute because of the very different songs with which the cycles commence. But we should not overlook the fact that 11 of the 12 songs stay in the later version exactly where they were in the earlier one. Both versions indeed have much in common, and the common features give us some clues about Schumann's ordering principles when he prepared the Eichendorff songs for publication not as individual songs with some vague notion of group identity but as a cycle. (See Table 3)

Table 3: Opus 39 in its 1842 and 1849 Versions

1842	1849
Der frohe Wandersmann	In der Fremde [I]
Intermezzo	Intermezzo
Waldesgespräch	Waldesgespräch
Die Stille	Die Stille
Mondnacht	Mondnacht
Schöne Fremde	Schöne Fremde
Auf einer Burg	Auf einer Burg
In der Fremde [II]	In der Fremde [II]
Wehmut	Wehmut
Zwielicht	Zwielicht
Im Walde	Im Walde
Frühlingsnacht	Frühlingsnacht

The cycle – most writers agree – falls into two halves: songs nos. 1-6, containing by-and-large songs of an upbeat nature, and songs nos. 7-12, containing settings with largely darker hues. The concluding songs of each half, "Schöne Fremde" and "Frühlingsnacht" clearly are articulated as climactic statements providing closure to their respective sections and, in both poetry and music, they are shaped as corresponding or related units. "Schöne Fremde" speaks ecstatically of some "great happiness to come" ('wie von künftigem großen Glück'), and this prophecy is fulfilled in the last song's jubilation "She is yours, is yours!" ('Sie ist deine, sie ist dein!'). And as if to underscore this relation, Schumann provides both climactic statements with similar music. (See Examples 1a and 1b)

Example 1a: Robert Schumann, Liederkreis, *Opus 39: "Schöne Fremde", mm. 18-26.*

Example 1b: Robert Schumann, Liederkreis, *Opus 39: "Frühlingsnacht", mm. 24-26.*

Promise and fulfillment, a glimpse of utopia and final happiness are highlighted through musical means. Both songs are also set into a relationship
through the keys of B major and F sharp major (with 5 and 6 sharps, respectively), keys that in Schumann's perspective were appropriate for capturing
the intensity and ecstasy expressed in the poetry. 'Simple feelings', he felt,
'demand simple keys; the more complicated ones require those which are
less frequently heard.' (Robert Schumann, *On Music and Musicians* 60-61)[4]

Another ordering principle for the cycle is that of pairing adjacent songs:
nos. 7 and 8 are linked by commencing with the same vocal line, albeit
transposed and given a completely different character in the latter song by
means of thematic transformation. (See Examples 2a and 2b)

Example 2a: Robert Schumann, Liederkreis, *Opus 39: "Auf einer Burg", mm. 1-4.*

Example 2b: Robert Schumann, Liederkreis, *Opus 39: "In der Fremde"
[II], mm. 1-4.*

---

[4] "Einfachere Empfindungen haben einfachere Tonarten; zusammengesetzte bewegen
sich lieber in fremden, welche das Ohr seltener hört." (Robert Schumann, "Charakteristik
der Tonarten" 106)

Moreover, these same two songs are linked tonally. For one thing, both are arguably in A minor (the key signature of the first speaks for A minor, though it seems to begin in E minor). For another, "Auf einer Burg" ends its archaic melodic and harmonic path with the dominant of A minor, which finds its resolution in song no. 8, "In der Fremde" [II]. Similarly, in songs nos. 5 and 6, the incipits of the vocal part outline an ascending fourth and a falling fifth; while the initial interval is stated in skeletal form in "Schöne Fremde", it is filled in through a stepwise motion in "Mondnacht". (See examples 3a and 3b)

Example 3a: Robert Schumann, Liederkreis, *Opus 39: "Mondnacht", mm. 1-5.*

Songs nos. 2, 3 and 4 establish a special unit in the cycle because of the 'dialogue' character of the poems. "Intermezzo" is a love song addressed by a man to a woman, "Die Stille" a *Rollengedicht* spoken in the persona of a woman in love, and both songs frame "Waldesgespräch", a dialogue between a male rider in the forest pursuing a beautiful female appearance and the Lorelei, also on horseback, trapping her stalker. (Some singers, e. g., Christa Ludwig and Walter Berry, have utilized the different personae of these poems as a point of departure for rendering the entire cycle as a dialogue between a male and a female singer – a solution not to be dismissed outright in view of the collaborative nature of the work and the biographical circumstances of Robert and Clara Schumann during the genesis of the cycle.)

Example 3b: Robert Schumann, Liederkreis, *Opus 39: "Schöne Fremde",* mm. 1-5.

A factor contributing to the cyclic nature of Opus 39, no doubt, is the rather uncomplicated key-sequence in the succession of songs. Keys with sharps prevail in the first half, and the number of sharps in the key-signature increases as we progress. Darker hues and subsequently minor keys prevail in the second half, until the last song tops the key-sequence pursued in the first half with an ecstatic F sharp major. (See Example 4)

Example 4: Key Sequence in Opus 39

Note: Keys for the songs of happiness, jubilation, ecstasy, etc. are listed in the upper stave, keys for songs displaying darker emotional hues in the lower stave; a plus sign indicates major keys, a minus sign keys in minor.

Stages 3 and 4: Differences

Despite a significant number of features common to both versions, including the various internal connections just listed, the differences are profound. The songs with which the two versions begin could not be more contrasting. In the 1842 version, a happy-go-lucky song of wandering recalls, as Finson (cf. 160) has pointed out, the beginning of Schubert's *Die schöne Müllerin,* with its evocation of *Volkston* and marching patterns, and the carefree optimism and confidence with which the wanderer starts his journey, perhaps in typical song-cycle fashion in search of a beloved, casts a light on subsequent songs. While most of the songs of the first half as well as the ecstatic conclusion bear out the optimism of our traveler, he also encounters situations of a more disturbing nature, especially in the cycle's second half. In the words of Finson, the initial song "provides a point of reference against which we can view other songs […]. Many take on a more ironic air [in light of 'Der frohe Wandersmann'], for the disparity between its cheerful confidence and the unhappy confusion in other parts of the cycle is acute" (167). One thinks of the ironic treatment of cheerfulness in other cycles of Schumann, such as "Ich grolle nicht" and (until its explicit last line) "Ein Jüngling liebt ein Mädchen" in *Dichterliebe.*

The 1849 version also commences with the song of a wanderer, but he is a wanderer who has seen considerably more of the world than our chap of the 1842 version. If the wanderer in the 1842 version 'begets' history (to stay in the conceptual framework with which Werner Wolf approaches Schubert's *Winterreise* elsewhere in this volume), the wanderer in the 1849 version 're-enacts' history (see 121 passim). He has returned to his homeland after many years on the road, only to find out that he has become a stranger. The feeling of alienation and estrangement cause in him a longing for being united with Nature, in short: for death. "In der Fremde" [I] casts a completely different light on the songs that immediately follow: they almost appear as retrospectives, flashbacks, as it were, displaying a trajectory from melancholy nostalgia and alienation to jubilant exultation and ecstastic union with the beloved. "In der Fremde" [I] prepares us for the more disturbing part of the journey in the second half of the cycle (better perhaps than "Der frohe Wandersmann"), but the ecstatic finale following nearly half a dozen songs evoking disturbing encounters comes out of the blue – a veritable *deus ex machina*, at most hinted at in the anticipation of future happiness in "Schöne Fremde", the last song in the cycle's first half[5].

The differences between the 1842 and 1849 versions pose some problems for commentators and analysts who usually have made a case for the musical coherence of the cycle on the basis of the second edition. "Der frohe Wandersmann" disturbs the tonal closure of the cycle; the D major beginning indeed does away with the F-sharp minor (of "In der Fremde" [I]) that, in the later version, corresponds so well with the F-sharp major at the end of the cycle. But it has the advantage of setting up more clearly the cycle's overall motion from relatively 'plain' keys to ones with increasingly more sharps. Perhaps more a fly in the ointment is that "Der frohe Wandersmann" does not feature the motive of the ascending and descending fourths and fifths which very subtly emerges in the middle section of "In der Fremde" [I] and which analysts (such as Turchin [cf. 240-241], McCreless [cf. 14-17], Daverio [cf. *Robert Schumann* 215-216], and Thym [cf. 215-216]) have identified as the germ for other occurrences in subsequent songs. We do not have to deny that Schumann indeed imbues some of his songs in *Liederkreis* with motivic and thematic correspondences (and we even can admit that the fourth/fifth motive takes on considerable significance in this context), but its absence in the first song of the 1842 version casts at least some doubt on the often unspoken teleological and organicist theories that seem to underlie the claims of motivic coherence.

Epilogue

"Ihre Worte über meine Claviercompositionen haben mich wieder erfreut", Schumann wrote on June 11, 1840 to W. H. Rieffel. "Fände ich nur mehr,

---

[5] Finson's proposal (cf. 168) to record both first songs on a CD to enable audiences to choose between the 1842 and 1849 versions requires, of course, a neutral rendition of the songs that follow. That, however, is not an option for the responsible artist. A performer selecting "In der Fremde" [I] as initial song may well feel the need to cast a different spell on subsequent numbers than the one who choses "Der frohe Wandersmann".

die mich verständen, wie ich Alles meine. Mit Gesangscompositionen hoffe ich soll es mir leichter fallen." (Jensen, ed. 164)[6]

Schumann draws in this letter an explicit connection between the writing of keyboard works of the 1830s and his vocal music of the Liederjahr 1840, suggesting that his compositional and aesthetic principles had not changed as much as the trope of the completely new Schumann emerging in the year of song implies. He was aware of the difficulties of comprehension which his keyboard cycles can create for audiences, because of the often bizarre juxtaposition of contrasting miniatures in the music. (The series of short, almost fragmentary movements in a work such as *Carnaval* are a case in point.) Schumann hoped to do better in terms of comprehensibility (and perhaps also in terms of financial rewards) with vocal compositions, in which a poetic text provides a key for aiding comprehension. The surface discontinuities and apparent non-sequiturs we discovered in the *Liederkreis*, as we traversed the compositional and publication history of this cycle in flux, are perhaps not different in quality from those encountered in the keyboard works of the 1830s. Indeed, the existence of two different first songs reminds us of Schumann's willingness in other works to remove whole pieces at a late stage (*Dichterliebe* comes to mind, but also *Symphonische Etüden* for piano). If no other Schumann work goes so far as to propose two alternative pieces for a single movement, perhaps this simply shows how radical an instance Opus 39 is of a more general tendency in his *œuvre*.

The recognition of Schumann as a master of the piano character piece and of vocal miniatures has often been coupled, in the reception of his work, with a verdict of a different and less flattering kind, namely that he was just a miniaturist who had problems creating large-scale musical structures, especially of the organicist Beethovenian kind. During the last decade a number of authors, among them Newcomb, Daverio ("Schumann's *Im Legendenton*" and *Nineteenth-Century Music and German Romantic Ideology*), and Reiman have questioned this interpretation by showing that keyboard cycles such as *Papillons*, *Carnaval*, *Kreisleriana*, and others are indeed essays in large-scale structures, albeit inspired by Romantic concep-

---

[6] 'I was again delighted with your remarks about my piano works. If I only could find more people who understood my meaning! I hope I shall succeed more easily with vocal compositions.'

tions of narrative that harken back to Jean Paul and Friedrich Schlegel. Anthony Newcomb has pointed out in a seminal article in 1987 that "Schumann, like Jean Paul, avoids clear linear narrative through a stress on interruption, embedding, digression, and willful reinterpretation of the apparent function of an event" (165). About the same time John Daverio ("Schumann's *Im Legendenton*") began looking at Schumann's instrumental works with the tools provided him by aesthetic categories ("Arabeske" and "Fragment") developed by German Romantics such as Friedrich Schlegel – a project that has led him to view many (and perhaps the most significant) works in the nineteenth century as works which are generic and structural hybrids, engaging in discontinuous, open-ended, and self-reflective constructs – in short, as works resisting rather than measuring up to the classical yardstick.

Romantic approaches to narrative indeed may help us in our quest to understand the nature of Schumann's song cycles, explain or account for the features that puzzle us in the *Liederkreis*. In his letter to Rieffel, written shortly after he had composed most (or even all) of the Eichendorff settings of what later would become his Opus 39, Schumann himself seems to have sanctioned such an approach to a work whose conception, genesis, and publication history reveal an unusual degree of uncertainty and flux. These features may be considered signatures of Romanticism in its most emphatic sense.

References

Boetticher, Wolfgang. *Robert Schumann in seinen Schriften und Briefen.* Berlin: Hahnefeld, 1942.
Daverio, John. "Schumann's *Im Legendenton* and Friedrich Schlegel's *Arabeske*". *Nineteenth-Century Music* 11 (Fall 1987): 150-163.
—. *Nineteenth-Century Music and the German Romantic Ideology.* New York: Schirmer Books, 1993.
—. *Robert Schumann: Herald of a 'New Poetic Age'.* Oxford: Oxford Univ. Press, 1997.
Finson, Jon. "The Intentional Tourist: Romantic Irony in the Eichendorff *Liederkreis* of Robert Schumann". R. Larry Todd, ed. *Schumann and His World.* Princeton: Princeton Univ. Press, 1994.

Hallmark, Rufus. "Die Rückert Lieder of Robert and Clara Schumann". *Nineteenth-Century Music* 14 (Summer 1990): 3-30.

Hofmann, Kurt. *Die Erstdrucke der Werke von Robert Schumann.* Tutzing: Schneider, 1979.

Jensen, F. Gustav, ed. *Robert Schumanns Briefe: Neue Folge.* Leipzig: Breitkopf und Härtel, 1904.

Kaldewey, Helma. "Die *Gedichtabschriften* Robert und Clara Schumanns". Josef A. Kruse, ed. *Robert Schumann und die Dichter: Ein Musiker als Leser.* Düsseldorf: Droste, 1991.

Knaus, Herwig. *Musiksprache und Werkstruktur in Robert Schumanns Liederkreis.* Munich: Katzbichler, 1974.

McCreless, Patrick. "Song Order in the Song Cycle: Schumann's *Liederkreis,* Op.39". *Music Analysis* 5/1 (1986): 5-28.

Newcomb, Anthony. "Schumann and Late Eighteenth-Century Narrative Strategies". *Nineteenth-Century Music* 11 (Fall 1987): 164-174.

Reiman, Erika. "Formal Strategies in Schumann's Piano Cycles and Their Counterparts in German Romantic Literature". PhD Dissertation, Univ. of Toronto, 1999.

Sams, Eric. *The Songs of Robert Schumann.* New York: W. W. Norton, 1969.

Schumann, Clara, ed. *Jugendbriefe von Robert Schumann.* Leipzig: Breitkopf und Härtel, 1886.

Schumann, Robert. "Charakteristik der Tonarten". Schumann. *Gesammelte Schriften über Musik und Musiker.* Vol. 1. Ed. Martin Kreisig. Leipzig: Breitkopf & Härtel, 1914.

—. *On Music and Musicians.* Transl. Paul Rosenfeld. Berkeley: Univ. of California Press, 1946.

Thym, Jürgen. *The Piano-Accompanied Solo Song Settings of Eichendorff's Poems by Schumann and Wolf.* PhD Dissertation, Case Western Reserve Univ., 1974.

Turchin, Barbara. "Schumann's Song Cycles: The Cycle within the Song". *Nineteenth-Century Music* 8 (Spring 1985): 231-244.

Walsh, Stephen. *The Lieder of Schumann.* New York: Praeger, 1971.

Hugo Wolf's Seventeen *Divan*-Settings
An Undiscovered Goethe-Cycle?

Harry E. Seelig, Amherst, MA

Hugo Wolf's half-hour sequence of brief yet richly diverse settings selected from Goethe's vast collection of west-eastern poetry has heretofore elicited almost no interest among even those musicologists who have given special weight to literary aspects of the lied, nor have any extensive cyclic features of these succinct *Kunstlieder* been considered, even by Wolf scholars. Drawing particularly on the recent culturally based literary-musical hermeneutics of C. Hamlin, L. Kramer, J. Neubauer and others, this paper demonstrates that not only the half-dozen explicitly 'duodramatic' (Goethe's characterization of 1816) *Divan* poems but also the eleven implicitly interrelated poetic soliloquies (or solo settings) in Wolf's selection are intricately composed to form a miniature cycle of seventeen songs that constitutes a microcosmic distillation of major themes and central concerns expressed in the 250 poems of the macrocosmic *West-östlicher Divan*.

Given the attention Wolf lavished on the universally celebrated love poems contained in the "Buch Suleika", it is similarly perplexing that the crucial inspiration and actual poetic contributions of Marianne von Willemer have – since their discovery in 1869 – often been overlooked. Her lyric voice in the guise of 'Suleika' is therefore given particular analytic emphasis; the 'feminine discourse' she provides vitally energizes the duodramatic symmetry of Wolf's idiosyncratic and unorthodox but profoundly expressive cycle.

In his *Word and Music Studies*-paper (1999), entitled "The Romantic Song Cycle as Literary Genre", Cyrus Hamlin argues persuasively "that criteria of memory – specifically re-cognition by the audience through the dynamics of performance –" (113) are vital means for understanding that the generic forms of (Romantic) song cycles – though **also** musical structures – are fundamentally **literary**. Elsewhere in that seminal study Hamlin points to the paradox that, while the *West-östlicher Divan* is generally regarded as Goethe's "most complex and supremely powerful achievement [...] in the genre of lyric cycle", it (along with all of Goethe's other larger lyric cycles) "has never been set to music as a song cycle" (130).

Hugo Wolf, however, some seventy years after the *Divan*'s publication (in 1819) selected just seventeen from among almost 250 poems in Goethe's

original collection and, as I shall argue below, succeeded in fashioning a
musical cycle that serves simultaneously as a **literary** microcosm of the
vast macrocosm Goethe himself could not quite complete according to his
original cyclic plan[1]. Moreover, Wolf's overall musical structure, in
addition to incorporating many traditional devices long recognized as
canonical in the song cycle tradition, also makes twofold use of the listeners' memory as "implicit hermeneutical consciousness" (to use Hamlin's
phrase, 121) and as allusion to other salient poems in the larger poetic
context of Goethe's entire collection.

   To better understand this twofold responsibility of listeners in the hermeneutics of cyclic consciousness, however, we must anchor Hugo Wolf's
sequential musical structure within the larger context of recent theoretical
studies of song cycles by Suzanne Lodato, Walter Bernhart, and Werner
Wolf. Their generically complementary contributions to the Ann Arbor
conference in August of 1999 – documented in this volume – establish
interdisciplinary song cycle parameters that clarify our understanding of
Hugo Wolf's compositional approach in his *Divan* settings. To begin with,
Lodato provides concise characterizations – based on Arthur Komar's
Authoritative Norton Critical Score (1971) of Schumann's *Dichterliebe* – of
the fundamental criteria that undergird most song cycles by analyzing the
limits of the so-called organicist view among recent song cycle critics such
as David Neumeyer, Patrick McCreless, and Christopher Lewis. These
limits in effect legitimize or justify – very much in the manner of John
Neubauer's timely call (cf. 66) for a methodological blending of formal
properties **and** cultural discourse in analyzing Bartók's use of folk music –
the contrasting analytic procedures of Lawrence Kramer and Amanda
Glauert, which are particularly germane here, as we shall see. Walter
Bernhart, who emphasizes "literary song cycles" ("song cycles with a dominant literary coherence" [see below 217]) as a seminal category that both
harmonizes with Hamlin's 'retrospective cyclicity' and also includes such
aspects as "a lyric persona with his/her flux of mental states, or a central

---

[1]   That plan foresaw thirteen more or less equally long 'books' of poems that in myriad
ways document the 65-year-old poet's experience synthesizing his own 'western' cultural
heritage with the 'eastern' wisdom he was then enthusiastically culling from the translated
poetry of the fourteenth-century Persian mystic Hafiz.

mental attitude, or a common suggestive theme" (see below 222), also elucidates characteristic aspects of Wolf's *Divan* settings. Finally, by questioning the true "cyclicity of song cycles" even while demonstrating that the "metatextual" retrospectivity (see above 121) of Schubert's *Winterreise*-settings cannot be grasped by the listener until he or she experiences the final rhetorical question posed by the traveler to the hurdy-gurdy man (namely "Willst zu meinen Liedern deine Leier drehn?"), Werner Wolf demonstrates to me – by way of 'intermedial' analogy and 'self-reflexive cyclic re-enactment' – that Suleika's climactic couplet "Denn das Leben ist die Liebe, / Und des Lebens Leben Geist" in the final *Divan* duodrama text (Goethe 75) is an equally fruitful point of departure for perceiving the cyclic integrity of all seventeen settings. The literary **and** musical manner in which this succinct poetic formulation – containing as it does the 'quintessence' (cf. Trunz in Goethe 514) of the entire *Divan* and the triadic embodiment of Goethe's cardinal concepts of life, love, and spirit – relates **retrospectively** to many of the earlier poems in the cycle will become explicit below.

As indicated above, there are theoretical viewpoints beyond those considered at the first two WMA-conferences that bear on Hugo Wolf's accomplishment. One is John Daverio's recent definition (1996) of song cycle as an "aesthetic claim" that requires "musicopoetic cohesiveness extending beyond the individual lied to encompass the entire set" (279)[2]. Another is Lawrence Kramer's evolving insight into the social dimensions of *Goethelieder* generally, beginning with his study (1995) of Felix Mendelssohn's emancipation from artistic "tutelage" (150) vis-à-vis Goethe in the young composer's two *Divan*-settings from the "Buch Suleika" and extending into his analysis of Hugo Wolf's "Subjectivity in the Fin-de-Siècle Lied" (1996), which probes well beyond the partisan legend of Wolf's "preternatural" ability to "understand" first-rate literary texts and to "express" them to "perfection by repeating their sound and meaning in the form of music" (186). In the former, Kramer makes important observations about gender and desire as "cultural practice" in the lied and views

---

[2] Ironically, however, while he correctly asserts that "a microcosmic history of the song cycle can be read out of [Wolf's settings of Goethe's] *Wilhelm Meister* lieder alone" (299), Daverio neglects utterly to mention the structural and semantic interrelatedness of Wolf's *Divan* settings.

Mendelssohn's choice of lyrics by Marianne von Willemer in the "Buch
Suleika" as crucial for his analysis of 'feminine discursive power' within
these settings (cf. 164-173). In the latter, Kramer deconstructs the conventional legend of Wolf's uncanny ability to "repeat" poetic nuance in succinct
musical detail by analyzing the composer's oedipal battle with his father as
part of the impetus for the "framing trilogies of the Goethe songbook" that
"deal exclusively with men"[3] and then concluding that Wolf's seventeen
Divan-settings constitute but "a group of amatory-exotic numbers" (200-
201). He thereby disregards entirely the seminal role played here by the
same Marianne von Willemer who wielded the 'feminine discursive power'
seen as crucial in Mendelssohn's choices.

Yet in spite of his dismissive attitude toward Wolf's musical renderings
of Goethe's 'exotic' love poems and high-spirited drinking revelries,
refrains, and ghazels, Lawrence Kramer has nevertheless provided a
refreshing and stimulating cultural construction of at least two competing
hermeneutic paradigms germane to the cyclical *Divan*-settings here
considered. His Mendelssohn and Wolf studies have inspired Amanda
Glauert's perceptive insights into Marianne von Willemer's vital role in
truly 'feminizing' the heretofore imbalanced Suleika-Hatem 'duodrama-
turgy' and into the immediacy of spiritual experience for Goethe as
expressed in the "shocking replacement of wine for the Koran as the door to
eternity in 'Ob der Koran von Ewigkeit sei'" (80-81). Moreover, Kramer
has extended retrospective 'deconstructive support' to Susan Youens's
analysis of the peculiarly 'divanesque' version of Biblical humor in Noah's
giving wine to "Hans Adam" in Wolf's setting of this deliberate *Divan*
spoof (cf. Youens 111-114).

An analogy drawn from Charles Rosen's chapter on "Mountains and
Song Cycles" in *The Romantic Generation* of 1995 serves both to connect
the preceding theoretical perspectives to a detailed consideration of Hugo
Wolf's actual *Divan*-settings and to reinforce Cyrus Hamlin's hermeneutic

---

[3] Namely the three "Harfenspielerlieder" at the beginning and "Prometheus",
"Ganymed", and 'der uralte heilige Vater' of "Grenzen der Menschheit" at the conclusion
of the fifty-one *Goethelieder* in their original published sequence (Wiener Verlag Carl
Lacom 1889, cf. H. Wolf. *Sämtliche Werke*).

suggestion that memory and re-cognition be accepted as salient criteria of generic form in song cycle analysis generally:

> Just as the travelers of the last decades of the eighteenth century looked back and saw a landscape almost unrecognizable, astonishingly different from the one they believed themselves to have passed through, so the listener must listen back in his memory to the earlier songs, and only then can he perceive how the cycle is taking shape. (194)

In the case of Goethe's *West-östlicher Divan*, of course, the poetic landscape is both a vast mountain range and an intimate topography of lovers united in aesthetic-cultural-intellectual 'play' on the highest spiritual level, a level that puts both poetic language and its musical correlatives to the severest test.

Having mentioned Marianne von Willemer's feminizing role in the genesis of the *Divan* poems that Hugo Wolf chose to set, let us return to the summer of 1814, when she was just thirty years old and Goethe, on a stage-coach from Weimar bound for the Main, Rhein, and Neckar region around Frankfurt, began to write some of the very first poems of his nascent cycle. A precipitating event was a relatively rare meteorological phenomenon known as a **fog**bow, which is an infrequently seen variant form of the vastly more prevalent **rain**bow. Goethe saw in its whiteness a sign of immanent amatory experience in spite of his tell-tale white hair: "Sind gleich die Haare weiß, / Doch wirst du lieben." Written ten days before Goethe first met Marianne, this "Phänomen" (Goethe 13) is obviously a very significant link in the chain of events that inspired the hundreds of diverse west-eastern poems that Goethe composed over the next several years. Equally significant, Hugo Wolf places this crucial poem at the start of his musical sequence, followed by the irreverently humorous "Erschaffen und Beleben", although both were composed **after** the five drinking songs of the "Schenkenbuch" during Wolf's spate of white-hot creativity in the first month of 1889[4].

Hugo Wolf's most spontaneously generated but very deliberately ordered cyclic settings, as already suggested, manifestly deserve to be understood as

---

[4]   From the sixteenth to the twenty-first of January he set these seven poems from two smaller *Divan* 'books', the "Buch des Sängers" and the "Schenkenbuch"; from the twenty-first to the thirtieth Wolf composed the ten settings from the largest book in the *Divan*, the "Buch Suleika".

an epitome of the *West-östlicher Divan* in its essence. Although between 1935 and 1965 the literary scholars Elisabeth Reitmayer, Helen Mustard, Hans-Egon Hass, and Ingeborg Hillmann had called some critical attention to its cyclic nature, it wasn't until 1971, with the appearance of Edith Ihekweazu's comprehensive *Untersuchungen zur Struktur des lyrischen Zyklus*, that Goethe's *West-östlicher Divan* began to be taken seriously as an intentionally shaped collection of interrelated poems, poems that owed their lyric function and efficacy not to the biographical chronology of their genesis, but rather to purposeful continuities and contrasts in the sequences devised by the poet during a considerable gestation period lasting from 1814 through 1819.

When I began my study of Wolf's "Buch Suleika"-settings some decades ago, it seemed rash to suggest that Wolf's mere ten out of forty-eight choices seriously represented a microcosmic distillation of the macrocosmic four dozen original poems. But in the wake of recent literary scholarship and my own continuing research, this notion – expanded to include the remaining poems from the "Buch des Sängers" and the "Schenkenbuch" – deserves serious consideration. Furthermore, Wolf's cyclic *Divan*-microcosm signifies that the efforts of earlier Goethe scholars to pursue the biographical or chronological facts while refraining from any aesthetic or cultural analysis of the poetry has finally been superseded by taking cyclic structures like Goethe's and Wolf's seriously and letting their interdisciplinary aesthetic-cultural synthesis take center stage.

The poems set by Wolf are precisely those to which *Divan* scholars such as Edgar Lohner, Hannelore Schlaffer, and Katharina Mommsen have given greatest attention. On the musical side of the ledger, on the other hand, and particularly if one considers the repeated musicological and literary-musical treatment given to Wolf's fifty-three *Mörikelieder,* most of Hugo Wolf's fifty-one *Goethelieder* – except for the *Wilhelm Meister* songs – have been largely ignored by musicologists and scholars of poetry and music alike. A few notable exceptions are two earlier studies, namely Eric Sams's descriptive analysis of all the songs Wolf composed, and Jack Stein's inconsistent and often dismissive treatment of both poetic and musical aspects in some of them. And very recently, as mentioned above, both Susan Youens and Lawrence Kramer have applied a Freudian analysis to some of Wolf's *Goethelieder.*

So, given the substantial interest in the song cycles of Schubert and particularly of Schumann, as two WMA-conferences have now brought clearly to the fore, as well as the considerable stake recording companies still seem to have in marketing ever more comprehensive collections of historical reissues along with numerous new interpretations of the general nineteenth-century lieder canon, it is perplexing that Hugo Wolf's obviously interrelated and deliberately coordinated settings of certain poems from Goethe's *Divan* are repeatedly presented totally out of context as self-sufficient entities even though their texts are (at best) incomplete or (at worst) incomprehensible: this is most startling in very recent unrelated CD-recordings of the tenth and eleventh *Divan*-settings, "Als ich auf dem Euphrat schiffte" and "Dies zu deuten, bin erbötig", as performed by Elly Ameling and Stephan Genz, respectively. In the first instance, the closing question that clearly asks what the dream means ("Was bedeutet dieser Traum?") is left totally unanswered; in the second case, the demonstrative pronoun 'this' ("Dies") refers clearly to Suleika's dream, which Hatem is anxious to interpret, but his subsequent four quatrains are necessarily meaningless without the antecedent text. Nor are these isolated examples: both Ruth Ziesak (in 1992) and Sophie Koch (in 1999) have added "Hochbeglückt in deiner Liebe" (*Divan*-setting no. 9) to the 'incomprehensible-without-further-elucidation' roster simply because the very next line they both sing, "Schelt' ich nicht Gelegenheit", refers specifically to the proverbial opportunity Suleika's lover Hatem punningly cites as stealing his heart's remaining capacity for love in the preceding poem "Nicht Gelegenheit macht Diebe" (*Divan*-setting no. 8)!

This is most regrettable in the case of any of the 'duodrama'-poems, which were specifically intended by Goethe to be read and understood in conjunction with one another, and not simultaneously, as duets, but rather as consecutively interrelated yet autonomous miniature dialogues between lovers. There are three such duodrama-pairings among the seventeen *Divan*-poems set by Wolf, and their corresponding musical shapes alone are reason enough to credit the composer with admirable cyclic sensitivity and creativity.

In Goethe's original macrocosmic cycle of well over two hundred poems, the "Buch des Sängers" contains twenty poems, including the justly famous mystical and esoteric "Selige Sehnsucht" (Goethe 18-19) with its sage injunction "Stirb und werde", the "Buch Suleika" consists of forty-eight love poems, one of which is the cosmic celebration of lovers reunited in "Wiederfinden" (Goethe 83-84), and "Das Schenkenbuch" has twenty-six variations on themes involving a young cupbearer. By having chosen the particular poems he set, Hugo Wolf enables the perceptive listener to remember or 're-cognize' (Hamlin's usage) these more speculative and philosophic poems as a function of memory and hindsight (Rosen's travelers!) although they are not actually part of the musical microcosm that is being sung or heard, as we shall see below. But besides selecting so perceptively, Wolf also rearranged the order of the seventeen poems he set, as the following very abridged listing (in which only the first couplets of the solo *Divan* poems and several quatrains of the duodramas in the musical sequence are included) demonstrates[5]:

BUCH DES SÄNGERS   BUCH SULEIKA

(1) PHÄNOMEN   (13)
                                                  Komm, Liebchen, komm!
Wenn zu der Regenwand   umwinde mir die Mütze!
Phöbus sich gattet
                                                  (14)
(2) ERSCHAFFEN UND   [Duodrama I]   Wie sollt ich heiter bleiben,
     BELEBEN   Entfernt von Tag und Licht?
                             (8) Hatem
Hans Adam war ein Erdenkloß, Nicht Gelegenheit macht Diebe,   (15)
Den Gott zum Menschen   Sie ist selbst der größte Dieb; Wenn ich dein gedenke,
                   machte   Denn sie stahl den Rest der Liebe, Fragt mich gleich der Schenke:
                             Die mir noch im Herzen blieb.
                                                         [Duodrama III]
                             (9) Suleika
DAS SCHENKENBUCH   Hochbeglückt in deiner Liebe,   (16) Hatem
                             Schelt' ich nicht Gelegenheit;   Locken, haltet mich gefangen
(3)   Ward sie auch an dir zum Diebe, In dem Kreise des Gesichts!
Ob der Koran von Ewigkeit   Wie mich solch ein Raub erfreut! Euch geliebten braunen
                    sei?   Schlangen
Darnach frag' ich nicht!   Zu erwidern hab' ich nichts
                                                  [...]

---

5   Quoted from Goethe, 12-13, 89-90, 92, 93, 63-65, 69-70, 68, 76 and 74-75.

(4)
Trunken müssen wir alle sein!
Jugend ist Trunkenheit ohne
              Wein;

(5)
Solang man nüchtern ist,
Gefällt das Schlechte;

(6)
Sie haben wegen der
          Trunkenheit
Vielfältig uns verklagt

(7)
Was in der Schenke waren
          heute
Am frühsten Morgen für
          Tumulte!

[Duodrama II]

(10) Suleika
Als ich auf dem Euphrat schiffte,
Streifte sich der goldne Ring
Fingerab in Wasserklüfte,
Den ich jüngst von dir empfing.

(11) Hatem
Dies zu deuten bin erbötig!
Hab' ich dir nicht oft erzählt,
Wie der Doge von Venedig
Mit dem Meere sich vermählt?

(12)
Hätt' ich irgend wohl Bedenken,
Balch, Bokhâra, Samarkand,

Schenke her! Noch eine
          Flasche!

Diesen Becher bring' ich ihr!
Findet sie ein Häufchen Asche,
Sagt sie: "Der verbrannte mir."

(17) Suleika
Nimmer will ich dich verlieren!
Liebe gibt der Liebe Kraft.
Magst du meine Jugend zieren
Mit gewalt'ger Leidenschaft.

Ach! wie schmeichelt's meinem
          Triebe,
Wenn man meinen Dichter
          preist:
Denn das Leben ist die Liebe,
Und des Lebens Leben Geist.

In Goethe's original sequence the "Schenkenbuch" actually follows the "Buch Suleika"; however, Wolf has placed the five drinking songs from this 'cupbearer's book' ahead of the ten love poems from the "Buch Suleika". He has also reversed the order of the first two poems – (2) "Erschaffen und Beleben" and (1) "Phänomen" – for his musical sequence. He has thereby integrated the alternating themes of love-making and wine-drinking in a more symmetrical manner than would be possible in Goethe's order; this also counter-balances two poems – namely (14) "Wie sollt' ich heiter bleiben" and (15) "Wenn ich dein gedenke" – in the "Buch Suleika". Both of these contain another amatory theme normally found in the "Schenkenbuch", namely the loving mentor-youth relationship between the poet Hatem and the cupbearer Saki. The symmetry of Wolf's ordering is further enhanced by the fact that these two cupbearer-poems follow upon two solo (rather than duodrama) poems, namely (12) "Hätt' ich irgend wohl Bedenken" and (13) "Komm, Liebchen, komm!", so that the five 'solo' wine-drinking songs from the "Schenkenbuch" proper complement the four 'solo' settings within the "Buch Suleika", all of which is indicated on the abridged scheme above.

As I have argued elsewhere, particularly with regard to the duodramas in the "Buch Suleika" and two "Schenkenbuch"-settings of poems written in imitation of the oriental Ghazel-form (Seelig, "Hugo Wolf's Ghazel Settings", "Orientalism and the Feminine"), Hugo Wolf's achievement resides in his uncanny ability to match and project – detail by detail – countless poetic nuances by remarkable musical means. Such a point-by-point analysis can obviously not be undertaken in the present context, yet precisely because the cyclic aspects of all seventeen of Wolf's *Divan*-settings have heretofore been so completely neglected, I intend to focus on several settings in detail even while keeping the general interrelatedness of Wolf's cyclic choices and the central themes of the *Divan* in mind. Two poems taken from the "Buch des Sängers" contain (in "Phänomen") the complementary themes of rejuvenation and the potential for love expressed in mythological and meteorological terms; in "Erschaffen und Beleben" ("Hans Adam") we find a parody of the Old Testament creation myth merged with the theme of wine as an aid to creativity. In the five "Schenkenbuch" poems, further ramifications of wine drinking, ranging from the Koran's ambivalent prohibition to the tumult in the taverns, are given their due. Characteristically, Goethe's notion of intoxication is spirited in a dual sense (alcoholic and aesthetic) or, as Amanda Glauert aptly observes: in the "Schenkenbuch" Goethe "used wine as a symbol of divine creativity" and "characterised inspiration as an exaltation which could be summoned up by the will of the poet and experienced in the flesh as much as in the spirit" (81). And finally, the "Buch Suleika" contains some of Goethe's most personal evocations of love and, above all, its ramifications for **both** partners. In fact six of the poems chosen by Wolf form three intimate duo-dramas, as shown by the bracketed Roman numerals on the scheme above; the first two of them were probably written by Marianne von Willemer herself (cf. Trunz in Goethe 508 and 514).

I have attempted to provide a miniaturized and schematic overview of Hugo Wolf's entire cycle in "Table 1: Thematic Listing of the Songs", which contains the abbreviated titles, the respective key areas, and the initial vocal melodies of each song. Because the very first setting and the three duodramas serve both as cornerstones and main pillars of Wolf's quite symmetrical cyclic structure, a series of excerpts from these songs (Examples 1 – 9b) will help to illustrate why I consider the following poetic and musical features to be structurally and cyclically significant:

TABLE 1 Thematic Listing of the Songs
(including apparent key areas)

BUCH DES SÄNGERS

(1) *"Wenn zu der Regenwand"*
A (- E♭ - B♭ - A♭ - B♭ -) E

Sehr langsam.

Wenn zu der Re-gen-wand Phöbus sich gat-tet, gleich steht ein Bo-gen-rand far - big ge-schat-tet.

(2) *"Hans Adam war ein Erdenkloß"*
e (- F - G - b - F♯ -) E

Etwas gemessen, nicht schleppend.

Hans A-dam war ein Er - den-kloß den Gott zum Men-schen mach-te,

SCHENKENBUCH

(3) *"Ob der Koran von Ewigkeit sei?"*
a (- E♭ - D - B♭ -) A

Mäßig.

Ob der Ko - ran von E-wig-keit sei?   dar-nach frag ich nicht!

(4) *"Trunken müssen wir alle sein!"*
f♯ (- A - F♯ - A - C♯ - f♯ -) F♯

Bacchantisch.

Trun - ken müs - sen wir al - le sein!

(5) *"So lang man nüchtern ist"*
a (- G - g - e - G - g -) D

Sehr gemessen.

So lang man nüch - tern ist,   ge - fällt das Schlech - te;

(6) *"Sie haben wegen der Trunkenheit"*
g (- E - F - A -) g

Ziemlich gedehnt.

Sie ha - ben we-gen der Trun-ken-heit viel - fäl-tig uns ver-klagt,

(7) *"Was in der Schenke waren heute"*
d (- A♭ - C -) d

Äußerst rasch und wirbelnd.

Was in der Schen-ke wa-ren heu - te am früh-sten Mor-gen für Tu-mul-te!

BUCH SULEIKA

(8) *"Nicht Gelegenheit*
macht Diebe"
F (- A - B♭ - E -) **F**

Ziemlich bewegt und sehr innig.

p

Nicht Ge - le - gen-heit macht Die - be,   sie ist selbst der größ-te Dieb;

(9) *"Hoch beglückt*
in deiner Liebe"
B♭ (- E♭ - B♭ - E♭ -) **B♭**

Äußerst leidenschaftlich und sehr lebhaft.

p

Hoch beglückt in deiner Lie - be schelt ich nicht Ge - le - gen - heit,

(10) *"Als ich auf dem Euphrat*
schiffte"
A (-A♭ -) **A** [**C♯**]

Sanft fließend.

pp   Als ich auf dem Eu - phrat schiff - te,

(11) *"Dies zu deuten*
bin erbötig!"
A (- A♭ - G - B♮ - F [etc] -) **A**

Ziemlich lebhaft.

p Dies zu deuten bin er-bö-tig! Hab ich dir nicht oft er-zählt,

(12) *"Hätt' ich irgend*
wohl Bedenken"
A (- C♯ - A - C♯ -) **A**

Ziemlich lebhaft.

p

Hätt' ich ir-gend wohl Be - den-ken,   Balch, Bokha - ra,   Sa-mar-kand,

(13) *"Komm, Liebchen,*
komm!"
A♭ (- E♭ - B♮ - E♭ - C♯ -B♭ -) **A♭**

Lebhaft und innig.

p

Komm, Liebchen, komm!   um - win - de mir   die Müt-ze!

(14) *"Wie sollt ich*
heiter bleiben"
f (- A♭ - G - F - D♭ - F -f -) **F**

Mäßig bewegt, traumhaft.

pp

Wie sollt ich hei - ter blei - ben,   ent-fernt von Tag und Licht?

(15) *"Wenn ich dein*
Gedenke"
A♭ (- F♭ - B♭ - B♮ - E - C - A♭ -) **F**

Mäßig bewegt, traumhaft.

p

Wenn ich dein ge-den - ke,   fragt mich gleich der Schen-ke:

(16) *"Locken, haltet mich*
gefangen"
A (- F♯ - g - E - C♯ - A♭ -) **A**

Rasch und feurig.

f

Lok - ken, hal - tet mich ge-fan-gen in   dem Krei - se des Gesichts!

(17) *"Nimmer will ich*
dich verlieren!"
A (- E - D - B♭ -) **A**

Sehr lebhaft und leidenschaftlich.

f

Nimmer will ich dich ver-lie-ren!   Lie-be gibt der Lie - be Kraft.

To begin with, the first three settings form a larger unit delineated by the related key areas A-E-A inasmuch as "Phänomen (Wenn zu)" (1) ends in the dominant E, which key "Erschaffen und Beleben (Hans Adam)" (2) develops from minor to major, and "Ob der Koran von Ewigkeit sei" (3) brings back the tonic A, beginning in the minor and concluding in the major key. Because these three poems contain crucial references to mythology (Phöbus), meteorological metaphor (white **fog**bow = Hatem's white hair) and parodies of the creation myth in both Christianity (Hans Adam/Noah) and Islam (Koran/Angels), this unified key area of A-E-A forms an expressive counterpart to the even more consistently A-major key area (A-Ab-A and A-E-Bb-A) of the two latter duodramas. But the importance of "Wenn zu der Regenwand" for the cycle as a whole is at least twofold: not only do the poem's three quatrains delineate the range of experience the poet is able to shape artistically – mythology (the perceived 'pairing' of Phöbus with a rain shower or wall of rain), meteorology (a fogbow or arc of white mist), and personal imagery or metaphor (white-haired potential for love) –, but the melodic and harmonic structure of this first setting could be said to contain *in nuce* all the compositional elements of the sixteen that will follow:

Example 1: "Wenn zu der Regenwand" (1).

In Eric Sams's words,

> the phenomenon here is the lunar rainbow, the rim of which remains white though potentially containing all colours; an encouraging image of old age. [...] [This setting] is among the most intensely chromatic of all [Wolf's] songs; for [...] the concept of chromaticism [...] connotes the idea of colour. The music [...] uses a whole palette of tone-painting. Its sixteen bars contain major or minor chords on each of the twelve semitones, [which] entails some 160 accidentals [...]. (222)

As the many accidentals in bars 3-11 of Example 1 demonstrate, the color symbolism inherent in the ubiquitous musical chromaticism provides all the elements imaginable for the later cycle; moreover, the syncopatedly 'lingering' conclusion of the setting on the dominant E-major chord enhances the poet's expectation of being able to love (in the delayed tonic of A).

Noteworthy in the "Thematic Listing" are the wide intervals – fourths, fifths, and sixths, but particularly fifths – both in descending and ascending directions that characterize virtually all of Wolf's *Divan*-settings: the descending sixths and fifths in (1) and (2) are answered by the ascending scale tones delineating a sixth in (3). The ascending fifth in (5) on "nüchtern" is quickly followed by the descending diminished fifth on "das Schlechte"; this latter configuration is then repeated in the very same descending diminished fifths on "der Trunkenheit" and "verklagt" in (6). While these wide intervals are also prevalent in the settings from the "Buch Suleika", when used in this descending fashion and together with the 'lisping' effect of the added grace notes, they certainly lend a characteristic 'carousing' effect to the drinking songs (2-7) in both the "Buch des Sängers" and, above all, in the "Schenkenbuch".

The poetic bond between Hatem's challenge and Suleika's response in Duodrama I (8) and (9) is all but indelible in terms of musical structure: the identical melodic motifs in the dominant-tonic key relationship of F and B flat are varied ever so slightly to indicate the subtle difference in the lovers' attitudes: even the descending chromatic lines in the initial two bars and the rising sixths followed by descending fifths in Example 2b make an unmistakable gesture of amatory mood fluctuation:

Example 2a: "Nicht Gelegenheit macht Diebe" (8), bars 1-2.

Example 2b: "Nicht Gelegenheit macht Diebe" (8), bars 3-6.

Wolf's sophisticated duodramatic cyclic structure can also be glimpsed in the contrast between how the descending melody in Example 2b follows upon the 'strumming' or 'vamping' piano introduction of Example 2a; Suleika's response to Hatem's witty proverb-inspired 'challenge' uses his tonic key as the dominant for her answer a fourth higher in Example 3c; Examples 3a and 3b indicate how Suleika's piano introduction begins with Hatem's melody – ever so poignantly nuanced with a dotted-quarter-and-eighth-note rhythmic change – over dominant seventh-chord harmony – and proceeds in the new tonic key:

Example 3a: "Hoch beglückt in deiner Liebe" (9), bars 1-2.

Example 3b: "Hoch beglückt in deiner Liebe" (9), bars 11-14.

Hoch   be - glückt   in   dei - ner   Lie - be   schelt   ich   nicht   Ge - le - gen - heit,

Example 3d 'telescopes' one-bar 'frames' to demonstrate the cumulatively developing 'Beethovenesque' aspects of this exuberant postlude (beginning in Example 3c) wherein Suleika's passion reaches its climax with a brilliantly structured coda that rivals Hugo Wolf's arch-enemy Brahms's climactic fugal coda in his *Piano Variations on a Theme by Händel*, Op. 24:

Example 3c: "Hoch beglückt in deiner Liebe" (9), bars 62-67.

Example 3d: "Hoch beglückt in deiner Liebe" (9), bars 66, 68, 70, 72.

It is hard to exaggerate the significance of this extensive yet logically crafted postlude; only in two *Mörikelieder* – "Er ist's" (6) and "Der Abschied" (53) – does Wolf allow his otherwise evident penchant for interpretive postludes to assume similarly large proportions. This particularly explicit enhancement of Suleika's passionate response to Hatem is perhaps the clearest indication of the seriousness with which Hugo Wolf has emphasized the feminine side of the profound duodramatic equation with purely musical means.

Additional instances of the descending sixth in A-major are very visible in Thematic Listings (10), (11), (16), and (17). Only partially visible in Examples 4, 5, and 6, but nonetheless noteworthy is the fact that settings (10), (11), and (12) all share a very similar bass line that derives from Suleika's dream about losing her ring during a boat ride on the Euphrates:

Example 4: "Als ich auf dem Euphrat schiffte" (10).

By subtly transforming the bass melody's initial barcarole-like texture into
ever more spirited subsequent versions, Wolf underscores in clear musico-
literary terms that Hatem is effectively *re*-interpreting his beloved's dream
and, above all, changing her gloomy premonition into a confident assertion
of spiritual union (even marriage!) and the promise of lavish Oriental (and
spiritual) tokens and favors of love. Example 4 enables us to observe how,
in "Als ich auf dem Euphrat schiffte", Hugo Wolf has fashioned the transition from A to A flat to coincide with Suleika's ring slipping down into the
water (at "Ringfinger ab", bars 4-5) in this second duodrama, which in
effect projects Suleika's dream-realm entirely into the key of A flat. This
dream-realm is then **musically** alluded to by Hatem in "Dies zu deuten bin
erbötig" when his reference to the Venetian Doge's symbolic 'marriage' to
the sea is also cast into A-flat melodic-harmonic textures (bars 5-8), both by
an analogously submerged ring and enharmonic modulation:

Example 5: "Dies zu deuten bin erbötig!" (11), bars 1-9.

Another striking connective detail observable in the table of thematic listings is the descending A-flat melody of "Komm, Liebchen, komm" (13), especially in the bass line of Example 7, which couches Hatem's invitation to his beloved in a virtual inversion of Suleika's ascending melodic desire to know what her dream really means (Example 4, bars 15-17):

Example 6: "Hätt ich irgend wohl bedenken" (12), bars 1-3.

Example 7: "Komm, Liebchen, komm" (13), bars 1-5.

The initial vocal melodies for the third duodrama, "Locken, haltet mich gefangen" (16) and "Nimmer will ich dich verlieren" (17), contain two important intervallic features: the half-step alternation between F sharp and

F natural at the beginning and the descending sixths on "(ge)fangen" and "(ver)lieren" at the end of the first verse lines, respectively:

Example 8a: "Locken, haltet mich gefangen" (16), bars 1-3.

Example 9a: "Nimmer will ich dich verlieren!" (17), bars 1-3.

Examples 8a and 9a show how Hugo Wolf intensifies the emotion, from eighth-note triplets in the piano part underlying "Locken, haltet mich gefangen" to quadruple sixteenths propelling Suleika's impassioned response "Nimmer will ich dich verlieren" after Hatem's self-mocking last couplet: "Findet sie ein Häufchen Asche, sagt sie: Der verbrannte mir" in Example 8b. Although the chances of Suleika actually finding the rejuvenated Hatem reduced to ashes are slim, the allusion to the haunting, fatal couplet of "Selige Sehnsucht" – "Und zuletzt, des Lichts begierig, / Bist du, Schmetterling, verbrannt" (Goethe 19) – is virtually impossible to ignore, and listeners aware of this mystical poem's central role in the "Buch des Sängers" will 're-cognize' retrospectively this added dimension in Wolf's microcosmic cycle:

Example 8b: "Locken, haltet mich gefangen" (16), bars 48-54.

Divan listeners who are already 'wise' enough to be aware of their status as initiates into the 'west-eastern' wisdom Goethe celebrates in "Selige Sehnsucht", namely those singled out in the first line: "Sagt es niemand, nur **den Weisen**" (Goethe 18, my emphasis), will also 're-cognize' that another poem (not set by Wolf) in the "Buch Suleika", the equally admired "Wiederfinden", with its macrocosmic speculation on the eternally recurring realities of separation and reunion between lovers, has its microcosmic equivalent in Wolf's structurally related settings of "Als ich auf dem Euphrat schiffte" (Example 4) and "Dies zu deuten bin erbötig" (Example 5), in which Suleika's dream of a possible parting of lovers is confidently interpreted by her beloved nomadic and widely-traveled Hatem as symbolizing spiritual marriage.

But surely most notable for its cyclic implications (in precisely the hermeneutically retrospective and re-cognitive sense of the above theoretical reflections) is the melodic and harmonic shape of Suleika's final and 'quintessential' couplet: "Denn das Leben ist die Liebe und des Lebens Leben Geist" (Example 9b, bars 25-33). By setting the penultimate word "Leben" to (secondary) dominant-seventh and (Neapolitan) lowered supertonic harmony in B flat immediately before 'resolving' the climactic closing (with its high A on "Geist") in the tonic key of A major, Wolf makes a crucial cyclic connection with the first duodrama ("Nicht Gelegenheit macht Diebe" and "Hochbeglückt in deiner Liebe") unmistakably clear:

Example 9b: "Nimmer will ich dich verlieren!" (17), bars 25-41.

The highly intellectualized love-play enjoyed by both linguistically and proverb-savvy partners in Duodrama I is a vital part of the 'life' their love enhances and immortalizes aesthetically. By musical and cyclical means that are simultaneously literary in the hermeneutic and generic sense delineated above, this crucial relationship of life, love, and (aesthetic) spirit is made manifest to any listeners 're-cognizing' the myriad dimensions of this intermedial re-enactment of Goethe's quintessential west-eastern intercultural experience.

Given the nearly mathematical nature of Suleika's epigrammatic final couplet, perhaps we should not be surprised that Werner Heisenberg, in a conversation with his (then) physics student Friedrich von Weizsäcker, emphasized the connection he sensed between working out his theory of

Quantum Mechanics and memorizing love poetry from Goethe's *Divan* while he was climbing among the chalk cliffs of the North Sea in 1925. Whether quasi-mathematical or poetically elliptical, Goethe's deceptively casual culminating triad projects profound insight into love as the force that mediates between life and spirit for the sake of human creativity. Surely this couplet, and others like it, are what motivated Heisenberg to 'equate' the joyful creative spirit of the *Divan*'s love poetry with his own creative work of evolving the quantum theory (cf. Fritz 64)[6]. Although this quintessential couplet is all but untranslatable, I think its 'heightening' effect – to paraphrase inadequately Goethe's untranslatable concept of *Steigerung* – can best be expressed as a kind of mathematical-literary equation something like: 'The essence of life (raised to the first power) is love, but life raised to the second power or 'life-enhanced-by-love' is (in effect) spirit.' And for his part, Hugo Wolf has surely 'heightened' our awareness of the cyclic integrity of Goethe's macrocosmic west-eastern vision even as the music projects its necessarily more limited and deliberately crafted form of aesthetic microcosm.

As a final excursion into hermeneutic 're-cognition' and 're-enactment', bars 31-36 of Example 9b provide Hugo Wolf's final non-vocal word on his trans-biographical and culturally reflective cyclic-structural response to Goethe's cross-cultural challenge: the piano postlude. Just as Theodor W. Adorno – referring to the eighth chapter of Thomas Mann's *Doktor Faustus* – sees in Beethoven's last Sonata Op. 111 a merging of 'subjective' and 'objective' components that creates a transcending synthesis of the usual juxtaposition of 'inspiration' and 'conventional figuration' throughout this unusual 'farewell' to the sonata form, so, too, Hugo Wolf has here fashioned

---

[6] I am grateful to colleague Howard Nicholson of the Mount Holyoke College Physics Department for helping me 'understand' this striking analogy. To paraphrase Nicholson: Heisenberg's uncertainty principle in quantum theory changed physics from an 'exact' science where cause in nature could always, in principle, be directly linked to effect by well-understood scientific principles, into a 'statistical' science where cause and effect could only by linked at their most fundamental level probabilistically. The impact of this basic limitation on human reason's ability to understand the natural world was not lost on those humanists and philosophers who understood the profound implications of it. Suddenly all attempts in literature, poetry, and critical analysis to describe a whole range of human actions and emotions, which had never been subject to simplification or study with the systematic precision of the natural sciences, could now take on a validity in their very impreciseness that had – before the advent of quantum theory – been denied.

a final farewell to the traditional organic-narrative manner of cyclic composition: his startling amalgamation of conventional coda material, thematic
reminiscences, and typical closing bombast (particularly bars 33-36 of
Example 9b) makes the structural integrity and expressiveness of his microcosmic cycle musically complete and provides fitting final punctuation for
Suleika-Goethe's triadic synthesis of love mediating between life and spirit
for the sake of human creativity.

Wolf's literary-musical insight into a mere seventeen poems out of some
250 of the most diverse poems imaginable, poems that Goethe himself only
inadequately managed to organize into twelve books somehow containing
similar or related subjects, has ultimately yielded a microcosmic epitome of
astonishing coherence in terms of its own constituent parts **and** in regard to
the original macrocosmic whole. This is true not so much because the
individual poems of the *West-östlicher Divan* – seen in their entirety – are
so varied and multi-faceted as to defy even the poet's concerted efforts to
unify them, but rather precisely because of the vast differences **within** their
often equally striking similarities.

If there is a final word of theoretical wisdom that can somehow encompass and embrace the seemingly disparate and disjunctive features of both
Goethe's and Wolf's synthesizing cyclic project, perhaps a serendipitous
insight of the then 15 or 16-year-old Douglas R. Hofstadter about "leap[s] to
higher abstraction" (64-65) can help explain what is implicitly and (yet in
certain respects) ineffably cyclic about Hugo Wolf's seventeen interrelated
and duo-dramatic settings. Hofstadter's juxtaposed pair of paradoxical
formulations, namely "different-by-not-being-different" and "unique-by-
being-most-typical", as well as his discerning within a trio of three **different**
beach balls "the barest germ of a hint at some important mechanisms of
creativity" (64) strike me as graphically analogous to the way Hugo Wolf's
'mechanism of overarching cyclicity' seems to derive from lower level
characteristics – whether key relationships, motivic repetition, thematic
juxtapositions, or any other structural and semantic features – that point to
higher and larger connections and interactions of undeniably cyclic character, particularly if this description is understood as an integral hermeneutical
aspect of generic 're-cognition', 're-enactment', and 'cultural practice'. And
most important for a practical evaluation of the cultural dimension of Hugo
Wolf's achievement should be an ever increasing recognition – yet to be

echoed by critics and scholars generally – that the musical weight Wolf granted to the duodramatic feminine voice of Marianne von Willemer is absolutely vital to the aesthetic success of Goethe's cultural synthesis so readily 're-cognizable' in a detailed analysis and fair hearing of this heretofore unacknowledged and undiscovered literary-musical cycle.

References

Adorno, Theodor W. "Spätstil Beethovens". *Moments musicaux*. Frankfurt a. M.: Suhrkamp, 1964. 13-17.

Ameling, Elly. "Als ich auf dem Euphrat schiffte". *Hugo Wolf: Goethe-Lieder*. Globe CD-Recording. 1995.

Bernhart, Walter, Steven Paul Scher, Werner Wolf, ed. *Word and Music Studies: Defining the Field. Proceedings of the First International Conference on Word and Music Studies at Graz, 1997*. Word and Music Studies 1. Amsterdam: Rodopi, 1999.

Daverio, John. "The Song Cycle: Journeys Through a Romantic Landscape". *German Lieder in the Nineteenth Century*. Ed. Rufus Hallmark. New York, NY: Schirmer Books, 1996. 279-312.

Fritz, Walter Helmut. "Der *West-östliche Divan* – gedichtete Liebe". *Goethe-Jahrbuch* 97 (1980): 65-81.

Genz, Stephan. "Dies zu deuten bin erbötig". *Hugo Wolf: Goethelieder*. Claves CD-Recording. 1996.

Glauert, Amanda. *Hugo Wolf and the Wagnerian Inheritance*. Cambridge: Cambridge Univ. Press, 1999.

Goethe, Johann Wolfgang v. *Gedichte II*. Hamburger Ausgabe. Fischer Exempla Classica. Ed. Erich Trunz. Frankfurt a. M.: Fischer, 1964.

Hamlin, Cyrus. "The Romantic Song as Literary Genre". Bernhart et al., eds. 113-134.

Hass, Hans-Egon. "Über die strukturelle Einheit des *West-östlichen Divans*": *Stil- und Formprobleme in der Literatur. Vorträge des 7. Kongresses der internationalen Vereinigung für moderne Sprache und Literatur*. Paul Böckmann, ed. Heidelberg: Winter, 1959. 309-318.

Hillmann, Ingeborg. *Dichtung als Gegenstand der Dichtung*. Bonn: Bouvier, 1965.

Hofstadter, Douglas R. *Le Ton beau de Marot: In Praise of the Music of Language*. New York, NY: Basic Books, 1997.

Ihekweazu, Edith. *Goethes* West-östlicher Divan*: Untersuchungen zur Struktur des lyrischen Zyklus*. Hamburg: Hartmut Lüdke, 1971.

Koch, Sophie. *Schubert und Wolf: Goethe-Lieder*. Le Chant du Monde CD Recording. 1999.

Komar, Arthur, ed. *Robert Schumann: Dichterliebe. An Authoritative Score*. Norton Critical Scores. New York, NY: W. W. Norton, 1971.

Kramer, Lawrence. "Hugo Wolf: Subjectivity in the Fin-de-Siècle Lied". Rufus Hallmark, ed. *German Lieder in the Nineteenth Century*. New York, NY: Schirmer Books, 1996. 186-217.

—. *Classical Music and Postmodern Knowledge*. Berkeley, CA: Univ. of California Press, 1995.

Lewis, Christopher. "Text, Time, and the Tonic: Aspects of Patterning in the Romantic Cycle". *Integral* 2 (1988): 37-74.

Lodato, Suzanne M. "Recent Approaches to Text/Music Analysis in the Lied. A Musicological Perspective". Bernhart et al., eds. 95-112.

Lohner, Edgar, ed. *Studien zum* West-östlichen Divan *Goethes*. Darmstadt: Wissenschaftliche Buchgesellschaft, 1971.

—. *Interpretationen zum* West-östlichen Divan *Goethes*. Darmstadt: Wissenschaftliche Buchgesellschaft, 1973.

McCreless, Patrick. "Song Order in the Song Cycle: Schumann's *Liederkreis*, Op. 39". *Music Analysis* 5 (1986): 5-28.

Mommsen, Katharina. "*West-östlicher Divan und* Chinesisch-deutsche Jahres- und Tageszeiten". *Goethe-Jahrbuch* 108 (1991): 169-178.

Mustard, Helen. *The Lyric Cycle in German Literature*. Columbia Univ. Germanic Studies 17. New York, NY: King's Crown Press, 1946.

Neubauer, John. "Bartók and the Politics of Folk Music: Musico-Literary Studies in an Age of Cultural Studies". Bernhart et al., eds. 59-77.

Neumeyer, David. "Organic Structure and the Song Cycle: Another Look at Schumann's *Dichterliebe*". *Music Theory Spectrum* 4 (1982): 92-105.

Reitmeyer, Elisabeth. *Studien zum Problem der Gedichtsammlung mit eingehender Untersuchung der Gedichtsammlungen Goethes und Tiecks*. Sprache und Dichtung 57. Bern: Paul Haupt, 1935.

Rosen, Charles. "Mountains and Song Cycles". *The Romantic Generation*. Cambridge, MA: Harvard Univ. Press, 1995. 116-236.

Sams, Eric. *The Songs of Hugo Wolf*. Bloomington, IN: Indiana Univ. Press, [3]1992 ([1]1962).

Schlaffer, Hannelore. "Furor Poeticus: Die vier Trunkenheiten in Goethes *West-östlichem Divan*". *Poetica* 22 (1990): 303-323.

Seelig, Harry E. "Hugo Wolf's Ghazel Settings from 'Das Schenkenbuch' of Goethe's *West-östlicher Divan*". Gerald Chapple et al., eds. *The Romantic Tradition: German Literature and Music in the Nineteenth Century*. Lanham: Univ. Press of America, 1992. 377-405.

—. "Orientalism and the Feminine in Selected German Lieder from 1814 to 1889: Settings of Goethe's *West-östlicher Divan* by Schubert, Mendelssohn, Hensel, Schumann, and Wolf". Jeffrey L. High, ed. *Festschrift für Wilfried Malsch*. Göttingen: Schwerin [forthcoming].

Stein, Jack M. *Poem and Music in the German Lied from Gluck to Hugo Wolf*. Cambridge, MA: Harvard Univ. Press, 1971.

Wolf, Hugo. *Sämtliche Werke*. Vol. 3, Part 2: *Gedichte von J. W. von Goethe*. Ed. Hans Jancik. Vienna: Musikwissenschaftlicher Verlag, 1978.

—. *Gedichte von Goethe für eine Singstimme und Klavier*. Vols. 3 and 4. Edition Peters 3158 and 3159. Frankfurt a. M.: C. F. Peters [n. d.].

Youens, Susan. *Hugo Wolf: The Vocal Music*. Princeton, NJ: Princeton Univ. Press, 1992.

Ziesak, Ruth. *Hugo Wolf: Lieder*. Sony CD Recording. 1993.

Three Types of Song Cycles
The Variety of Britten's 'Charms'

Walter Bernhart, Graz

The great variety of Benjamin Britten's 'song-cycle' *oeuvre* forms the empirical basis for identifying three types of song cycles. Criteria for defining these types are both the strength of coherence among the individual songs of the cycle and the dominating features which establish coherence. In this essay the types are accordingly labelled as 'loose', 'literary' and 'musical' song cycles, and a substantial number of individual cohesive features, constituting these types, are discussed. Their defining properties are demonstrated by referring to representative examples from Britten's works. Contributions from Britten criticism to the song-cycle issue form the starting point for much of the theoretical discussion of this paper, which concludes on some general definitional considerations.

"Not since the days when musician and poet were the same person has there been a great composer whose art is as profoundly bound up with words as Benjamin Britten's." (Porter 271) These words by the prestigious Australian-born poet and critic Peter Porter indicate that Britten is an unavoidable 'victim' of Word and Music Studies, and as he was a prolific writer of songs which almost exclusively appeared in whatever kind of 'song-cycle' form, he is also bound to be a 'victim' of a conference devoted to this intermedial artform.

Britten wrote song cycles in every period of his creative life, and as they have such a wide range and show such an impressive variety of formations it is tempting to base one's reflections on the song cycle in general on some form of 'empirical' assessment of Britten's songs. If one takes as the crucial issue of song cycles the way in which they are able to achieve unity and coherence as a whole while at the same time preserving the autonomy and separateness of the individual songs, it seems justified to begin one's investigation by trying to identify the various cohesive features and devices that can be found in the cycles. It is a further 'empirical' element of this research to collect statements by critics of Britten's works about the song-cycle issue. Yet it is of interest to observe that the various careful book-length studies on

Britten deal with the song cycles **as** song cycles only in passing, although they occasionally contain very perceptive remarks on the issue. Following these research lines it is possible to arrive at three general types or categories of song cycles to be described and illustrated in this essay. The discussion of these types will be conducted, at least in part, in the light of Cyrus Hamlin's seminal definitional considerations to be found in the proceedings of the 1997 Graz conference on Word and Music Studies, and the paper will find its conclusion by presenting some further definitional observations of my own.

The main body of Britten's songs consists of 17 song collections (see Appendix below)[1]. This number does not include two groups of Britten songs: the folk-song arrangements, which came out in several collections, carefully selected by Britten himself, but which – though written in typical Britten style – cannot be considered original works; and the five Canticles, which in many ways are similar to the song cycles, both in length and general approach; yet they have to be left out of consideration as they are all based on single texts and not on sequences of separate poems[2].

All the 17 collections are written for a single voice (mostly a high voice, having Peter Pears in mind), and 13 of them have a single accompanying instrument, in most cases the piano; a guitar is used in *Songs from the Chinese* (1957) and a harp in Britten's last cycle, *A Birthday Hansel* (1975), based on texts by Robert Burns. Four of the cycles have an orchestral accompaniment, including Britten's then scandalous first cycle of 1936, *Our Hunting Fathers* (created in collaboration with W. H. Auden), which is also

---

[1] This list does not include ambiguous cases of 'song cycles' such as the Owen settings in the *War Requiem*, for which, as a song cycle in its own right, Donald Mitchell recently has found eloquent words (it "authentically represents Britten's final orchestral song-cycle"; "Violent Climates" 196). Yet it is so intricately linked up with the rest of the requiem (a fact which Mitchell equally acknowledges, cf. ibid. 207f.) that it defies comparison with the main body of Britten's cycles as here discussed. Similarly, the *Spring Symphony* is outside the scope of the present investigation. ("Commentators have called the *Spring Symphony* a cantata, a song-cycle, and a latent opera. In truth, the work is all and none of these"; Ashby, 224.) Finally, the juvenile *Quatre chansons françaises* (1928), written by the fourteen-year-old Britten, are left out of consideration for their lack of artistic independence (although they have recently found their advocate in Christopher Mark; cf. 25-27).

[2] Yet Graham Johnson calls *Canticle I*, based on a poem by Francis Quarles, "a sort of continuous song-cycle"; "Voice and Piano" 292.

the only work which was named a cycle by Britten: he calls it *Symphonic Cycle*; no other collection was given a genre description by the composer himself. The titles sometimes refer to the kind of texts used in the cycle – e. g., *Lyrics, Rhymes and Riddles by William Soutar*, the subtitle of *Who Are These Children?* – but mostly they only give the musical cast (e. g., *Songs and Proverbs of William Blake. For Baritone and Piano*).

Twelve of the 17 collections are based on texts by a single poet, and the range of poets – in various languages, with one exception (Chinese) composed in the original is impressive. In five of these twelve collections the texts are selections from original poetry cycles (such as Donne's *Holy Sonnets* or Rimbaud's *Illuminations*), but in no case Britten preserved the original order. Only five sequences contain texts by different poets. Again, *Our Hunting Fathers* is a special case as the subtitle says *Text Devised by W. H. Auden*: it contains two poems by Auden himself and three typically weird choices by Auden, animal poems of a satirical political intent. One critic observes that "Auden provided a libretto" for *Our Hunting Fathers* (Kennedy 228), which is a rather unusual – and not very convincing – use of the term 'libretto'.

A brief remark is in place on how Britten found and used his texts. He was in the habit of wandering about the house and randomly picking books from the shelves (cf. Carpenter 185). He would later remember what he had read and use it for his compositions. He once marked over twenty poems in a Goethe edition, "which suggests he was considering a Goethe cycle" (ibid. 259). (However, the only Goethe poem Britten actually set was "Um Mitternacht"; cf. ibid.) Britten also "usually composed more items than he needed, excluding some because they did not fit into his final scheme" (Kennedy 258). This is a remark pertinent in our context, as one is bound to wonder by which criteria (of coherence, we can assume) they would 'not fit into his scheme'. To my knowledge he, regrettably, never expressed himself more specifically on this issue.

Before discussing the three types of song cycles to be distinguished, two of the 17 collections will have to be excluded from the list as they cannot be considered 'song cycles' in any meaningful way as they are only **editorial collections**. Four *Cabaret Songs* were published posthumously in 1980, and Donald Mitchell, in charge of the Britten legacy, reports that at least seven were written between 1937 and 1939 and "more may still turn up" ("[Intro-duction]"). They were "composed with [the singer Hedli Anderson] in mind" (Kennedy 18); but this fact alone does not, as such, give any artistic unity to the collection. Equally, the stylistic similarity of the songs, as caba-ret songs, is not sufficient to establish a 'song cycle'.

The other collection to be excluded from the list is *Tit for Tat*, again a later publication of songs written early in Britten's life. As a schoolboy he wrote over fifty songs, most often based on texts by Walter de la Mare, from which Britten chose five to be published – in a partly revised shape – in 1969. He says himself that he chose them according to 'completeness of expression' (cf. "Prefatory Note"), i. e. on the basis of their individual qual-ity, and not in view of any coherence among them.

The first type are what can be called **'loose song cycles'**, which show a weak form of coherence if coherence at all. It comprises the following collections: *On This Island* (1937), *A Charm of Lullabies* (1947), *Songs from the Chinese* (1957), *Who Are These Children?* (1969) and *A Birthday Hansel* (1975). The most popular and characteristic of these is *On This Island*, based again on texts by Auden, and it has elicited interesting, con-tradictory remarks from critics as to the issue here pursued. Michael Kennedy states that the songs "are often wrongly called a song-cycle, implying a formal unity they do not possess" (133), while Peter Evans observes that "even *On This Island* feels like a cycle because it reveals a consistent response to Auden" (355) and because each song is "neatly real-ized within a simple structural frame" (73).

Two very different criteria for cyclicity are here invoked, that of **'formal unity'** and that of **'unity by a single poet'**. For Kennedy, the "formal unity" established by the collection's "simple structural frame" – as it is attributed by Evans – is not sufficient for cyclicity: an introductory "Maestoso" song is followed by a slow, a fast, another slow and a final fast song, whereby the finality of that last song is emphasised by the fact that it ends on a sixfold repetition of the word "final". (Such a structure reminds us, e. g., of Schu-mann's *Myrthen*, whose final song, after a freely structured, contrastive sequence of songs, is tellingly called "Zum Schluß".) I agree with what is implied in Kennedy's statement, namely, that such a **'linear structural**

frame' alone – which is determined by contrasts[3] and finality (and ultimately follows basic rhetorical principles) – is insufficient to establish
cyclicity as otherwise any well-structured song recital, offering contrasts in
the programme to keep the audience awake and bringing the evening to a
marked conclusion, would become a 'song cycle'.

The second option for cyclicity offered by Peter Evans is what he calls
"that unity which the verse of a single poet can bring to the most diverse
subjects" (355). Following this statement, even *Tit for Tat*, which I have
previously excluded as a mere editorial collection, would qualify as a cycle
as all its texts are by Walter de la Mare. So Evans's statement about '**a
single poet**' needs some qualification. It can only be convincing when it
refers to a particular form in which the poet manifests himself in his poetry,
i. e. when the texts share a common **tone** and the common **speaker role** of a
unified '**lyric I**'. Such a lyric I is not identical, but has an affinity with the
poet, it shares some of his or her views, thoughts and feelings (they share
common attitudes and have a similar 'set of mind'), and it lives – as the
critical jargon has it – 'on the same level of existence' as the poet without
being coextensive with his or her biographical person. A strongly defined
common 'lyric I' in this sense, being reflective of some essential aspects of
the poet's own personality, may very well establish some form of unity and
cyclicity among individual poems.

Whether this applies to *On This Island*, however, is another case. Auden
is not a poet whose texts are generally characterized by such a strong lyric I
(although some of them are). Particularly his early, often experimental work
of the thirties shows a great variety of speaker roles, a kaleidoscopic versa-
tility as to lyric voices, which fundamentally undermines the notion of a
unified tone of his texts. This is also true for *On This Island*, where, as an
example, we have the sharp contrast of the tender, lullaby-like "Nocturne"
and the jazzy, cabaret-style "As it is, plenty" in the two final songs. In addition, while we find a typical Audenesque diction in both these texts, a common lyric attitude, or 'set of mind', as a unifying factor is difficult to identify. Thus one is tempted to argue that a common **diction**, i. e., a similar
way of handling language, is not a factor that contributes essentially to

---

[3]   Ralph Woodward observes "contrasts of mood and, indeed, technique" in *On This
Island*, which are "features common to many Britten song-cycles" (262).

cyclicity on the literary level. As a consequence, I tend to agree with Michael Kennedy and object to calling *On This Island* a song cycle in any but a loose sense.

Another case of a loose cycle is *A Charm of Lullabies*. Here the texts were written by several poets, and as the five songs are all separate entities the question of what holds them together significantly arises. Of course, they are all lullabies, but it is again Kennedy who observes that the cycle, "lacking a central theme", "makes a patchwork effect" (175). Thus, inter-estingly, the lullaby is considered the **subject**, but not a **theme** of the cycle, which attitude, in this case, is backed by Peter Evans, who observes that the lullaby does not offer a "rich visionary world", as, e. g., the subjects of 'sleep' or 'night' so often do in Britten, and he quotes Peter Pears as saying, "a lullaby is – a lullaby, *sonst nichts* or almost *nichts*" (Evans 355). Thus we may conclude that a subject, to be productive as a unifying 'theme', needs to be richly suggestive of a wider range of experience. *A Charm of Lullabies* is characterized by a diversified 'linear structural frame' in the sense described above (by strong internal contrasts among the songs) but this, again, – along with the lack of a suggestive unifying theme – does not yet constitute a song cycle in any but a loose sense.

Such a judgement may sound rather restrictive, but Peter Porter is even more restrictive, as the following quotation shows: "A distinction should always be made between a true cycle, dramatically organized and telling a story (*Die schöne Müllerin*)[,] and a collection of poems by the same author or one illustrating a theme (*Dichterliebe*, Britten's *Nocturne*)." (279) In the light of what has already been said this statement needs to be qualified: both 'unity by author' and 'unity by theme' do establish cyclicity on the specific conditions given above. (On the dramatic and narrative elements see below.)

The other collections of this first group of 'loose song cycles' are similar in their setup to the ones already discussed. They show a 'linear structural frame' through contrasts and the 'sense of an ending' (cf. Johnson, "Voice and Piano" 304) – which alone are insufficient to establish cycles –, but they are given a cycle quality by the unified tone of a single author's poems. However, their cyclicity appears only in a loose form, as striking facts of **performance** and **publication** illustrate: *Who Are These Children?*, based on Soutar texts, was first performed by Pears and Britten in a version com-

prising only seven of the twelve songs; and, similarly, Britten himself published a shorter, piano version of the seven songs of *A Birthday Hansel*
(which was originally written for the harp) as *Four Burns Songs*. Apparently
he did not conceive of these two works as organic units. This is particularly
interesting to note, as in *A Birthday Hansel* we have instrumental links
between the individual songs which, however, – for lack of a common
theme of the poems – perform no 'meaningful' function as they do, e. g., in
Nocturne, as will be shown later.

The second group of Britten song collections comprises the Rimbaud
(1939), Michelangelo (1940), Donne (1945), Hardy (1953), Hölderlin
(1958), and Pushkin (1965) cycles, and the *Serenade* (1943), which is based
on texts by different poets. All these cycles, except for the popular *Serenade*
with its horn and strings, are for voice and piano. They represent a type of
song collection which can be called 'song cycles with a dominant literary
coherence' or, for easier reference, **'literary song cycles'**. They are characterised by a distinctive cyclicity which is primarily established by coherence
on the literary level, which does not exclude the existence of musical cohesive devices as well; yet these are not the principal unifying factors.

As not all Britten cycles belonging to this type can here be discussed, the
Hardy cycle, *Winter Words* – which, according to Graham Johnson, is "at
the centre of Britten's song *oeuvre*" ("Voice and Piano" 295) – shall be used
for demonstration. It is a great artistic achievement, and no-one has as yet
doubted its 'unity in diversity'. Yet its unity is not obvious to trace: there are
nine clearly separated and strongly contrastive *Lyrics and Ballads*, as the
subtitle indicates, such as the narratives of "The Choirmaster's Burial" and
"Journeying Boy", the satire of "Wagtail and Baby", or the very lyrical "At
Day-close in November". Evans sees the cycle's unity and "focus through
the poet" (355), which is a vague statement. Kennedy is more specific when
he says: "Britten's insight into Hardy's melancholy fatalism and naive
imagery gives an overall unity to one of his most satisfying works for voice
and piano" (196). Thus it is not vaguely "the poet" who unifies the work but
a specific **mental disposition** or set of mind, a particular **lyric attitude** of a
'lyric I' – in this case, "melancholy fatalism" – that does so (most likely
reflecting a facet of the poet's own personality).

Even more illuminating about the factors establishing the unity of *Winter Words* is Humphrey Carpenter's observation that "the meaning of *Winter Words*" lies in the last song, "Before Life and After" (331). This song – Peter Porter thinks it is Britten's "greatest single song" (280) – has, very perceptively, been compared to the final song of *Die schöne Müllerin* (cf. Johnson, *Die schöne Müllerin* 65f.): both – in the words of Hardy's poem – share the vision of "A time [...] / Before the birth of consciousness, / When all went well" and the vision of a time before "[...] the disease of feeling germed, / And primal rightness" was. It is this vision of an innocent earlier and of a later idealized state, "released from all human concerns and sufferings" (Johnson, *Die schöne Müllerin* 63), that binds the songs of *Winter Words* together and in a profounder sense gives the collection a cyclic quality.

This observation is clearly in congruence with, and fundamentally asserts, Cyrus Hamlin's definition of the song cycle as a literary form in terms of a "retrospective understanding" (123), "a 'recognitive' [...] awareness of the meaning of the cycle as a whole" (121), achieved by the workings of memory in the listener during the receptive act in performance. Similarly, Peter Porter, who has a less 'technical' view of song-cycle coherence than most other critics, asserts that selections from experience form what he calls "a shape in memory" (275), giving it a *gestalt* on a secondary level. The same idea is expressed by Peter Evans when he comments on Britten's Michelangelo, Donne, Hölderlin and Hardy cycles that in each of them the composer has "striven to make the final song a statement [...] of some fundamental philosophical tenet of his poet, one that could in retrospect embrace all that had gone before" (370).

Yet only twice in Britten's song cycles do we find literal **cyclic returns** (modelled on Beethoven's *An die ferne Geliebte* or Schumann's *Frauen-Liebe und -Leben*), i. e. in the Pushkin cycle (*The Poet's Echo*) and in the *Serenade*, where the "Epilogue" repeats the impressive "Prologue", played by the natural horn. What prevails in the second group of 'literary song cycles' is the **'retrospective cyclicity'** in Hamlin's terms.

I am aware of only one Britten cycle as having been described in terms of a "'**storyline**'" (Carpenter 158): Humphrey Carpenter detects an "implied narrative" (159) in the *Seven Sonnets of Michelangelo*. The supposed story

element consists in the narrative presentation of the progress of a love relationship from courting through some form of happy togetherness to the
anticipation of its dissolution in death – all this of course being reminiscent
of *Frauen-Liebe und -Leben*. I strongly share Cyrus Hamlin's conviction
that to conceive of song cycles in narrative terms, as here attempted, and in
terms of "a unified and rounded slice of time and experience", as Anthony
Newcomb does (167, quoted in Hamlin 117), is "in direct conflict with the
principle of the lyric as an autonomous and self-contained effusion"
(Hamlin ibid.). This position conforms with the views on the generic distinction of lyric and narrative which I have expressed elsewhere (cf. Bernhart 369f.), namely to consider it unjustified to look for plot-like sequences
in lyric texts; lyric texts are characterized by a primary emphasis on the
presentation of mental/emotional states. Nonetheless, a set of poems in a
song cycle may form a sequence of such mental states, a sequence that may
imply a temporal order, which, however, does not mean that necessarily a
story in the traditional sense is being told. Such a **flux of mental states**,
often leading to a final – mostly fatal – condition, is a genuinely lyric form
of experience which is extremely suitable for song cycles and can be
observed in several of its most prominent representatives. In this respect it
forms a further cohesion factor in song cycles – in addition to the 'recognitive' factor and the factor of the common 'mental disposition' discussed
before.

What the 'flux' element implies, however, is that the agency of the unifying process is not only – as discussed above – a fairly abstract 'mental
disposition' manifesting itself in the text (as, e. g., the "melancholy fatalism" of *Winter Words*), but that it becomes more tangible in the conception
of a **'lyric persona'** behind the text which experiences the sequence of
mental states. It needs to be stressed, however, that this does not mean that a
quasi real-life 'person' appears 'on the stage', as it were, a 'character' with a
full psychological setup and development, which is also rejected by Hamlin
(cf. 118); it only implies that the lyric consciousness can appear at a higher
or a lower degree of concreteness in the text. In other words, when a song
cycle presents a 'flux of mental states' the lyric consciousness appears in a
middle position on a scale of varying concreteness of manifestation: it manifests itself as a 'lyric persona', which is a more concrete manifestation than

a mere 'mental disposition', but it is not as concrete as a 'character'. (Only rarely in a song cycle, if at all, the lyric consciousness appears as a fully realized 'person' or 'character'; which does not rule out that listeners to song cycles may be inclined, to varying degrees, to establish in their minds such a full 'character' from the clues the text gives. Yet to do so runs counter to the generic frame of a lyric text.)

What all this amounts to is a rejection of Peter Porter's conception of "a true cycle", as quoted above, namely that a true cycle is "dramatically organized and telling a story" (279). The basic misunderstanding of this conception rests in the fact that a song cycle, whatever shape it may take, will always primarily belong to the lyric genre, which implies that, in individual cases, it may incline, to different degrees, to the dramatic or to the narrative mode, but it will never be 'dramatic' or 'narrative' in the generic sense.

In the 'literary song cycles' of the second group the primary cohesion factors work on the literary level but, as briefly mentioned before, there are additional musical factors of cohesion in this group as well. They are basically of two kinds: either there is a **basic musical motif** which keeps recurring in the work; this is, e. g., true of Britten's Michelangelo cycle (cf. Kennedy 146) and especially the Donne cycle, where such a motif "runs through the piano part in ever-changing form" (Johnson, "Voice and Piano" 241); or there are **musical links** between individual songs which serve as subtle cohesive factors. A very fine example of this latter device can be found in Britten's *Serenade*, where the "Elegy", based on Blake's famous poem "The Sick Rose", is intricately linked to the following "Lyke-Wake Dirge", which begins with a reversed version (G – A flat – G) of the semitone motif on which the "Elegy" is based and also ends (G sharp – G – G sharp).

It is in the third group of song cycles that musical elements predominate as cohesive factors, which is why they can be called 'song cycles with a dominant musical coherence' or, for easier reference, **'musical song cycles'**. Britten's cycles of this type are the early *Our Hunting Fathers* (1936), *Nocturne* (1958), and the *Songs and Proverbs of William Blake* (1965). The defining factor in these cases is that all three are through-composed, not necessarily also that they are orchestral. (*Les Illuminations* is orchestral but does not belong here.) Yet, *Our Hunting Fathers* and *Nocturne* **are** orchestral, and in the Blake cycle the piano has been accredited with a particularly forceful orchestral character (cf. Johnson, "Voice and Piano" 300). Thus the orchestral disposition is not indispensible but conducive to a musical dominance in the cycle.

These 'musical song cycles' have a symphonic texture, as already implied by the title Britten gave to *Our Hunting Fathers* (*Symphonic Cycle*). To quote Michael Kennedy: "[...] its 'symphonic' epithet [is] fully justified by the derivations and transformations of a motto-theme – a major arpeggio falling to the tonic and ascending to the minor third – which binds and unifies the cycle." (129)[4] Similarly, the *Nocturne* has been called a "symphonic dreamscape" (Palmer 322) or a "song cycle in the guise of symphony" (Kennedy 96), and it is characteristically dedicated to Alma Mahler. The well-known linking feature of the *Nocturne* is what has frequently been called "the 'breathing' motif", which refers to the sleeping persona of the cycle, and "the interludes of peaceful, deep-breathed slumber in a succession of dreams" (Evans 371). In Palmer's words, it "is the motif of muted strings, divisi, breathing gently in and out in [...] dactylic rhythm" ("Voice and Piano" 322)[5]. The point is that here, as in the other cycles of that type, we have **ritornelli** (cf. Woodward 271f.) as links which – in contrast to *Tit for Tat* (see above) – are meaningful links also in terms of the literary dimension of the work.

Another 'symphonic' feature of these cycles is the fact that here the sequence of the songs tends to remind one of the sequence of **movements** in a symphony. It is telling that Kennedy talks about the setting of the famous poem "The Tyger" in the Blake cycle as "the scherzo of the cycle" (228; similarly, on *Our Hunting Fathers*, cf. 129). We can observe that the 'linear structural frame' referred to earlier quite often reflects, as a musical cohesive device, the overall pattern of symphonies or sonatas.

As a final remark, before reaching the conclusion, it can be observed that in a cycle like *Nocturne* the musical coherence becomes such a strong

---

[4] Woodward observes that *Our Hunting Fathers* is "unified by a five-note cell, its juxtaposition of major and minor infiltrating many structural moments" (262).

[5] In fact, the smooth long-short sequences of the eighth and sixteenth notes form a trochaic, rather than a dactylic rhythm.

element of the work that it tends to lose its character of a song cycle because the sense of a collection of individual songs disappears. A very telling indication that this is the case, and that it is also part of the composer's overall conception of the work, lies in the fact that, in the score, – in contrast to all other cycles – the beginning of a new poem is not marked in the singer's text. Thus we find a continuous flow of words, not only for those who listen to the work but also for those who sing it. This is a situation familiar from the *Canticles*, which are based on single texts, and thus *Nocturne* appears as a borderline case of cyclicity, at the other end of *Tit for Tat*, which – as was pointed out above – shows no real **unity** of the songs: in contrast, *Nocturne* shows no real **separateness** of the songs; and whatever one may be inclined to call 'true' song cycles: what defines them is that combination of unity and separateness which can be found, in various forms, in all the types of song cycles here discussed.

The conclusion can be brief. The New English Dictionary (NED) does not give a definition of 'song cycle', only the Supplement of 1987 defines it as "a series of songs intended to form one musical entity and having words dealing with related subjects". The "one musical entity" applies, as a defining element, only to the third group here discussed, and the reference to "related subjects" is vague and certainly insufficient. Webster's Third is wiser and no doubt more careful when it defines the song cycle as "a group of songs based on the same general subject [again!] or having some other unifying feature" – which answers no question either. The investigations presented in this paper have brought definitional results which are substantially in harmony with Cyrus Hamlin's findings. Yet, in the light of the three types here discussed, it can be argued that, though 'retrospective understanding' is identifiable as the central force behind cyclicity, there are literary elements (such as a lyric persona with his/her flux of mental states, or a central mental attitude, or a common suggestive theme) as well as musical elements (such as motivic, harmonic/tonal etc. links between the songs, or a symphonic texture) which may function as other, or additional, unifying factors in a cycle. Further, there are sequences or collections of songs which are not inherently unified cycles at all but only appear to be so on the basis of external factors, such as editorial or performative conditions.

Thus the term 'song cycle' proves – like most terms do upon closer scrutiny – to be rather problematic: in most cases it is too specific, especially considering the fact that only relatively few examples of so-called 'song cycles' show the circularity which the term basically implies (the same is true for the term 'garland', which is sometimes used for similar works); the dictionaries prefer terms like 'group' or 'series' or 'sequence' which, by contrast, are too general and neutral[6]. The term I prefer, maybe rather idiosyncratically – it is used in the title of this paper –, is 'charm', which is taken from Britten's song collection called *A Charm of Lullabies*. As Eric Crozier's introductory commentary in the score of this song collection tells us, "'charm' is the collective noun for a flight of goldfinches" (similar to 'a flock of finches'). According to the NED, 'charm' is an alternative form of 'chirm', which also – significantly – refers to the din or noise that birds make. 'Charm' is derived from the Latin *carmen* ('song'), which, in the present context, is very pertinent, even more so as the word 'charm' in the sense of magic or spell also goes back to the same root of *carmen*. Thus I find it particularly attractive to reflect on types of 'charms' which Benjamin Britten's prolific song output teaches us to distinguish.

Appendix

1928-31 *Tit for Tat. Five Settings from Boyhood of Poems by Walter de la Mare.* (Re-written 1968, published 1969).

1936 *Our Hunting Fathers. Op. 8. Symphonic Cycle for High Voice and Orchestra. Text Devised by W. H. Auden.* [2 poems by Auden and 3 others].

1937 *On This Island. Op. 11. Words by W. H. Auden.* [For high voice and piano]. [5 poems].

---

[6] A term worth considering is 'composite', as used in the following recent study: Rolf Lundén. *The United Stories of America. Studies in the Short Story Composite*. Amsterdam: Rodopi, 1999. (The publisher's note states that the book "discusses the American short story composite, or short story cycle, a neglected form of writing consisting of autonomous stories interlocking into a whole".)

1937-39 *Cabaret Songs. For Voice and Piano.* [Words by W. H. Auden]. [4 poems]. (Published 1980).

1939 *Les Illuminations. Op. 18. For High Voice and Strings. Poems by Arthur Rimbaud.* [In French]. [9 poems].

1940 *Seven Sonnets of Michelangelo. Op. 22.* [For high voice and piano]. [In Italian].

1943 *Serenade. Op. 31. For Tenor Solo, Horn and Strings.* [6 poems by various poets].

1945 *The Holy Sonnets of John Donne. Op. 35. High Voice and Piano.* [9 poems].

1947 *A Charm of Lullabies. Op. 41. For Mezzo-Soprano and Piano.* [5 poems by various poets]. (Published 1994).

1953 *Winter Words. Op. 52. Lyrics and Ballads of Thomas Hardy for High Voice and Piano.* [9 poems].

1957 *Songs from the Chinese. Op. 58. For High Voice and Guitar.* [6 poems by various poets; Engl. tr. A. Waley].

1958 *Nocturne. Op. 60. For Tenor Solo, Seven Obligato [sic] Instruments and String Orchestra.* [8 texts by various poets].

1958 *Sechs Hölderlin-Fragmente. Op. 61.* [For voice and piano]. [In German].

1965 *Songs and Proverbs of William Blake. Op. 74. For Baritone and Piano. Selected by Peter Pears.* [14 texts].

1965 *The Poet's Echo. Op. 76. For High Voice and Piano. Poems by Alexander Pushkin.* [In Russian]. [6 poems].

1969 *Who Are These Children? Op. 84. Lyrics, Rhymes and Riddles by William Soutar. For Tenor and Piano.* [12 poems].

1975 *A Birthday Hansel. Op. 92. For High Voice and Harp. Poems by Robert Burns.* [7 poems]. (Selection for voice and piano: *Four Burns Songs,* 1975.)

References

Ashby, Arved. "Britten as Symphonist". Cooke, ed. 217-232.

Bernhart, Walter. "Überlegungen zur Lyriktheorie aus erzähltheoretischer Sicht". Herbert Foltinek, Wolfgang Riehle, Waldemar Zacharasiewicz, eds. *Tales and 'their telling difference'. Zur Theorie und Geschichte der Narrativik. Festschrift zum 70. Geburtstag von Franz K. Stanzel.* Anglistische Forschungen 221. Heidelberg: C. Winter, 1993. 359-375.

Britten, Benjamin. "Prefatory Note". Britten. *Tit for Tat. Five Settings from Boyhood of Poems by Walter de la Mare.* London: Faber Music, 1969. [n.p.].

Carpenter, Humphrey. *Benjamin Britten: A Biography.* London: Faber, 1992.

Cooke, Mervyn, ed. *The Cambridge Companion to Benjamin Britten.* Cambridge: Cambridge Univ. Press, 1999.

Crozier, Eric. "Introduction". Benjamin Britten. *A Charm of Lullabies. Op. 41. For Mezzo-Soprano and Piano.* London et al.: Boosey & Hawkes, 1994. 2.

Evans, Peter. *The Music of Benjamin Britten.* London/Melbourne/Toronto: Dent, 1979.

Hamlin, Cyrus. "The Romantic Song Cycle as Literary Genre". Walter Bernhart, Steven Paul Scher, Werner Wolf, eds. *Word and Music Studies: Defining the Field. Proceedings of the First International Conference on Word and Music Studies at Graz, 1997.* Word and Music Studies 1. Amsterdam/Atlanta, GA: Rodopi, 1999. 113-134.

Johnson, Graham. "Voice and Piano". Palmer, ed. 286-307.

—. *Die schöne Müllerin. The Poems and Their Background.* The Hyperion Schubert Edition. Complete Songs 25. London: Hyperion Records, 1996.

Kennedy, Michael. *Britten.* 2nd. ed. London: Dent, 1993 ([1]1981).

Lundén, Rolf. *The United Stories of America. Studies in the Short Story Composite.* Amsterdam: Rodopi, 1999.

Mark, Christopher. "Juvenilia (1922-1932)". Cooke, ed. 11-35.

Mitchell, Donald. "[Introduction]". Benjamin Britten, W. H. Auden. *Cabaret Songs. For Voice and Piano.* London: Faber Music, 1980. 1.

—. "Violent Climates". Cooke, ed. 188-216.

Newcomb, Anthony. "Structure and Expression in a Schubert Song: Noch einmal 'Auf dem Flusse' zu hören". Walter Frisch, ed. *Schubert: Critical and Analytical Studies.* Lincoln: Univ. of Nebraska Press, 1986, rpt. 1996. 153-174.

Palmer, Christopher. "Embalmer of the Midnight: The Orchestral Song-cycles". Palmer, ed. 308-328.

—, ed. *The Britten Companion.* London/Boston: Faber and Faber, 1984.

Porter, Peter. "Composer and Poet". Palmer, ed. 271-285.
Woodward, Ralph. "Music for Voices". Cooke, ed. 260-275.

Concept Albums
Song Cycles in Popular Music

Martina Elicker, Graz

This paper consists of two parts: the first section is devoted to a definition of the term 'concept album' – the term used in popular music to refer to a song cycle. It also provides a brief assessment of the importance and success of concept albums in the music business.

The second part looks at one particular concept album in more detail, namely Paul Simon's 1986 Grammy Award winning album *Graceland*. This case study serves to illustrate the definitions proposed in Part I and furthermore describes the dynamics at work on a concept album. The discussion is approached from a semiotic angle and encompasses an analysis of musical and textual elements as well as the music making process itself.

Defining the term 'Concept Album'

When trying to define the term 'concept album' in popular music, one is by no means confronted with an easy task. As Peter Kaminsky points out at the beginning of his excellent analysis of Paul Simon's album *Still Crazy After All These Years*, "[...] assertions of cyclic principles are both controversial and difficult to prove [...]" (38). That is possibly one of the reasons why scholarly discussions of popular concept albums are extremely rare[1].

Let us first look at the term 'concept': according to Webster's *New World Dictionary of the American Language*, the term 'concept' refers to "an idea or thought, esp. a generalized idea of a class of objects; abstract notion" (293). Similarly, *The New Oxford Dictionary of English* defines 'concept' as "an abstract idea; a general notion" (380). The latter also includes a defini-

---

[1] As a matter of fact, I know of only two papers focusing on the aspect of coherence within pop albums, the above-mentioned analysis by Kaminsky and Robert W. Butts's 1988 article "More Than a Collection of Songs: The Concept Album in Country Music" (which, in contrast to Kaminsky's paper, primarily looks at themes providing unity in country music concept albums). For more detail see References.

tion of the term 'concept album': it is described as "a rock album featuring a cycle of songs expressing a particular theme or idea" (ibid.).

Of course, the problem of defining the concepts underlying a song cycle is not unknown to scholars of classical/Western art music. In the nineteenth century, "a poetic relationship among the songs — be it a narrative design, or a grouping of poems that radiate out from a central idea in monologue or dialogue format — was basic to the concept of a song cycle. However, [...] relatively little attention was given to the possibility of relating the songs by musical means" (Turchin 231). According to Turchin, this all changed with Robert Schumann, who, along with his fellow song reviewers on the staff of the *Neue Zeitschrift für Musik*, stressed the desirability of musical as well as poetic coherence and integrity in a song cycle (cf. 232).

Scholars and reviewers of popular music alike have come up with a variety of definitions of what accounts for a record's classification as a concept album. Mike Boehm of *The Los Angeles Times* proposed an extremely broad definition: according to him, a concept album is "an effort to turn the simple rock 'n' roll album into something much bigger: a story, a play, an opus" (Boehm F1). Similarly, his fellow reviewer at *The Los Angeles Times*, Don Heckman, refers to concept albums as "projects centered on a specific point of view or a related collection of materials [...]" (Heckman F3).

These very open definitions are echoed in all the newspapers I have looked at (i. e. *The Los Angeles Times, The New York Times, Der Kurier* for the years 1990 to 1999). They also mirror the usage of the term by the average music fan, as can easily be seen when looking at music-related newsgroups on the internet.

When applying these extremely broad definitions to pop albums one is, however, faced with several problems. Broad definitions include basically any album that has some sort of underlying theme tying the songs together; that is, it also includes soundtrack albums, Broadway show recordings, greatest hits albums, tribute albums, charity records, Christmas albums, compilation and live albums. And indeed, among the concept albums reviewed in the three newspapers mentioned above, I found discussions of The Who's *Tommy* (a rock opera); Elton John and Tim Rice's most recent collaborative effort, *Aida* (a contemporary Disney musical, based on Verdi's opera); Frank Sinatra's *The Complete Capitol Singles Collection* (a greatest hits double album); Various Artists' *Red, Hot and Rio* (an informal tribute to the music of Brazil, released by the AIDS organization Red Hot to raise money for AIDS research); Various Artists' *Tammy Wynette Remembered* (a tribute album to the late country singer).

Neil Rosenberg narrows down this broad view of concept albums some-what by stressing that popular song cycles are "albums bringing together a body of music unified by something more than the simple presentation of a musical artist's or group's work [...]. [T]hey *represent* in the sense of standing for ideas like history, tradition, biography, or religion. And they do this by *representing* texts, tunes, and the facts that accompany them [...]" (450). Robert W. Butts argues along the same lines, pointing out that in addition to having/containing a clear musical and/or thematic focus, concept albums should also be the recognizable work of a single person or group of persons (cf. 90-92).

Thus, both Rosenberg and Butts automatically rule out an inclusion of soundtracks, tribute albums, Christmas and Gospel/sacred records. Butts states that "[a]lthough superficially conceived around a single theme, few, if any Christmas or sacred albums attempt to relate any one song to any other beyond the general categorical designation" (91). The same holds true for most tribute albums, which are traditionally dedicated to the works of a single songwriter or to an earlier recording artist and usually feature many contemporary artists. Beyond the general framework of a tribute there is generally little attempt at album unification (cf. ibid.).

According to Wicke and Ziegenrücker (cf. 264), the most common type of concept album is a song cycle in which the song sequence contains a thematic and musical thread and in which the last song refers back to the beginning of the album. Other forms of concept albums include the mere presentation of a fictional story or a purely musical connection between the individual songs (e. g. Mike Oldfield's 1973 album *Tubular Bells*).

Taking all those classifications into consideration, I propose the follow-ing definition: a concept album in popular music is an album by either one artist or a group which contains a unifying thread throughout the songs – be it musical, thematic, or both.

An example of thematic unity are the so-called 'songs of the working man', especially popular in country music but also found in rock music. Dave Dudley's mid-60s record *Songs of the Working Man*, Johnny Cash's 1963 *Blood, Sweat and Tears*, and rocker Bruce Springsteen's *Nebraska* are only three examples. Sometimes a running commentary is used, especially in country music, in order to emphasize the concept of unification, as on Johnny Cash's 1960 album *Ride This Train*. In this case, sound effects (i. e. a train rumbling along with a whistle blowing throughout the record) are used as an additional means of unification (cf. Butts 93-94).

But what are the musical particularities of a concept album? In art song cycles, close key relationships between adjacent songs constitute one of the primary means of musical coherence. Frequently the first and last songs within the song cycle are written in the same key, literally making the cycle come full circle (e. g. Schumann's *Liederkreis* op. 24; cf. Turchin 232). As in collections of art songs, key relationships, motivic returns, long-range structural patterns, and some sort of coherent compositional plan and correlation between the narrative and the music feature prominently in popular concept albums as well (cf. Kaminsky 38-39). Musical coherence may also be achieved by a homogeneous approach to arrangement/instrumentation and production style.

Assessing the importance of concept albums in popular music

In order to assess the importance of concept albums in popular music, we will have to take a look back in history, to an album which has often been credited with being the first concept album in rock and pop music history – namely the Beatles' *Sgt. Pepper's Lonely Hearts Club Band*, which was released on June 1st, 1967. Both the cover and the music/lyrics reflect the notion of the 'summer of love'. At the time of its release the album was considered a novelty, with its experimental sounds, its songs segueing into each other, with an album sleeve that was the first to feature printed lyrics. Interestingly, George Martin, the producer of the album, has maintained over the years that *Sgt. Pepper* was not initially conceived of as a concept album at all because "[...] all the songs [...] don't really have a great deal of connection with each other. We made it appear whole by editing it closely and by tying it up with the idea that the band, themselves, were another band, [a]nother alter ego if you like [...]. To heighten that effect, I used sound effects of audiences and laughter [...]" (*George Martin Interview*).

One year prior to the Beatles' *Sgt. Pepper*, Pete Seeger, one of the leading figures of the American folk movement, had released an album called *God Bless the Grass*, which featured environmental songs exclusively. The Beach Boys also recorded their *Pet Sounds* album in 1966, which tells the tale of young love that blooms, staggers, and ends in crushing disillusionment, and captures much of the idealism, anxiety, self-doubt and elevated passion that come with growing up. Mike Boehm of *The Los Angeles Times* has called it the "first rock album to hang together as a story" (F1). It was not until 1967, however, that, with the release of *Sgt. Pepper*, pop/rock critics and fans alike became familiar with the idea of a concept and unified structure underlying a pop album. The term 'concept album' was born.

Ever since then, a number of pop artists have taken up the challenge of writing and/or recording concept albums. In the following, I would like to list some of the milestones of popular concept albums which have been critically acclaimed and commercially successful. This selection of albums will also serve to illustrate the musical and thematic variety and diversity of popular song cycles. All the albums I am going to mention are concept albums according to the definition given above.

The British band The Kinks released several concept albums throughout their career in the late 1960s and 1970s. *Lola Versus Powerman & the Moneygoround (Part One)*, released in 1970, was probably their most successful attempt at a unified concept, which also spawned the hit single "Lola". The album tells the story of a young British rocker of humble beginnings and high ambition who achieves stardom only to wind up feeling used and abused by the music business in particular and modern life in general (cf. Boehm F1).

David Bowie's 1972 *The Rise and Fall of Ziggy Stardust and the Spiders From Mars* depicts the meteoric career of a decadent, sexually ambiguous, possibly extraterrestrial Ziggy. This album helped Bowie and his image of a mock-extraterrestrial persona to stardom (cf. ibid.).

In 1973, two artists who had formed the alternative band Velvet Underground earlier in their careers, recorded two highly acclaimed concept albums: Lou Reed's *Berlin* depicts a couple bent on mutual humiliation and destruction and sets the story to a combination of edgy, sparse rock songs and bombastic orchestrations (cf. ibid.). In the same year, John Cale released *Paris 1919*, an interesting album about longing, nostalgia, and melancholy, mixing different musical styles, which prompted Diedrich Diederichsen to call it the best collection of songs since Schubert's *Winterreise* (cf. 28-30).

More mainstream artists have not shied away from the challenge of creating song cycles either. Neil Diamond, for instance, released *Beautiful Noise* in 1976, a tribute to Tin Pan Alley, a district of music making in New York City which housed such well-known musicians as the Gershwins and Alan J. Lerner. The entire album deals with the beauty and hassles of writing and performing music, and it displays different musical styles, from Dixieland jazz and gospel-fueled blues to mainstream pop.

The British rock band Pink Floyd portrays an isolated rock star sinking into madness and megalomania on their 1979 album *The Wall*, which produced the legendary hit single "Another Brick in the Wall". With its unique arrangement and production, the album blended melodic fragments and sound effects and consequently helped promote the extensive use of synthesizers in rock music (cf. Erlewine).

Most of Bruce Springsteen's records qualify as concept albums in the sense that they contain some underlying theme or story. 1982's *Nebraska*, mentioned before, focuses on the isolation, loneliness, and dark thoughts of small time criminals, desperate people, and those who love them. The entire album is actually made up of demo versions, recorded with only acoustic or electric guitar, harmonica, and vocals, which furnishes the record with an additional layer of unity. *Born in the USA*, one of Springsteen's most successful albums, was released in 1984 and depicts the economic decline and the decline of American society in general as its unifying theme. However, as opposed to Springsteen's earlier albums, the characters on *Born in the USA* are not defeated, they have a family or friends to fight for and defend. This more optimistic outlook on life is mirrored in the more up-beat music, complete with galloping rhythms and chiming guitars.

Another artist who built his career on concept albums is Meat Loaf, who together with his songwriter Jim Steinman created a rock opera-like record, *Bat out of Hell*, in the late 1970s. The fast-moving, sweeping melody lines,

Meat Loaf's smooth voice, the overwrought, bombastic instrumental arrangements, and the cryptic lyrics about love make for a unified work and add considerably to the overwhelming effect of the album on its audience when listened to in its entirety. The 1993 sequel, adequately titled *Bat out of Hell II*, works with the same tricks and sound effects, and although not a novelty any more, was an equal commercial success.

British rock icon David Bowie resurfaced in the 1990s as well, with his 1995 album *Outside*, which is a concept album designed to be a kind of virtual soundtrack, experimenting with modern technological means of music production and creating futuristic sound effects with the help of synthesizers.

Similarly, concept albums by heavy metal artists make use of modern technology, taking advantage of manifold methods of distortion, from the wailing sound of an electric guitar to synthesized drum machines. The Seattle-based heavy metal band Queensryche, like Springsteen on *Born in the USA*, chose the decline of American society during the Reagan administration as the starting point of their 1988 record *Operation: Mindcrime*. It tells the story of a fortune hunter whose disillusionment with Reagan-era US society leads him to join a shadowy plot to assassinate corrupt leaders.

British metal band Iron Maiden also released a concept album, *Seventh Son of a Seventh Son*, in 1988, which depicts the life of a very special child from birth to death with all the stages in-between. The boy is blessed with very unusual talents, such as the power to heal and the ability to see the future, all of which raises the suspicion of other people and ultimately leads to his own early death. The album showcases the extensive use of keyboard and synthesizer guitars and drums throughout.

Possibly as a kind of countermovement to rock and heavy metal artists' experiments with synthesized sounds and topics such as alienation, apocalyptic visions, and destruction, another completely unamplified, 'acoustic' form of popular music emerged in the 1990s, that is, pop and folk music with clearly ethnic tinges. Thus, several albums drawing on Irish, Celtic, or other traditional musics have been released in the last decade. Canadian singer-songwriter Loreena McKennitt, for example, explores her own Irish/Celtic roots on many of her albums, most notably on 1992's *The Visit* and 1997's *Book of Secrets*, on which she sets her own mythic tales and poems by Yeats, Tennyson, Blake, and Shakespeare to music. The songs are characterized by a traditional Celtic sound, dominated by her own superb harp playing.

Like McKennitt, American folk singer-songwriter Tom Russell traces his own ethnic and musical roots on his latest album, *The Man from God Knows Where*, released in early 1999. Russell himself has called the 26-track double album an "immigrant song cycle", an "epic record with American sounds and stories of my ancestors" (quoted in Bessman). The album features Irish pipes and the Norwegian fiddle worked into the texture of American folk music.

One of the most intriguing and critically acclaimed albums of recent years was the collaborative effort of English alternative rocker Billy Bragg and the American folk-rock band Wilco, who teamed up on 1998's *Mermaid Avenue* to set to music a collection of poems written by the late Woody Guthrie between 1939 and 1950. The collaboration between Bragg and Wilco furnished the album with a more contemporary, alternative kind of folk music than folk legend Woody Guthrie himself would have, without, however, taking away from the many different layers of meaning of the poems about love and life.

The last genre of popular music I would like to look at in this context is American country music. Pop/rock/folk music on the one hand, and country music on the other, began to venture down separate paths in the 1920s, and with the exception of some cross-over artists, this development has continued to this day. This fact may explain why from the early 1960s on — that is, almost a decade before rock music's acknowledgment of concept albums — concept albums have featured highly in country music but have largely been ignored by rock and pop fans and critics.

Willie Nelson and Johnny Cash are certainly among the best-known country artists who have released a great number of artistically and commercially successful concept albums. Many of these records draw on old American myths, such as the American railroad (the aforementioned Cash album *Ride This Train*), the old West in general (Marty Robbins's *Gunfighter Ballads and Trail Songs*), or the American Indian (Johnny Cash's 1964 album *Bitter Tears*). Others simply tell everyday stories from different points of view, as does Willie Nelson's 1974 *Phases and Stages*, which tells the story of a marriage breakup from the woman's viewpoint on side one, and from the man's on side two (cf. Butts 92-96). It is characterized by a low-key, simply arranged, almost folkish musical style — a far cry from the overblown production style common in 1970s Nashville. Similarly, Nelson's follow-up album, *Red Headed Stranger* (1975), displays a stripped-down production style underscoring the tale of redemption. It tells the story of a fictitious hero who, upon romantic betrayal, goes on a bloody rampage throughout side one, gunning down his wife, her lover, and a prostitute. On side two he then finds a new love and a new lease on life. A more recent Nelson CD, *Spirit*, from 1996, continues in Nelson's story-telling mold, yet adds a more spiritually tinged edge to the general storyline of heartbreak and loss.

Another artist belonging to the new generation of country singer-song-writers, k.d.lang, recorded an eclectic array of familiar tunes that use tobacco and smoking as central metaphors for her 1997 concept album *Drag*. All songs examine addiction and the act of love, and musically cover a wide range of styles, from traditional country to rock. Lang says there is no political motivation in the smoking concept, stressing that "[...] what fascinates me is that tobacco and alcohol and whatever else we get addicted to is really a form of emotional cover-up, an escape that stems from deprivations of love" (quoted in Flick 1).

I have provided a list of well-crafted, successful concept albums that for the most part have also spawned at least one hit single, which shows that individual songs ideally are strong enough to stand on their own outside the realm of the concept. All those examples serve to emphasize the notion that when done well these albums gain stature over time. Very often it takes intent and repeated listening to reach a deeper understanding of the artists' words and music, especially in places where the connections may be extremely subtle. However, as Butts points out, the temptation towards self-indulgence or pretentiousness is extremely high in such artistic endeavors (cf. 98) — and this is usually when a concept album fails with both critics and the public.

Paul Simon's *Graceland*: a case study

After its release in 1986 *Graceland* became an instant critical and commercial success, earning Paul Simon several Grammy Awards in 1987. At the same time, however, *Graceland* was regarded as highly controversial in sociopolitical respects: the album features South African musicians, was recorded partly in South Africa, draws on South African styles of music, yet almost entirely lacks direct reference to South Africa in the lyrics, although at the time of the album's production and release the struggle against apartheid was at its height. Simon's extensive liner notes exclude sociopolitical discussion as well, and even the album graphics represent nothing South African: the front cover depicts an Ethiopian effigy, Simon's name and the album title.

Paul Simon himself has pointed out on several occasions that he was not so much interested in a political statement as in a musical one. And as a matter of fact, bringing different kinds of music together on one album is a process Simon has always been familiar with: as a member of the so-called folk revival of the late 1950s and 1960s, he, as well as most of the other folk performers of his time, drew heavily on folk tunes from around the world and performed them in harmonic, rhythmic, and instrumental arrangements consonant with the style of mainstream American pop. In that way, many critics have argued that *Graceland* merely continues the tradition of American folk music by borrowing elements from South African music and at the same time bringing it in line with contemporary American pop styles through overdubbing, mixing, or other technological procedures (cf. Hamm 304; DiMartino 233). However, with his *Graceland* project Simon reinvented himself as a true world musician and helped get his stalled career back on track (cf. DiMartino ibid.).

But what makes this album a concept album? What are the elements that provide the record with coherence and unity?

The first, probably most obvious concept underlying *Graceland* is that of collaboration, on the musical, lyrical, and social planes, between one white American, Paul Simon, and several Black South African musicians, among them the well-known group Ladysmith Black Mambazo. Most of the instrumentalists are Black Africans or African-Americans (with the exception of Los Lobos, an East Los Angeles band of Mexican descent), thus exemplifying a theme that dominates the album, namely Simon's conscious use of various African materials in his own artistic pursuits – Simon's tribute to his own musical 'roots'[2]. The fact that the song "Homeless" was co-written with Ladysmith Black Mambazo lead singer Joseph Shabalala reinforces the collaborative effort. The album was recorded in South Africa, the U.S., and England.

Table 1 below briefly summarizes the most important features discussed in the following.

song title	key / meter	instrumental / vocal arrangement	progression of theme and setting
1. The Boy In the Bubble	G major 4/4	drums/percussion; bass; accordion; guitars; synthesizers	general introduction to the modern western world
2. Graceland	E major 4/4	drums/percussion; bass; guitar; pedal steel; backing vocals (bv): The Everly Brothers	general + personal perspectives; setting: American South
3. I Know What I Know	C major 4/4	synclavier; bv: The Gaza Sisters with General M.D. Shirinda	personal account; setting: the U.S., probably a city
4. Gumboots	D major 4/4	drums/percussion; guitars; accordion; tambourines; saxophones; synclavier; with The Boyoyo Boys	personal account; setting: a U.S. city, probably New York
5. Diamonds On the Soles of Her Shoes	E major/ F major 4/4	drums/percussion; bass; guitar; saxophones; bv: Ladysmith Black Mambazo	story; setting: New York City; with the Zulu intro-duction set in Africa
6. You Can Call Me Al	F major 4/4	drums/percussion; bass; guitar; saxophones; trumpets; trombones; synthesizer; penny whistle	story; setting: unspecified place in the Third World
7. Under African Skies	Eb major 4/4	drums/percussion; bass; guitar; bv: Linda Ronstadt	general perspective; setting: Africa
8. Homeless	F# major 4/4	a cappella: Paul Simon with Ladysmith Black Mambazo	general perspective + story; setting: Zulu story set in Africa

---

[2] For a more detailed discussion of this point, see Bennighof 231-232.

9. Crazy Love, Vol. II	Gmajor/ F major 4/4	drums; bass; guitar; soprano sax; guitar synthesizer; with Stimela	story; setting: probably the U.S.
10. That Was Your Mother	F major 2/2	drums; bass; accordion; guitar; soprano sax; washboard; with Good Rockin' Dopsie and the Twisters	personal account; setting: American South (Louisiana)
11. All Around the World or The Myth of Fingerprints	G major 4/4	drums/percussion; bass; guitars; accordion; sax; with Los Lobos	general perspective (2 examples); setting: the U.S., Africa

Table 1: Outline of musical and textual features of Paul Simon's Graceland

As can be seen, the idea of collaboration is embedded in many levels of the music and the music making process. Undoubtedly, the degree of African influence on the music of *Graceland* varies greatly: while "Homeless" is a fully integrated collaboration between Simon and Ladysmith Black Mambazo, the last two tracks on the album, "That Was Your Mother" and "All Around the World", "each connect with South Africa only by using American bands [...] that use saxophone and accordion, which Simon associated with some of the South African bands that he had heard" (Bennighof 231). Nevertheless, the structural integration of diverse musical elements and styles is central to the album: the rhythm section (drums, percussion, guitars, bass) and vocals dominate the album's musical texture. The strikingly different vocal styles and voices of Paul Simon and the African singers are blended perfectly; the foregrounded drums and percussion provide a strong, heavy beat, which clearly functions as the album's 'heartbeat'. Additionally, accordion and saxophones are featured in many of the songs, the combination of which makes for an unusual, African-tinged sound.

In his characterization of *Graceland*'s musical collaboration and its signification, Erlman stresses that the songs are about "the fashioning of an authentic identity from the margins, from the position of the subaltern" (9), i. e. from the music of South African townships of the 1980s, which reminded Simon of the 1950s rock 'n' roll of the Atlantic Records School.

This musical identity is mainly achieved by Simon's skillful integration rather than juxtaposition of distinct musical styles. To illustrate this point, I would like to give one example. In the instrumental interlude of the Top 40 hit "You Can Call Me Al", the featured instruments, the penny whistle and bass guitar, index three Black South African genres of music: the penny whistle references *kwela*, a Black urban genre in the 1950s and 1960s, sometimes credited with being a foundation of South African jazz; the bass guitar makes reference to *mbube*, a Zulu choral style, characterized by a call and response pattern in the bass line and a great number of glides; the way the two instruments are combined is then typical of *mbaqanga*, a township instrumental jive, which incidentally provides the basic backing on "You Can Call Me Al" and several other tracks on *Graceland*. The most obvious features taken from *mbaqanga* and incorporated in Simon's songs are the translation of vocal lines into instrumental lines and the foregrounding of instrumental tracks and vocals in the mix (cf. Meintjes 43-44). The penny whistle is automatically linked to South African music by the mere inclusion of the instrument, but simultaneously also to a western contemporary context by its polished timbre. Thus, the instrumental interlude of "You Can Call Me Al" is "compacted with meanings associated with Simon's personal style and various South African styles" (ibid. 45). This example is representative of the collaboration and production of the entire album.

In addition to the choice of instruments and the instrumental and vocal arrangements permeating the entire album, the key progression, outlined in Table 1, is also interesting to look at. It starts out in G major on the first track, "The Boy In the Bubble", and comes full circle on the last song, "All Around the World", which is again written in G major. Track number 5, "Diamonds On the Soles of Her Shoes", contains a modulation from E major to F major, which is then the key used in the first cut on side two, "You Can Call Me Al". As these two songs tell two totally unrelated stories, the common key serves as a means to connect not only the two songs but the two sides of the LP.

Similarly, Simon creates an additional link between "Crazy Love, Vol. II" and "That Was Your Mother": the verses of "Crazy Love" are composed in G major, the chorus in F major – the same key "That Was Your Mother" is written in. Here again, the stories told and the musical styles are very different, so that the common key has a unifying effect.

An aspect related to keys concerns chord progressions within the individual songs. Most tracks start out on the tonic (I) chord and are based on either a I-IV-V-I or a I-V-IV-I progression, which is very common in popu-

lar music in general. Non-tonic and minor chords used frequently throughout the album supply a richer, more exotic sound.

With the exception of "Homeless", a track sung a cappella, and "That
Was Your Mother", which ends with a fermata on the tonic F chord, all the
songs on *Graceland* have fades. This particular feature[3] is associated with a
certain sense of incompleteness and therefore ties in with the idea of a concept album: the individual songs are seen as complementing each other,
almost leading into one another.

Other musical elements which provide additional coherence and unity are
song structure and meter. All songs are written in 4/4 time, except for "That
Was Your Mother", which is composed in cut time (2/2). All tracks on
Graceland are written in a mostly irregular verse − chorus form, some with,
some without bridge.

Paul Simon has repeatedly described *Graceland* at its broadest level as a
search for truth. The songs have "a very similar theme: acceptance, aiming
at some state of peace, looking for some state of redemption or grace"
(Simon quoted in Humphries 131). The title of the album, *Graceland*,
already points in that direction: following Elvis Presley's death in 1977,
Presley's Tennessee retreat, Graceland, had symbolized the first lost
promise of rock 'n' roll. Paul Simon's appropriation of the name 'Graceland' for his 1986 album, according to him, "offered the possibility of the
dream being reborn" (Simon quoted ibid. 132). Of course, the literal meanings of 'grace' and 'land' underscore the notion of the hope of redemption at
this particular place.

Looking at how the textual content progresses from song to song, we find
that, for the most part, Simon has abandoned his trademark linear, narrative
approach to his words and instead draws on "highly poetic ('Diamonds On
the Soles of Her Shoes'), abstract ('The Boy In the Bubble'), and satiric ('I
Know What I Know') portraits of modern life [...]" (Ruhlmann). Consequently, the album doesn't tell a story, as is the case with so many pop
concept albums, but it provides glimpses of modern society by introducing
several different characters in the various songs and by placing them in
diverse locations, such as the urban jungle of New York City, the American

---

[3]   Cf. Citron (207) for a more detailed discussion of the role of fades in popular music.

South, the Third World, and Africa in particular. As varied as the characters, situations, and settings are in the individual songs, there are, however, two narrative threads running through the entire album, a feature Bennighof refers to as "the dual focus on personal and general perspectives" (220).

The first track, "The Boy In the Bubble", serves as a general introduction, depicting an 'automatic', completely artificial world as its setting. Track two, "Graceland", combines a more general thread with a personal narrative, involving the narrator, his son, and his former wife, and relating the lyric I's own life experiences and destiny to his culture, to other people, to God. The narrator's physical journey to Graceland in Memphis, Tennessee, unfolds parallel to "his mental pilgrimage, winding inward from external cultural awareness to the engagement of personal concerns, yet without final resolution" (Bennighof 221).

The third cut, "I Know What I Know", continues the personal theme and delves into satire. It describes the encounter of the narrator with a woman, both obviously belonging to the upper echelons of American urban society, dominated and corrupted by money and societal obligations.

"Gumboots" again tells a personal story about the breakdown of the narrator's friend. Like "I Know What I Know", it is set in a U.S. city, possibly New York. According to the liner notes, the song title makes reference to a "term used to describe the type of music favored by miners and railroad workers in South Africa. The term refers to the heavy boots they wear on a job [...]" (*Graceland* liner notes).

Track number five, "Diamonds On the Soles of Her Shoes", introduces a third textual thread, namely that of a story taking place outside the narrator's world, reducing the lyric I's role to that of a witness and/or commentator, reminiscent of the omniscient narrator in fiction. With that it links the last song on side one of the LP with its first track, "The Boy In the Bubble". "Diamonds" is set in New York City and tells about the relationship of a rich girl and a poor boy. The introduction of the song is sung in Zulu, it is based on a wedding song and forms part of the choral tradition known as *isicathamiya*. It was "written by Joseph Shabalala as a response to Simon's lyrics ('awa, awa' expressing amazement at the unusual Manhattan story), [but] [...] in reality echoes some of the patriarchal concerns of migrant workers about the increasing independence of women in South African society" (Erlman 11). Hence, the primary setting of the song is New York, yet the Zulu reaction to the story is deeply rooted in South African life and mirrors the majority of *isicathamiya* lyrics, which celebrate and reconstruct a vanished world of regional identity, domestic cohesion, and specific gender hierarchies. Thus, in the opening lines we hear a voice deploring the growing independence of women, which stands in stark contrast to the English lyrics which follow the Zulu introduction. The contrast is effectively reinforced by the use of both languages, Zulu and English.

Side two starts out with yet another story. The song "You Can Call Me Al" is set somewhere in the Third World and tells the tale of a man, Al, who is looking for a purpose in life and for redemption. It connects the life of an American, Al, to an unspecified place in the Third World which is obviously foreign to him. Thus, on the content level, "You Can Call Me Al" achieves what was accomplished in the previous song by the combination of two languages.

The following track, "Under African Skies", is more explicit with regard to the setting and places its account in Africa. Similar to the first track of the album, which introduces the western world and its technologically ruled society, this song is again very general and non-narrative. It depicts the African continent as the cradle of rhythm and reinforces Simon's claim of having recorded an album unifying the musics of two continents, Africa and America. It also taps into the old stereotype of western music providing the melody and African music supplying the rhythm.

The eighth cut, "Homeless", shifts the focus of the album even more toward South Africa by including a story told in Zulu. According to Simon's liner notes, the Zulu lyrics tell of "people living in caves on the side of a mountain, cold and hungry, their fists used as pillows" (*Graceland* liner notes). It ties in with Simon's English lyrics, in which he sings of poor people in general: "We are homeless, we are homeless / The moonlight sleeping on a midnight lake", and "Strong wind destroy our home / Many dead, tonight it could be you"). The Zulu story unquestionably takes place in Africa, whereas the English lyrics bring in a more universal angle.

"Crazy Love, Vol. II", track number nine, contains more narrative aspects again and moves the setting back to the U.S. It depicts the relationship between two people, Fat Charlie the Archangel and his wife, who have grown apart and are getting divorced. The story carries general implications, such as the notion of lost love, indifference, passivity, and the inability to change one's life. This particular element connects to the title track, "Graceland", which describes the same kind of passivity of the characters toward redemption.

The tenth cut on the album, "That Was Your Mother", is another narrative song, with the narrator telling his son about the time before he was born. The story takes place in the American South, in Louisiana, and relates to dancing and music, Zydeco music in particular.

The final track, "All Around the World or The Myth of Fingerprints", unites the more universal strand with two short accounts and two settings, namely that of a former talk show host living alone and isolated in the U.S. and that of a former army post in the Indian Ocean, also long gone, deserted, and abandoned. Thus, the last song provides a climactic and final link between two continents, two traditions, two forms of society. The universal notion of loneliness, the search for life's deeper meaning, grace, and redemption are the central ideas dealt with in "All Around the World". It becomes clear at this point that the song lyrics too come full circle, adding layers of meaning along the way, telling individual stories and giving examples.

A point which goes hand in hand with content progression is the point of view the songs are written from. In all the songs, the narrator appears either explicitly as 'I' or implicitly as 'we/us', hence stressing the American point of view. It is safe to say that Paul Simon's own societal and musical backgrounds serve as the starting point of this album. Consequently, the stories, the music, the collaborations, the musical styles, the production are all mediated and seen through the eyes of an American.

The last aspect I would like to draw attention to is Simon's integration of the Zulu language into the English lyrics. As in musical terms, this is most notably and skillfully achieved on "Homeless", which comprises alternate Zulu and English sections: the first and third sections are modeled – as already referred to – after a traditional Zulu wedding song, while the second, the fourth, and the sixth are written in English. A vocable transition, "too loo loo", bridges the third and fourth sections, which facilitates the linguistic transition from one language to the other. Additionally, these "too loo loo" sounds are similar to the familiar "ooh" vocables Simon sings on other tracks as well, such as "Graceland", "Diamonds On the Soles of Her Shoes", and "Under African Skies".

Concluding Remarks

As we have seen, a concept album needs to be scrutinized thoroughly on both the textual and the musical levels in order to gain a deeper understanding of the cohesive and unifying elements that run through the album as a whole. In popular music in particular, the actual music making process, the collaboration between individual musicians, songwriters, lyricists, arrangers, and producers becomes a primary element in the creation of a song cycle. More so than in most other genres of music, the aspect of the actual performance is foregrounded, so that vocal and instrumental arrangements, rhythmic and melodic motifs, phrasing, and the interaction between the different voices, the lead singer and the background singers, rather than the score, become central to the analysis of any piece of popular music, be it a song or an entire album. As the preceding case study has shown, those elements, together with a thematic thread running through the lyrics, make for a coherent album on which the individual songs are interrelated to form a unity.

References

Bennighof, James. "Fluidity in Paul Simon's *Graceland*: On Text and Music in a Popular Song". *College Music Symposium* 33/34 (1993/94): 212-236.

Bessman, Jim. "Tom Russell's Song Cycle Traces His Family's Roots". *Billboard*, Feb. 25, 1999: http://www.billboard.com/feature/tomrussell.html.

Boehm, Mike. "Plenty of Rock Albums Tell Story, Too". *The Los Angeles Times*, May 12, 1994: F1+.

Butts, Robert W. "More Than a Collection of Songs: The Concept Album in Country Music". *Midamerica Folklore, USA* 16/2 (1988): 90-99.

Citron, Stephen. *Songwriting. A Complete Guide to the Craft*. London: Hodder & Stoughton, 1985.

Diederichsen, Diedrich. "John Cale". *Sounds: Die Zeitschrift für Popmusik* 6 (1981): 26-30.

DiMartino, Dave. *Singer-Songwriters. Pop Music's Performer-Composer. From A to Zevon*. The Billboard Hit Makers Series. Billboard Books. New York: Watson-Guptill Publications, 1994.

Erlewine, Stephen Thomas. "Pink Floyd, *The Wall*". *All-Music Guide (AMG)*. http://www. allmusic.com.

Erlman, Veit. "'Africa Civilised, Africa Uncivilised': Local Culture, World-System and South Africa". *SAMUS: South African Journal of Musicology* 14 (1994): 1-13.

Flick, Larry. "Lang's Smoky Sound Shines on WB". *Billboard*, May 24, 1997: 1+.

George Martin Interview. http://members.tripod.com/taz4158/martin.html.

Hamm, Charles. "*Graceland* Revisited". *Popular Music* 8/3 (1989): 299-304.

Heckman, Don. "Joshua Redman 'Timeless Tales'" (CD Review). *The Los Angeles Times*, Oct. 11, 1998: F3.

Humphries, Patrick. *Paul Simon's Still Crazy After All These Years*. New York: Doubleday, 1989.

Kaminsky, Peter. "The Popular Album as Song Cycle: Paul Simon's *Still Crazy After All These Years*". *College Music Symposium* 32 (1992): 38-54.

Meintjes, Louise. "Paul Simon's *Graceland*, South Africa, and the Mediation of Musical Meaning". *Ethnomusicology* 34/1 (1990): 37-73.

Rosenberg, Neil V. "From the Sound Recordings Review". *Journal of American Folklore* 106/422 (1993): 450-461.

Ruhlmann, William. "Graceland". *All-Music Guide (AMG)*. http://www.allmusic.com.

Simon, Paul. *Graceland*. Warner, 1986. [sheet music]

Turchin, Barbara. "Schumann's Song Cycles: The Cycle Within the Song". *Nineteenth- Century Music* 7 (1985): 231-244.

Webster's New World Dictionary of the American Language. Second College Edition, Deluxe Color Edition. New York: Simon & Schuster, 1984.

Wicke, Peter, Wieland Ziegenrücker. *Rock Pop Jazz Folk. Handbuch der populären Musik*. Leipzig: VEB Deutscher Verlag für Musik, 1985.

The New Oxford Dictionary of English. Oxford: Clarendon Press, 1998.

Discography

Beach Boys, The. *Pet Sounds*. Capitol, 1966.

Beatles, The. *Sgt. Pepper's Lonely Hearts Club Band*. EMI/Apple Records, 1967.

Bowie, David. *The Rise and Fall of Ziggy Stardust and the Spiders from Mars*. Virgin/EMI, 1972.

—. *Outside*. Virgin/EMI, 1995.

Bragg, Billy, & Wilco. *Mermaid Avenue*. WEA/Elektra, 1998.
Cale, John. *Paris 1919*. Warner, 1973.
Cash, Johnny. *Ride This Train*. Sony/Columbia, 1960.
—. *Blood, Sweat and Tears*. Sony/Columbia, 1963.
—. *Bitter Tears*. Sony/Columbia, 1964.
Diamond, Neil. *Beautiful Noise*. Sony/Columbia, 1976.
Dudley, Dave. *Songs of the Working Man*. Mercury, [n.d.].
Iron Maiden. *Seventh Son of a Seventh Son*. Capitol, 1988.
k. d. lang. *Drag*. WEA/Warner, 1997.
Kinks, The. *Lola Versus Powerman & the Moneygoround (Part One)*. WEA/Warner, 1970.
McKennitt, Loreena. *The Visit*. WEA/Warner, 1992.
—. *Book of Secrets*. WEA/Warner, 1997.
Meat Loaf. *Bat out of Hell*. Sony/Columbia, 1977.
—. *Bat out of Hell II*. MCA/Uni, 1993.
Nelson, Willie. *Phases and Stages*. WEA/Atlantic, 1974.
—. *Red Headed Stranger*. Sony/Columbia, 1975.
—. *Spirit*. Uni/Mercury/Polygram, 1996.
Pink Floyd. *The Wall*. Sony/Columbia, 1979.
Queensryche. *Operation Mindcrime*. Capitol/EMI, 1988.
Reed, Lou. *Berlin*. BMG/RCA, 1973.
Robbins, Marty. *Gunfighter Ballads and Trail Songs*. Sony/Columbia, 1959.
Russell, Tom. *The Man from God Knows Where*. WEA/Atlantic/Rhino/HighTone, 1999.
Seeger, Pete. *God Bless the Grass*. Sony/Columbia, 1966.
Simon, Paul. *Graceland*. WEA/Warner, 1986.
Springsteen, Bruce. *Nebraska*. Sony/Columbia, 1982.
—. *Born in the USA*. Sony/Columbia, 1984.

Notes on the Contributors

Frédérique Arroyas is Assistant Professor at the University of Guelph, Canada, where she teaches 19th- and 20th-century French fiction. Her research interests include a reader-based approach to the study of music in literature, interart analogies, and gendered descriptions of music in the works of contemporary French women writers. She is the author of *La lecture musico-littéraire: À l'écoute de* Passacaille *de Robert Pinget et de* Fugue *de Roger Laporte*, to be published by the Presses de l'Université de Montréal in 2001.

Walter Bernhart is Professor of English Literature at the University of Graz, Austria, and chairman of the university's research unit on Literature and the Other Media. His main research interests are intermedia studies, word and music studies, theory of lyric, metrics and rhythm studies, iconicity, Elizabethan and twentieth-century English poetry. He is founding and current president of the International Association for Word and Music Studies (WMA). His numerous publications include *'True Versifying': Studien zur elisabethanischen Verspraxis und Kunstideologie. Unter Einbeziehung der elisabethanischen Lautenlieder* (1993), and more recently he edited *The Semantics of the Musico-Literary Genres* (Festschrift Ulrich Weisstein) and *Leoš Janáček: Konzeption und Rezeption seines musikdramatischen Schaffens*.

Mary Breatnach studied French at the universities of Cork and Edinburgh, and viola in London and Germany. An academic and professional musician, she teaches French at the University of Edinburgh and viola at the Royal Scottish Academy of Music and Drama. She is the author of *Boulez and Mallarmé: A Study in Poetic Influence* (Scolar Press, 1996) and has published a number of articles on the relation between French literature and music.

Peter Dayan is Reader in French at the University of Edinburgh (and in 2000-2001, Visiting Fellow at the University of New South Wales). He began his career with research on the aesthetics of French authors of the 19th century, from Sand to Mallarmé. Having realized that these authors find it impossible to define literature without reference to music, he began to investigate the way they present the connections, distances, and inter-dependencies between the two arts, particularly through the notion of translation from one to the other; he has written articles on translation into music according to Sand and Baudelaire, is now working on musical translation in Proust, and, with the help of a grant from the Arts and Humanities Research Board, will be spending most of the academic year 2001-2002 working on the same concept in the texts of Barthes and Derrida.

Martina Elicker studied English and French at the University of Graz, Austria; Rider University, NJ; Columbia University, NY; Indiana University, Bloomington, IN; and UCLA, Los Angeles, CA. In 1995, she received her doctorate degree from the University of Graz. She has been working at the English Department of the University of Graz since 1994, teaching linguistics and language proficiency. Her main fields of research include semiotics (with a focus on the analysis of the connection between language and music), sociolinguistics, dialectology and phonetics. She is the author of *Semiotics of Popular Music. The Theme of Loneliness in Mainstream Pop and Rock Songs* (Tübingen 1997), and has published several articles on the relationship of language and music in popular music.

Michael Halliwell studied literature and music in South Africa and completed his operatic studies at the London Opera Centre and with Tito Gobbi in Florence. He pursued a career in opera as principal baritone for the Netherlands Opera, Nuremburg Opera, and the Hamburg State Opera, as well as giving guest performances in opera and recitals in many European countries. He was artistic director of music theatre in Durban, South Africa, in the late 1980s and early 1990s. Since 1996, he has been Graduate Co-ordinator of Performance at the Sydney University Conservatorium of Music and was recently appointed Chair of Vocal Studies and Opera. He still performs regularly in opera, concert, radio and television and has recently released a CD of vocal settings of Kipling's *Barrack-Room Ballads*. He has lectured and published widely on music and literature and his research speciality is operatic transformations of the novel.

Suzanne M. Lodato received her PhD from Columbia University, after which she served as a Fellow in the Society of Fellows in the Humanities at Columbia University. Currently, she is on the Scholarly Communications program staff at The Andrew W. Mellon Foundation. Her research interests concern the music of Richard Strauss, particularly his lieder; vocal music (opera and art song) of the nineteenth and early twentieth centuries; and literary/musical relationships. She is a contributor to the recently published new edition of *The New Grove Dictionary of Music and Musicians*, as well as to volume 1 of the Word and Music Studies series, *Word and Music Studies: Defining the Field*. In addition, she maintains an active career as a professional singer.

John Neubauer taught at various universities in the US; since 1983 he has been Professor of Comparative Literature at the University of Amsterdam. His publications include *The Emancipation of Music from Language* (Yale 1986), *The Fin-de-siècle Culture of Adolescence* (Yale 1992), and extensive contributions to the Hanser edition of Goethe's works. He is presently Editor of the comparatist journal *Arcadia* and of a large international project on the history of literary cultures in East-Central Europe.

Leon Plantinga is Henry L. and Lucy G. Moses Professor of Music, Yale University. He has been Chair of the Yale Music Department for a total of 11 years and Director of the Humanities Division at Yale for 6 years. He gave lectures and lecture-recitals at many places in the United States, Canada, England, Germany, France, and Spain. His publications include: *Schumann as Critic* (1966), *Muzio Clementi: His Life and Music* (1977), *Romantic Music: a History of Musical Style in Nineteenth-Century Europe* (1985) and *Beethoven's Concertos* (1999).

Harry E. Seelig, Associate Professor at the University of Massachusetts at Amherst, has degrees in German (BA) and piano (BM) from Oberlin

College and Conservatory, and the MA and PhD (in German) from the University of Kansas. While teaching all levels of German Language and Literature at Amherst for more than three decades and a lied-course (from Schubert to Schoenberg) for the Music Department, he has published translations of contemporary German poetry and articles on musical-literary subjects ranging from Goethe's poetry ("Wanderers Nachtlieder" and *Divan* lyrics) in the music of Hensel, Schubert, Schumann, Weigl, and Wolf to Hofmannsthal's prose in an opera of Strauss (a comparative study of *Die Frau ohne Schatten* and Mahler's Symphony No. 8).

His recent scholarship includes a chapter on the literary context of *German Lieder in the Nineteenth Century* (1996) and a survey-article of Rilke's poetry in chiefly American musical settings published in *Rilke-Rezeptionen / Rilke Reconsidered* (1995) that compares six settings of the poet's popular "Liebes-Lied". He is currently completing research on his chief scholarly interest, a book-length literary-musical study of Hugo Wolf's settings of seventeen poems from Goethe's *West-östlicher Divan*, for which the present paper is a prelude.

Jürgen Thym is Professor of Musicology at the Eastman School of Music (University of Rochester). Having taught there since 1973 and serving as chair of the musicology department from 1982 to 2000, he contributed to the field in three distinct areas: 1) as translator of music theory treatises (Kirnberger, *Die Kunst des reinen Satzes in der Musik*, with David Beach, Yale University Press 1983; Schenker, *Kontrapunkt*, with John Rothgeb, Schirmer Books 1987); 2) as editor of several volumes in the Schoenberg Gesamtausgabe, with Nikos Kokkinis, Schott/Universal Edition 1984-94; 3) as author of numerous essays on text-music relations in the German lied, partly in collaboration with the late Ann C. Fehn. A book *Of Poetry and Song: Approaches to the Nineteenth-Century German Lied*, gathering articles by Rufus Hallmark, Harry E. Seelig, Fehn and himself, will be published in 2002 by the University of Rochester Press.

Werner Wolf is Professor of English and General Literature at the University of Graz, Austria, and member of the executive board of the International Association for Word and Music Studies (WMA). His main areas of research are literary theory, especially narratology and literary self-referentiality, functions of literature, 18th- to 20th-century English fiction, 18th- and 20th-century drama, and intermedial relations between literature and other media, notably music. His recent publications include *Ästhetische Illusion und Illusionsdurchbrechung in der Erzählkunst* (1993), *The Musicalization of Fiction: A Study in the Theory and History of Intermediality* (1999) and several articles on intermediality. He is also co-editor of *Word and Music Studies: Defining the Field. Proceedings of the First International Conference on Word and Music Studies at Graz, 1997.*

SIGLIND BRUHN

Musical Ekphrasis
in Rilke's *Marien-Leben*

Amsterdam/Atlanta, GA 2000. 235 pp.
(Internationale Forschungen zur Allgemeinen und Vergleichenden Literaturwissenschaft 47)
ISBN: 90-420-0800-8   Hfl. 100,-/US-$ 43.-

Contents: Introduction. The "Life of Mary". Rilke and Christian Devotion. Ekphrasis in Rilke's Work: Poems on Depictions of Mary and Jesus. Hindemith: From Expressionism to the Ethos of Art. Outline of the Poetic and Musical Cycles on the "Life of Mary". Geburt Mariä (no. 1). Die Darstellung Mariä im Tempel (no. 2). Mariä Verkündigung (no. 3). Mariä Heimsuchung (no. 4). Geburt Christi (no. 7). Vor der Passion (no. 10). Pietà (no. 11). Stillung Mariä mit dem Auferstandenen (no. 12). Vom Tode Mariä I (no. 13). Vom Tode Mariä II (no. 14). The Five "Picturesque" Songs. Conclusion: Hindemith's Ekphrastic Response to Rilke's Marien-Leben. Bibliography. List of Illustrations. Indes of Names. Index of Literary and Musical Works Cited. About the Author.

--------------------------------   *Editions Rodopi B.V.*
USA/Canada: 6075 Roswell Rd., Ste. 219, Atlanta, GA 30328, Tel. (404) 843-4314, *Call toll-free* (U.S.only) 1-800-225-3998, Fax (404) 843-4315

All Other Countries: Tijnmuiden 7, 1046 AK Amsterdam, The Netherlands. Tel. ++ 31 (0)20 6114821, Fax ++ 31 (0)20 4472979
orders-queries@rodopi.nl ----- http://www.rodopi.nl

STEPHANOS STEPHANIDES WITH KARNA SINGH

Translating Kali's Feast
The Goddess in Indo-Caribbean
Ritual and Fiction

Amsterdam/Atlanta, GA 2000. XII,200 pp.
(Cross/Cultures 43)
ISBN: 90-420-1381-8   Bound Hfl. 100,-/US-$ 55.50
ISBN: 90-420-1371-0   Paper Hfl. 45,-/US-$ 25.50

Translating Kali's Feast is an interdisciplinary study of the Goddess Kali bringing together ethnography and literature within the theoretical framework of translation studies. The idea for the book grew out of the experience and fieldwork of the authors, who lived with Indo-Caribbean devotees of the Hindu Goddess in Guyana. Using a variety of discursive forms including oral history and testimony, fieldnotes, songs, stories, poems, literary essays, photographic illustrations, and personal and theoretical reflections, it explores the cultural, aesthetic and spiritual aspects of the Goddess in a diasporic and cross-cultural context. With reference to critical and cultural theorists including Walter Benjamin and Julia Kristeva, the possibilities offered by Kali (and other manifestations of the Goddess) as the site of translation are discussed in the works of such writers as Wilson Harris, V.S. Naipaul and R.K. Narayan. The book articulates perspectives on the experience of living through displacement and change while probing the processes of translation involved in literature and ethnography and postulating links between 'rite' and 'write,' Hindu 'leela' and creole 'play.'

---------------------------------   *Editions Rodopi B.V.*

USA/Canada: 6075 Roswell Rd., Ste. 219, Atlanta, GA 30328, Tel. (404) 843-4314, *Call toll-free* (U.S.only) 1-800-225-3998, Fax (404) 843-4315

All Other Countries: Tijnmuiden 7, 1046 AK Amsterdam, The Netherlands. Tel. ++ 31 (0)20 6114821, Fax ++ 31 (0)20 4472979
       orders-queries@rodopi.nl ----- http://www.rodopi.nl

ON TRANSLATING FRENCH LITERATURE AND FILM II

Ed. by Myriam Salama-Carr

Amsterdam/Atlanta, GA 2000. XI,241 pp.
(Rodopi Perspectives on Modern Literature 22)
ISBN: 90-420-1451-2   Bound Hfl. 125,-/US-$ 53.-
ISBN: 90-420-1441-5   Paper Hfl. 45,-/US-$ 19.-

Editions Rodopi B.V.

USA/Canada: 6075 Roswell Rd., Ste. 219, Atlanta, GA 30328, Tel. (404) 843-4314, *Call toll-free* (U.S.only) 1-800-225-3998, Fax (404) 843-4315

All Other Countries: Tijnmuiden 7, 1046 AK Amsterdam, The Netherlands. Tel. ++ 31 (0)20 6114821, Fax ++ 31 (0)20 4472979

LITERATURE AND HOMOSEXUALITY

Ed. by Michael J. Meyer

Amsterdam/Atlanta, GA 2000. VII,274 pp.
(Rodopi Perspectives on Modern Literature 21)
ISBN: 90-420-0529-7   Bound Hfl. 140,-/US-$ 60.-
ISBN: 90-420-0519-X   Paper Hfl. 45,-/US-$ 19.-

Editions Rodopi B.V.

USA/Canada: 6075 Roswell Rd., Ste. 219, Atlanta, GA 30328, Tel. (404) 843-4314, *Call toll-free* (U.S.only) 1-800-225-3998, Fax (404) 843-4315

All Other Countries: Tijnmuiden 7, 1046 AK Amsterdam, The Netherlands. Tel. ++ 31 (0)20 6114821, Fax ++ 31 (0)20 4472979

MUSICO-POETICS IN PERSPECTIVE
CALVIN S. BROWN IN MEMORIAM

Ed. by Jean-Louis Cupers and Ulrich Weisstein

Amsterdam/Atlanta, GA 2000. XVII,313 pp.
(Word and Music Studies 2)
ISBN: 90-420-1532-2   Bound Hfl. 150,-/US-$ 64.-
ISBN: 90-420-1522-5   Paper Hfl. 50,-/US-$ 21.-

The volume is dedicated to the memory of the late Calvin S. Brown of the University of Georgia, author of the first systematically conceived survey - Music and Literature: A Comparison of the Arts (1948) - of the branch of interart studies now generally known as Melopoetics. Part One consists of six original contributions by experts from Austria, Belgium, France, and the United States, authored by a novelist and a composer/scholar, respectively, the first two essays - Jean Libis's "Inspiration musicale et composition littéraire: Réflexions sur un roman schubertien" and David M. Hertz's "The Composer's Musico-Literary Experience: Reflections on Song Writing" - focus, not surprisingly, on the creative process. The third piece - Francis' Claudon's review of the pertinent research done between 1970 and 1990 - complements the honoree's analogous report on the preceding decades, reprinted in the present volume, whereas the fourth - Jean-Louis Cupers' "Métaphores de l'écho et de l'ombre: Regards sur l'évolution des études musico-littéraires" - surveys the plethora of metaphorical applications, in music and literature, of two significant natural phenomena, the one acoustic and the other optical. Linked to each other, the two remaining papers - Ulrich Weisstein's "The Miracle of Interconnectedness: Calvin S. Brown, a Critical Biography" and Walter Bernhart's "A Profile in Retrospect: Calvin S. Brown as a Musico-Literary Scholar" - offer critical accounts of the honoree's theoretical and methodological stance as viewed, in the first case, from a biographical angle and, in the second, in the light of subsequent scholarly practice.

Part Two bundles eleven of Professor Brown's previously uncollected articles, covering a period of nearly half a century of significant scholarly activity in the field. The selection demonstrates Brown's poignant interest in transpositions d'art exemplifying the "musicalization" of literature in the formal and structural, rather than thematic, domain as culminating in his trenchant critique of "music in poetry" as understood, somewhat naïvely, by Mallarmé and his critics, and, to a slightly lesser extent, by his translation of Josef Weinhebers' variations on Friedrich Hölderlin's ode "An die Parzen". Just as Professor Brown's successive anatomies of melopoetic theory and practice illustrate his steadily growing sophistication and the maturing of his mind, so his Bloomington lecture "The Writing and Reading of Language and Music: Thoughts on Some Parallels Between two Artistic Media" reflects his unique ability to assemble, and organize, vast materials and comprehensive data in such a way as to reveal the underlying pattern.

--------------------------------   *Editions Rodopi B.V.*
USA/Canada: 6075 Roswell Rd., Ste. 219, Atlanta, GA 30328, Tel. (404) 843-4445, *Call toll-free* (U.S.only) 1-800-225-3998, Fax (404) 843-4315

All Other Countries: Tijnmuiden 7, 1046 AK Amsterdam, The Netherlands. Tel. ++ 31 (0)20 6114821, Fax ++ 31 (0)20 4472979
orders-queries@rodopi.nl ----- http://www.rodopi.nl

WERNER WOLF

The Musicalization of Fiction
A Study in the Theory and History
of Intermediality

Amsterdam/Atlanta, GA 1999. XI,272 pp.
(Internationale Forschungen zur Allgemeinen und
Vergleichenden Literaturwissenschaft 35)
ISBN: 90-420-0457-6   Hfl. 90,-/US-$ 38.-

This volume is a pioneering study in the theory and history of the imitation
of music in fiction and constitutes an important contribution to current
intermediality research.
Starting with a comparison of basic similarities and differences between
literature and music, the study goes on to provide outlines of a general
theory of intermediality and its fundamental forms, in which a more
specialized theory of the musicalization of (narrative) literature based on
contemporary narratology and a typology of the forms of musico-literary
intermediality are embedded. It also addresses the question of how to
recognize a musicalized fiction when reading one and why Sterne's *Tristram
Shandy*, contrary to what has been previously said, is not to be regarded as
a musicalized fiction.
In its historical part, the study explores forms and functions of experiments
with the musicalization of fiction in English literature. After a survey of the
major preconditions for musicalization - the increasing appreciation of
music in 18th and 19th-century aesthetics and its main causes - exemplary
fictional texts from romanticism to postmodernism are analyzed. Authors
interpreted are De Quincey, Joyce, Woolf, A. Huxley, Beckett, Burgess
and Josipovici. Whilst the limitations of a transposition of music into fiction
remain apparent, experiments in this field yield valuable insights into
mainly a-mimetic and formalist aesthetic tendencies in the development of
more recent fiction as a whole and also show to what extent traditional
conceptions of music continue to influence the use of this medium in
literature.
The volume is of relevance for students and scholars of English,
comparative and general literature as well as for readers who take an
interest in intermediality or interart research.

Editions Rodopi B.V.

USA/Canada: 2015 South Park Place, Atlanta, GA 30339, Tel. (770)
933-0027, *Call toll-free* (U.S.only) 1-800-225-3998, Fax (770) 933-9644

All Other Countries: Tijnmuiden 7, 1046 AK Amsterdam, The